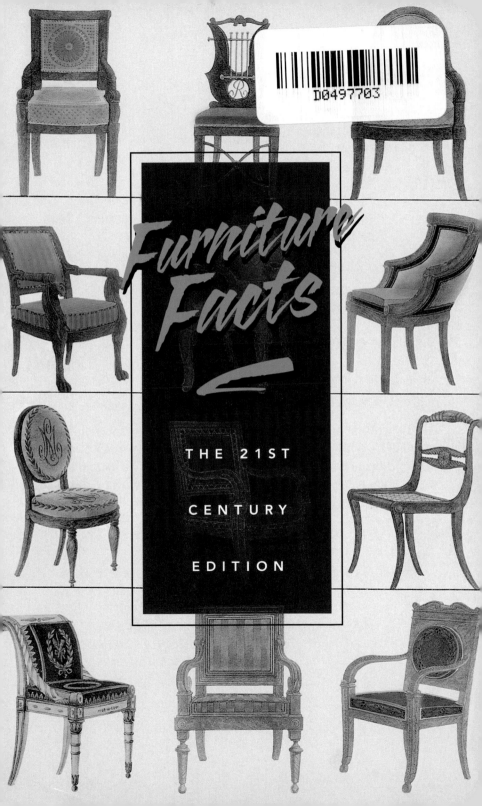

Furniture Facts

THE 21ST

CENTURY

EDITION

Furniture Facts © is published
in the interest of the
Furniture Industry by

J. Franklin, Publishers, Inc.
Furniture Facts ~The 21st Century Edition
28th Edition, Copyright, 1999; Second Impression,, 2003
ISBN#0-9616736-6-4

Furniture Facts© 28th Edition,
Library of Congress Catalog Card Number: 99 075825
Printed in U. S. A.

Distributed exclusively by:

Selling Retail International™Inc.
1-800-444-6141

*The editors of Furniture Facts urge manufacturers to send pictures
and descriptions, philosophy of design, introductions and innovations
for review and possible inclusion in the next printings of Furniture
Facts©. The manufacturers' wares shown in this printing of Furniture
Facts© are not paid advertisements, but selected as representative of
industry trends in the spirit of the best interests of furniture industry.*

Foreword

FURNITURE FACTS© ~ AN INDUSTRY TRADITION

In 1874, Wendalin Seng realized that the future of mass production depended on a reliable source for metal parts. He founded The Seng Company in Chicago, Illinois as a one-man operation, developing a metal highchair lock and soon became deluged with orders. For over 100 years, the people of his company pioneered the development of metal component parts for sofas that made beds, bed units concealed in the sofa, chairs that recline and so on for furniture manufacturers. Further, this pioneer instilled in his company one simple principle: The men and women on the firing line -- the people who do the selling to the retail customer -- are essential to the success of every industrial enterprise--and accurate and factual information is the basis of selling for the retail salesperson. It was agreed that a handy reference book was needed that would help the retail salesperson and Interior Designer to sell more furniture. Seng's Furniture Facts was first published in 1924 as a small guide for salespeople. Through the next 50 years, it became a small dictionary, glossary and encyclopedia for the producers, buyers, and sellers of furniture.

The Seng people continued to update and publish Furniture Facts through its 24th Edition which was published for the 100th Anniversary of the Seng Company. Soon after, Selling Retail International ™ Inc. purchased all rights to Furniture Facts©(1980). Extensive updating and upgrading ensued. Thus, Selling Retail International ™ introduced the 26th and 27th Edition which has been reprinted four times. Since then, hardly a single element in the design, construction, distribution and retailing of home furniture that has not undergone some change. The publishers of Furniture Facts© considered it a sacred trust to perpetuate the legacy The Seng Company left the furniture industry. The 28th Edition for the 21st Century, reflects those changes with the most recent developments and updated technical terms in easy to understand text and descriptions, as well as early 21st Century predictions, while the historical elements of Furniture Facts©, so vital to the heritage of the furniture industry and its future, have been preserved.

Furniture Facts© ~the 21st Century Edition ~ is published with great pride in the interest of the furniture industry.

John F. Lawhon
Chief Executive Officer
Selling Retail International ™ Inc.

CONTENTS

SECTION II: THE CONSTRUCTION OF FURNITURE
75

SECTION III: INTERIOR DESIGN
119

Continued, next page

SECTION IV: SLEEP EQUIPMENT
145

SECTION V: FURNITURE & DESIGN TERMS & DEFINITIONS
157

❖

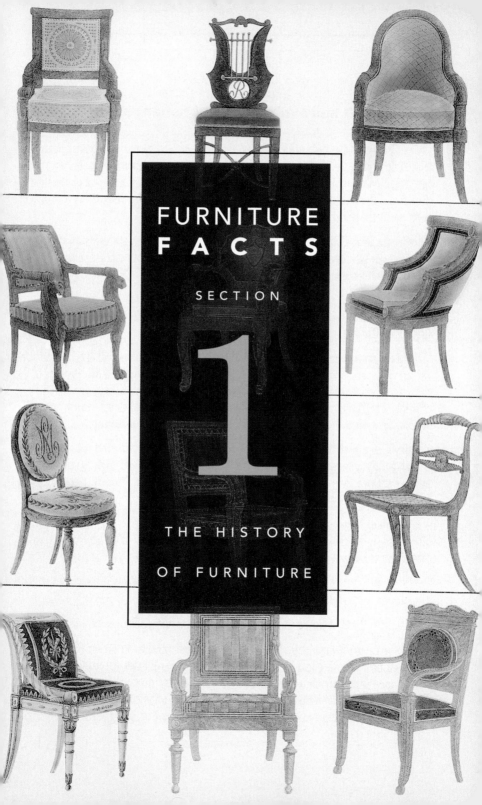

FURNITURE FACTS

SECTION

1

THE HISTORY

OF FURNITURE

Period Furniture
How it has evolved to meet changing needs.

Furniture styles have always run in cycles, their designs and general attributes affected by related decorative trends. Whims and preferences of reigning monarchs and their courts have traditionally influenced styles. Hence major periods bear a king's or a queen's name (Georgian, Queen Anne), the name of a reigning house (Tudor), the designation of a type of government (Regency).

Rome, the Near East and the Orient developed furniture which indirectly affected later designers, but scant attention is given here to styles prior to the 16th century since they have had minor influence on today's furniture.

The first significant major period, the Gothic, prevailed from 110 to 1500 A.D. Massive and ornate, designed by churchmen and produced principally in monasteries, the furniture of this era was similar to all parts of Europe.

The 16th century witnessed the flowering of the Renaissance -- the revival of classic culture. The arts prospered. Furniture and cabinet-making became honored crafts. Because of its classical origin all Renaissance furniture has common characteristics, regardless of country of origin. Following this era the use of furniture grew and individual craftsmen began developing styles with national characteristics keyed to people's preference.

Today's furniture descends from the great styles of the 17th and 18th centuries. Contemporary designers have borrowed from these traditional styles...improved on them...increased their comfort...scaled them to modern homes. Modern technology has brought well-designed furniture within the reach of all.

In common practice, the terms "period," "style," even "period style," are used interchangeably. Because we are dealing here with identification of design characteristics, "style" is used wherever applicable.

◆ A style relates to design characteristics identifying the work of a famous designer or school of designers.

◆ A period is a measure of historical duration.

In some cases (William and Mary) style and period coincide. In others (Georgian) the period includes several styles (Sheraton, Chippendale). In still others, styles like Gothic and Renaissance were common to many countries and extended through several historical periods. Certain individual features mark period designs. Legs and chair shapes are the easiest to recognize. The charts and information following should aid in speedy initial identification.

CHRONOLOGICAL TABLE OF PERIOD SYYLES				
TIME	ENGLAND	FRANCE	AMERICA	OTHER COUNTRIES
EARLY STYLES	Gothic (1100-1500)	Gothic (1100-1500)		Gothic (1100-1500) in Germany, Spain, Italy, etc.
16TH CENTURY	Renaissance Tudor (1509-1558) Elizabethan (1558-1603)	Renaissance (1500-1610)		Early Renaissance (1500-1600)in Italy, Holland, Spain, Germany
17TH CENTURY	Jacobean (1603-1649) Commonwealth (1649-1660) Carolean (1660-1688) Wm & Mary (1689-1702)	Louis XIII (1610-1643) Louis XIV (1643-1715) Early French Provincial (1650-1800)	Early Colonial (1620-1700)	Late Renaissance (1600-1700) in Italy, Holland, Spain, Germany
18TH CENTURY	Queen Anne (1702-1715) Early Georgian (1714-1754) Late Georgian (1754-1795) including: (Chippendale ,1740-1779) (Hepplewhite, 1770-1786) (Sheraton, 1780-1806) (Adams Bros. 1760-1792)	French Regency (1715-1723) Louis XV (1723-1774) Louis XVI (1774-1793) Directoire (1795-1804) Early French Provincial (1650-1800)	Late Colonial (1700-1790) (copies of English, French and Dutch styles) Duncan Phyfe (1790-1830)	European furniture of this time greatly influenced by French, Dutch, English craftsmen.
19TH CENTURY	English Regency (1793-1830) Victorians (1830-1890) Eastlake (1879-1895)	French Empire (1804-1815) Late French Provincial (1800-1900)	Federal (1795-1830) (Duncan Phyfe) Victorian (1830-1900)	Biedermeier (1800-1850) in Germany
20TH CENTURY	Arts & Crafts (1900-1920) Modern Utility (1939-1947)	L'Art Nouveau (1890-1905) (1926) Modern	Mission (1895-1910) Modern	Swedish Modern in Sweden. Modern in other countries.

NOTE: Since furniture styles have a tendency to overlap, it is almost impossible to determine the exact date when one period ends and another begins. The dates listed above are approximately correct, however, and they delineate the years of maximum popularity for each style. This table should serve as a quick reference to the leading styles in each century and as a guide to the interrelation of styles in the countries shown.

DUNCAN PHYFE

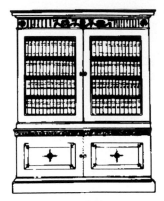

ADAM

COLONIAL

QUEEN ANNE

VICTORIAN

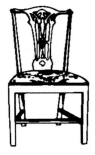

SHERATON

HEPPLEWHITE

CHIPPENDALE

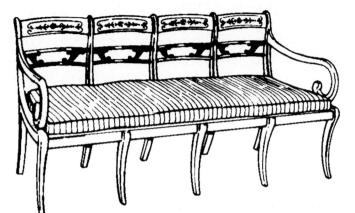

REGENCY

| FRENCH PROVINCIAL | CHIPPENDALE | LOUIS XV | TUDOR | QUEEN ANNE |

| CHINESE CHIPPENDALE | LOUIS XV | SHERATON | HEPPLEWHITE |

| ADAM | DUNCAN PHYFE | JACOBEAN | COLONIAL |

WILLIAM AND MARY 1689-1702

HISTORICAL. When Mary Stuart ascended the English throne, she brought with her a Dutch husband and many new ideas, new customs and new standards for furniture. William III and Mary popularized the Dutch idea of comfort. For the first time, beautiful furniture was brought within reach of the public. The monarchs brought with them craftsmen and cabinetmakers from Holland, Flanders and France who introduced ideas of their own and motifs borrowed from Spain, China and India. The era is also noted for the number of new pieces which were introduced.

GENERAL ATTRIBUTES. Use of upholstery appears extensively for the first time. Traditional English oak is replaced with walnut. Carving features motifs of flowers, foliage, cupids, wreaths, C-scrolls and serpentine designs (5), often gilded, painted or lacquered (11). Marquetry is used extensively, as is veneering, but most furniture of this period depends more on graceful lines and curves than on decoration for its pleasing effect. Among characteristic turnings on legs is the "Inverted Cup"- a bell-shaped detail (6) which appears near the top of the leg (4,9,12). Upholstery fabrics are tapestry, petit point, embroidery, damasks, brocades, velvets, figured chintzes. Trumpet shaped (2) and octagonal legs (3) are common. All types of feet are used: bun, pear, club and hoof-shaped (4,7). All are equipped with stretchers often set x-wise between the legs (12), with a finial at the conjunction.

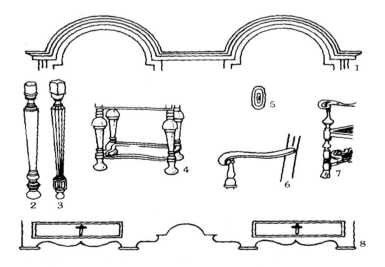

TABLES. In rectangular tables, stretchers are governed by the size of the table, but are always flat and curved. Stretchers are also used on small tables. Veneers are common on table tops, with occasional use of elaborate marquetry. Legs are elaborate as in chairs. Cabriole legs appeared on later occasional tables. Round and oval gate-legged tables are found as are splay-legged butterfly tables.

OTHER PIECES. Stools have upholstered tops, heavy, elaborately carved legs and characteristic, heavy stretchers. Cabinets and desks have shaped skirts or aprons (8) and drop handles on drawers (9). Top rails of cabinets are hooded with arched tops (1). Cabinets have six or eight legs, all connected with curved, flat stretchers (9). Bedsteads are canopied with rich hangings, the four corner posts often surmounted with plumes. Upholstered settees or love seats (10) resemble joined chairs with elaborately carved stretchers.

SUGGESTIONS FOR USE. William and Mary furniture is reproduced only rarely today, but, because of its grace and lightness, it goes well with 18th century and Queen Anne, especially occasional pieces.

QUEEN ANNE 1702-1715

HISTORICAL. The reign of Queen Anne is often called the "first modern furniture period." This furniture had its beginnings in the William and Mary style, but the era produced many innovations, such as the highboy, Windsor and bannister-back chairs. It marked the first general use of upholstering in the "overstuffed" manner.

GENERAL ATTRIBUTES. Queen Anne furniture can be recognized by the almost universal cabriole leg (4,5,6) and the undulating lines. Dutch influence is apparent, comfort is a primary consideration, and simplicity of ornament is the rule. Carving, when used, is simple and in low relief. Corners are rounded and pieces shaped to fit the body rather than to follow the straight lines of previous styles. Walnut is most generally used, although occasionally pieces were produced in oak, pine and ash. Mahogany began to appear in the later pieces. Gilding and lacquer were sometimes used as decoration. The principal motif for decoration is the scalloped shell (2,10) which appears at the knees of cabriole legs (5,6) the top of the chair splat (2) or the center of the seat frame. Acanthus and floral motifs are also used. Favored upholstering fabrics are brocades and embossed leather.

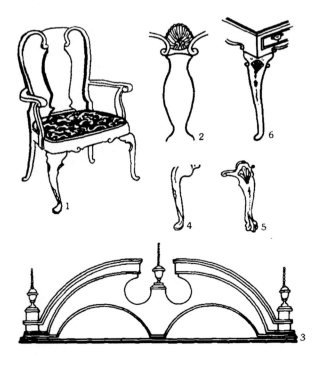

CHAIRS AND TABLES. Typical chairs have high rounded backs and cabriole legs (I). Early models have delicate, turned stretchers recessed between the front legs, but these gradually disappeared. The cabriole leg was derived from China via Holland. Originally, it represented the claw of a dragon holding a jewel. It had many variations, such as the claw and ball (5) and the Dutch foot (4). The single curved splat is also distinctive. These were fiddle-shaped or vase-shaped (7,11) and were spooned to fit the body. Wing chairs have sturdy, comfortable lines. Chair back posts are continuations of the rear legs. Seats have rounded front corners, and backs of seats are considerably narrower than the front. The lower edge of the seat frame is often shaped (I).

MISCELLANEOUS PIECES. Highboys generally have cabriole legs, connected with stretchers in early pieces. Five and six-legged pieces are common. In early models, the tops are flat (9), in later ones, highboys and tall cabinets have broken pediments (3) with shaped finials at outer edges and center.

Popular pieces in this period include the china cabinet (borrowed from the Dutch), lowboys, bureaus, wardrobes and secretaries, and have the same general characteristics as the highboys. Drawers are usually equipped with plain brass ball handles (8) and pierced escutcheons. Settees or "love seats" have upholstered seats, and two joined chair backs, usually with five legs. Queen Anne beds were cumbersome, of the poster type, with wood canopies and curtains of damask and velvet.

SUGGESTIONS FOR USE. The simplicity of line and absence of flamboyant decoration make Queen Anne fit well with contemporary or 18th century walnut pieces.

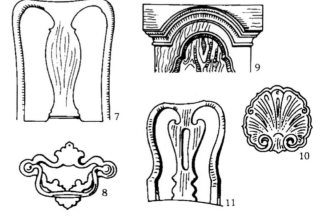

GEORGIAN 1714-1795

HISTORICAL. The Georgian period covers the reigns of George I, George II and George III up to the time of the Regency. This era, especially in its later years, was dominated by individual craftsmen who created styles which bear their own names: Chippendale, Sheraton, Adam, Hepplewhite.

GENERAL ATTRIBUTES. It is chiefly notable for the introduction of mahogany. Furniture was curved with limited use of straight lines. French and Oriental influence is strong. Use of casters on chairs and tables distinguishes it from Queen Anne styles. Pieces are richly upholstered, often gilded. Cabinets, dressers, bookcases, desks (2) have heavy, dignified lines with carving, pilasters, columns and broken pediments (1). Cabriole legs are decorated with masks and heads of lions, satyrs, cabachon, leaf designs. Claw and ball feet, paws and open splats characterize chairs. Carving is often elaborate (4).

Chippendale, Adam, Hepplewhite, Sheraton, masters of the era, dominated and influenced other craftsmen through their published works as well as actual pieces. Thomas Shearer created dainty pieces similar to Sheraton and Hepplewhite. He is credited with inventing the sideboard (5). Ince and Mayhew specialized in chairs similar to Chippendale but less elaborate (3). Manwaring produced heavy chairs similar to Chippendale. Locke and Copeland followed the Adam style.

SUGGESTIONS FOR USE. See recommendations for other 18th century styles on preceding and succeeding pages of Furniture Facts©.

LOUIS XV 1723-1774

HISTORICAL. During the early years of Louis XV (Louis Quinze) France was ruled by a regent and furniture produced then was called French Regencé. When Louis actually began his reign, he encouraged new designs. Furniture became more ornate and luxurious, more feminine, smaller in scale, is often referred to as rococo.

GENERAL ATTRIBUTES. Comfort, luxury and beauty are stressed. Curves appear wherever possible. Chairs have cabriole legs, carved knees, scroll feet (1,6); seats are broad and rounded; arm supports are carved and joined to elaborately carved seat rails which are always exposed (1,6). Tables have curved legs (2,7,8), onyx or marble tops. Stretchers are infrequent but when used are elaborately carved (10). Cabinets and chests have bombe fronts and sides, carved aprons, cabriole legs. The Bureau du Roi (desk) of Louis XV is one of the most elaborate pieces of furniture ever built. Decoration includes carving (3,4,5,9) metal inlay, ormolu mounts, painted panels, gilt, lacquer. Upholstery fabrics are tapestries, brocades, velvets; woods are mahogany, walnut, oak, ebony, chestnut.

SUGGESTIONS FOR USE. It can be used with Chippendale and other early Georgian.

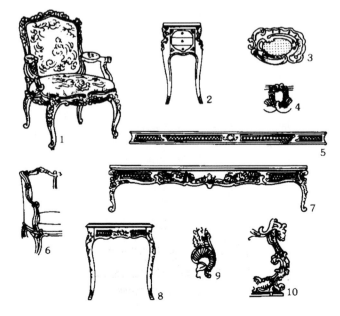

CHIPPENDALE 1740-1779

HISTORICAL. Chippendale is one of the outstanding styles of the Georgian period of the eighteenth century. Thomas Chippendale was the first man not a reigning monarch to give his name to a furniture style. He was both designer and master craftsman. His "Directory" published in 1754 opened a new era in furniture making-and is still consulted.

GENERAL ATTRIBUTES. Chippendale derived his inspiration from three principal sources: English (preceding styles), French and Chinese. He produced furniture of every kind-all graceful and well proportioned. Occasionally, however, comfort is sacrificed to appearance in some of his chairs with their sharply carved, decorative backs.

Early Chippendale pieces have cabriole legs and other features common to early 18th century furniture. Later pieces have straight legs. Pieces of French inspiration have been given English sturdiness of construction. Chippendale depended mostly on carving for decoration; it is delicate and intricate on some pieces, bold and lavish on others. Lion's paws, shells, acanthus, acorns, roses, dolphins, scrolls are familiar motifs. Fretwork is extensively used-veneering occasionally, also gilding and lacquering. He never used inlay, painting or applied ornament. Practically all Chippendale furniture is mahogany. Upholstering materials include leather in colors, French brocades, velours, satins, plushes.

CHAIRS. Chairs of French and Early Georgian inspiration have cabriole legs with carved knees and more pronounced curves than chairs of Louis XVI and are more slender in form than Queen Anne chairs (2,6). The feet vary, including claw and ball (6), scroll (14), leaf carved (13) hoof and splay. Front rails are slightly bowed or serpentine. In Gothic and Chinese styles, front legs are straight (9,12)

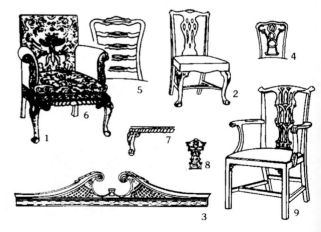

and the feet are plain. In all styles, Chippendale used back legs which were slender and plain. Chair seats are upholstered, usually square with tapering sides. Chair backs are of a variety of shapes (2,4,5,9). Backs usually are wider at the top than bottom. Splats invariably extend from top to rear seat frame. Original models also include "ladder backs" (5) and ribband (ribbon) backs (4,9). Chair arms generally join the back at an angle to give effect of roominess. Top rails are bow-shaped or irregular. Wing chairs are upholstered with flaring contours.

MISCELLANEOUS PIECES. Dining tables have either straight or carved cabriole legs. Divans have flaring arms and straight (11) or cabriole legs (7). Tea and tripod tables are trimmed with pie crust borders. Some have fretwork railings. Cabinets, bookcases and chests of drawers are characterized by graceful, swelling fronts and sides; occasionally fronts of serpentine. Large pieces have broken pediments (3,10). Fretwork decoration appears on bookcases. Lowboys have cabriole legs, curved skirts and carved decorations (15). Chippendale also made beds, settees (16), clock cases, screens, desk, and many other pieces, but no sideboards.

SUGGESTIONS FOR USE. Recommend earlier, heavier pieces with William and Mary and Queen Anne styles. Smaller pieces go well with Sheraton, French styles, and Hepplewhite. Chinese Chippendale fits well with modern.

CHINESE CHIPPENDALE 1750-1800

HISTORICAL. About 1740, Chinese influences were enjoying great popularity in England. Thomas Chippendale began to experiment with Chinese inspired furniture designs. The proportions of the original Chinese furniture were different from prevailing English standards, their craftsmen inclining to favor long sweeping curves with a disregard for symmetry and balanced lines. Chippendale combined Chinese decorations and motifs with English proportions to produce a style which enjoyed tremendous popularity in the middle eighteenth century.

GENERAL ATTRIBUTES. Open fret work and all-over lattice work (4) of Chinese pattern is a dominant characteristic of Chinese Chippendale pieces. It appears in chair backs (1,2) and in the angles formed between the legs and seat of chairs (1,5) and the legs and top of tables (3). Bookcases and china cabinets have latticed and trellis doors and upturned pagoda-roof tops. Legs on chairs and small tables are often straight with decorations of raised carving in Chinese designs (1,3,5). Dragon feet, clutching a "pearl" or ball, were frequently employed. Stretchers were used on many chairs. Extensive use of carving was employed for decoration. Many pieces were lacquered, gilded or enameled. Straight lines and long sweeping curves were generally used. Today's replicas of Chinese Chippendale favor the more restrained designs of small tables, chairs, cabinets and settees, employing fretwork and straight lines, fluted or carved legs.

SUGGESTIONS FOR USE. Chinese Chippendale replicas, because of their straight, clean lines, can be used with Chinese Modern, Swedish Modern, Contemporary pieces. It also goes well with other Chippendale pieces.

ACANTHUS

ACANTHUS

ARABESQUE

BOSS

ANTHEMIOM

CORNUCOPIA

ANTEFIX

CARTOUCHE

DENTIL MOLDING

DIAPER WORK

DOLPHIN

EGG AND DART

PALMETTE BAND

PENDENT

RINCEAU

FINAL

TUDOR ROSE

TREFOIL

PILASTER

ESCUTCHEON

QUATREFOIL

SPOOL BEAD

FRET

GRIFFIN

FESTOON

ROCOCO SHELL

ROSETTE

GUILLOCHE

LUNNETTE

SPIRAL WAVE

SWAG

HONEYSUCKLE

STRAPWORK

LINENFOLD

HUSKS

LAUREL LEAF

SHELL CARVING

WHEAT

LOTUS

LOZENGE

VOLUTE

MODILLION

URN

Here are some of the more common decorative details found on period furniture. Each craftsman, however, modified these basic designs to suit his own ideas. See "Furniture Terms" in Section V.

ADAM BROTHERS 1760-1792

HISTORICAL. Adam is not a period in itself but is one of the styles of the late Georgian period of the 18th century. The Brothers Adam-Robert, James, William-were primarily architects who turned to furniture design to develop a style to match the houses they planned. Robert traveled extensively, visiting Greece, Italy and the Pompeiian excavations to bring back ideas which seemed revolutionary in an era of curves.

GENERAL ATTRIBUTES. All Adam designs are characterized by restraint, delicacy, classic simplicity. Slender, straight lines, tapering legs and flat surfaces, ornamented with painting, gilding and inlay are recognizable earmarks. Inspiration comes from Classic Roman, Pompeiian and French styles. Construction is simple.

Occasional delicate low-relief carving is used. Classical motifs predominate: ornamental discs and ovals, spandrel fans, floral swags and pendants (3,8) drapery, acanthus, pineapples, human figures (6) and animal heads. The classic urn (2) is the most commonly used feature. Adam pieces are also famed for daintily carved moldings (4,5,10,16). Brocades, damasks, figured and striped satins and silks are favored upholstery fabrics. Mahogany and satinwood veneer are favored woods with occasional use of sycamore, ebony, other fancy woods.

CHAIRS. Chairs have slim, tapered legs, round or square (1,13,14) and often fluted (12). Splats have a variety of designs-some square (12), some curved (15), and open. Shield shape backs were occasionally used even before popularized by Hepplewhite. Adam shields are usually solid. Curved backs (13) and Greek legs also appear. Block or spade feet used on square legs, turned or molded feet on round legs. Frequently backs are solid panels (7) or caned-or have center panel of cane-or are upholstered (9). Arms are flattened and shaped and usually supported by an extension of front legs (9,12). Sometimes upholstered arm rests are used (13). Stretchers rarely appear.

TABLES. Tables are usually long and narrow with decorated side rails, under framings, moldings (11). Legs are straight and fluted or turned (11). More than four legs are sometimes used. Adam Brothers popularized the console tables which they designed in great numbers. They are frequently semicircular with four legs. Marble tops often appear.

OTHER PIECES. Adam Brothers scored their greatest success with larger pieces: mantels, sideboards, upholstered divans, settees and daybeds (6). These were extensively ornamented with motifs of a classical nature. Sideboards are regular in outline, occasionally semi-oval or six-sided-usually with six or eight slender legs. Pedestals, knife drawers, wine coolers, other accessories are built into sideboards, cupboards, cabinets.

Commodes have delicate inlay, painted decorations, Wedgwood plaques. Oval and round handles and classic brass ornaments are typical. Bookcases and cabinets have straight or classic pediment tops.

SUGGESTIONS FOR USE. Replicas of dining room and bedroom pieces now made in both walnut and mahogany. This style mixes well with Sheraton, Phyfe, Hepplewhite, Empire, Louis XIV, but requires harmonious background.

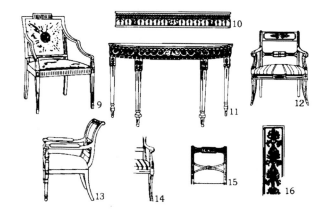

HEPPLEWHITE 1770-1786

HISTORICAL. Hepplewhite-like Adam, Chippendale, Sheraton-is not a period, but one of the styles of the Georgian period of the 18th century. George Hepplewhite, its creator, was a practical cabinet maker. His chief inspirations were French designs of Louis XIV period.

GENERAL ATTRIBUTES. Lines and proportions are graceful, refined and slender, though sturdy. Chairs, settees and other pieces are all built on a smaller scale than heretofore produced. Characteristic of his designs are their slender, fluted legs (1,5,7,13) and rather low backs which give pieces a somewhat fragile appearance. Spade feet are characteristic (4,6,7). Graceful curves predominate rather than straight lines. Dainty carving is sparingly used consisting mostly of classical motifs: wheat ears, ferns, pendant husks, urns, rosettes (8) and the Prince of Wales feathers (14) which he introduced. Veneer is skillfully employed. Mahogany is the favored wood, with satinwood, birch, sycamore and imported woods also used. Upholstery of striped damask, silk and satin, red and blue morocco is used with horsehair stuffing.

CHAIRS. The backs of Hepplewhite chairs are almost always open and seldom upholstered. The most individual designs are the hoop (3), shield and interlacing heart patterns (9,10). In the shield back (9) Hepplewhite kept the curve at the top unbroken, (in contrast to Sheraton, who also used shield designs). Oval backs have vase or lyre-shaped back splats (12). Hepplewhite backs never reach to the seat frame, always being supported above it by the back posts. Arms are usually short and serpentine or concave (9), curved, carried down to the front legs (2). Easy chairs have protecting wings, rolled arms and generous curved lines, with straight legs connected by stretchers.

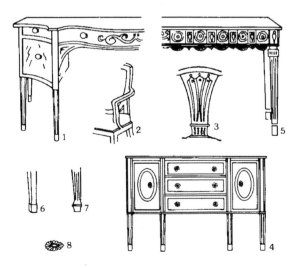

MISCELLANEOUS PIECES.   Hepplewhite tables have the same delicate legs as his chairs (5) slim, tapered, often fluted, and usually with spade feet. Some models have two slender legs at each corner instead of one. One type of settee is really a long chair with several shields or oval chair backs joined together. Upholstered sofas show strong French influence. The backs are a series of flowing curves building up to a central "hump"-or else are a simple low curve. Arms are upholstered or carved; some models have eight legs, some seven.

Hepplewhite did much to develop the modern sideboard. His models have serpentine fronts and graceful curves, with six legs, usually square and tapered, and spade feet (1,4). His designs have concave corner construction (1) differentiating them from similar Sheraton models which always have convex corners. Low "sideboard tables" have pedestal cupboards at each end surmounted by urns.

SUGGESTIONS FOR USE.   This style is recommended for use with other 18th century designs, especially Sheraton, Adam, Phyfe and Chippendale.

LOUIS XVI 1774-1793

HISTORICAL   Where the reign of Louis XIV (1643-1715) prompted an interest in florid baroque style that emanated from Italy and Louis XV's reign gave rise to a rococo style which was a further reaction to ancient plainness and simplicity; the tenure of Louis XVI (Louis Seize) injected still another influence into furniture design. Furniture of this period represents a counter reaction. The frills of Louis XIV and Louis XV now gave way to a resurgence of the classical age and its chaste, relatively unadorned spirit of design. Unearthing of the ruins at Pompeii and Herculaneum brought about renewed interest in antiquity, comparable to the similar rebirth prompted by the Renaissance. Furniture legs found expression as severe vertical members; flat, undecorated panels were often relieved only by moldings.

GENERAL ATTRIBUTES.   The character and function of individual pieces were reminiscent of the lines popular in Louis XV's reign. Style is refined, elegant in its simplicity, excellent in workmanship, restrained in its decoration. Curves yield to straight lines, scrolled surfaces to rectangular ones. Decoration consists of classic motifs (2,3) used largely to emphasize the authority and the beauty of line. A Marie Antoinette basket of flowers (5) is a typical embellishment.

TABLES AND CHAIRS. Chairs have straight, tapered legs (8,9) carved or fluted like Greek columns. Seat rails are gently curved (9) with backs that are square or medallion shape. Padded arm rests are common. Tables have the same straight legs as the chairs, sometimes carved or fluted (1,2) with carved aprons (2,6,7). Occasionally there are curved stretchers (6). Sofas, beds and cabinets, even tête-à-têtes and chaise lounges, have typical straight, column type legs. Painted work, on panels, is common. Striped and small-patterned upholstery fabrics are favored, in silks, tapestries and other materials common to the Louis XV era. Mahogany is a popular wood, as are ebony, tulipwood, rosewood and fruitwoods arranged in Arabic marquetry. Many of the woods were decorated with lacquers of black or of gold and Sèvres plaques were often inset into surfaces with flat planes.

Among the distinguished furniture designers of this period were Roentgen, Riesener, Aubert, Lalonde, the George Jacobses, père and fils, Lavasseur and Severin. All played an important part, with their emphasis of ideas and trends, in building a bridge between the styles of Louis XVI's reign and the Empire style which was to follow.

SUGGESTIONS FOR USE. The Louis XVI, or Louis Seize, period pieces can be mixed with Adam, Sheraton, Hepplewhite, and Directoire styles and, if care is exercised, they often blend well with Federal and French Provincial furniture.

SHERATON 1780-1806

HISTORICAL. Sheraton is one of the styles included in the 18th century Georgian period. Thomas Sheraton was a teacher, preacher, bookseller, fanatic and pamphleteer, in addition to being a designer of furniture. Not a master craftsman himself, he exerted a tremendous influence on furniture craftsmen through the designs in his four books. Orders for furniture were generally turned over to other cabinetmakers who worked out his designs. Sheraton built the first twin beds, roll-top desks, kidney-shaped tables, and dual-purpose furniture.

GENERAL ATTRIBUTES. Sheraton's designs are slender, refined and delicate in appearance but structurally sound and durable in construction. Legs are slender, usually round, sometimes square, tapered and reeded (1,4) but never cabriole. All pieces are well proportioned, straight lines predominating, although curves were used to good effect in pieces such as sideboards. Sheraton's designs are strongly influenced by Adam and the Louis XVI and French Empire styles. Ornamentation, however, is simple. Inlay and marquetry are extensively used for decoration, also carvings in classical tradition-ferns, shells, urns, ovals and floral swags. Sheraton produced mahogany furniture for dining rooms, bedrooms, libraries; rosewood, satinwood and painted furniture for drawing rooms. Upholstering fabrics included plain, striped and flowered satins, silks and damasks, with occasional use of cane.

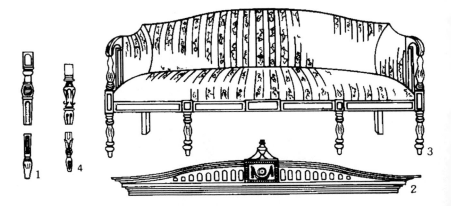

CHAIRS. Sheraton chairs are refined, graceful, beautifully proportioned. Most of them have square backs with delicately carved openwork in a wide variety of designs: fretwork panels (6,8) urns (5) lyre or turned posts (9) shield (11) or cane. In every case, splats rest on cross frames -never on the seat frame. Often the central panel rises above the top rail (5,9,10). Early chairs have tapered legs and spade feet. Later models have spiral turning. Rounded legs often splay outward (6). Some chairs have bowed or serpentine front seat rails. Arm rests curve gracefully out from back to front supports which are usually continuations of the front legs. Seats are rectangular, nearly square, but tapering a little toward the back. In upholstered chairs, Sheraton allowed the seat frame to show as visible support for cushioning.

SIDEBOARDS AND TABLES. Both have slender tapered legs, similar to chairs, usually without stretchers. General lines of sideboards are straight with convex curves on corners and front (in contrast to Hepplewhite's designs which have concave curves at corners). Sideboards have useful drawers, cellarets.

Sheraton designed many types of tables. Some have tripod pedestal bases, other have drop leaves. Oval tops appear on occasional pieces. Secretaries are delicate and well proportioned. Bookcases often have shaped pediments (2,7) and curved traceries on glazed doors. Sofas are graceful with light, slender legs (3).

SUGGESTIONS
FOR USE.
Sheraton's style is extensively repro-duced today. It combines well with other similarly scaled furniture: Late Georgian, Louis XVI, Duncan Phyfe, and Regency styles.

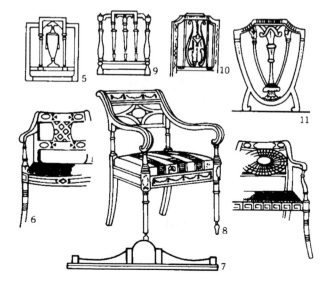

ENGLISH REGENCY 1793-1830

HISTORICAL. This is not a distinct period, but one of the styles of the late Georgian period. It is named for the years (1810-1820) when George IV ruled as regent for the aged George III, but it actually dates from the time when George was Prince of Wales and extends beyond his regency and through his reign which ended in 1830. It was a period of prosperity and luxury when decorations of palaces set the styles. Chief English designers were Holland, Tatham, Thomas Hope. In America, Duncan Phyfe turned out many pieces of Regency inspiration. Do not confuse English Regency with French Regencé 1715-1723.

GENERAL ATTRIBUTES. Regency evolved from the furniture of the 18th century. It was a return to classic principle of design, strongly influenced by the French Directoire and Empire styles and to some extent by Chinese and Egyptian inspiration. In general it was a style of simplification and functionalism, a mingling of classic simplicity of outlines with oriental richness of decoration. Furniture pieces were scaled down to smaller, more intimate sizes. Much of the furniture is lacquered (Chinese influence) with black as the favorite color (white and ivory

occasionally used) and trimmed with extensive gilding. Curves are simple but bold and used with straight lines. Surfaces are flat, decorated with carving and relief in classical and Chinese motifs, cornucopias, and floral designs usually gilded for emphasis. All pieces are beautifully proportioned and refined. Mahogany, satinwood and rosewood are favored woods, with inlays of ormolu, metal, exotic woods, holly, ebony. Metal work is usually of brass, with occasional galleries and grill work. Chinese influence is reflected in bamboo trimmings, occasional use of cane seats, back (9). Upholstery fabrics are damask, velvets, brocades, silk and usually in brighter colors: yellow, gold, white, cream, blue, etc.

CHAIRS. Regency chairs have both straight (5,9) and concave backs (4), ornamented with fretwork, relief, carving, gilding. Legs are usually straight, without underbracing (11), sometimes slightly curved (4,5) occasional use of classic double curves (1). Feet are continuation of legs (4,5) with straight collars or banding (6), occasional use of lion paws (1). Legs are sometimes fluted or carved. Flat, thin upholstery common on all seats, some full upholstered pieces (2).

OTHER PIECES. Tables often elaborately inlaid, lacquered, gilded. Straight legs on larger pieces. Small tables often have triangular bases (3), Roman tripods, gilt and metal feet. China cabinets and bookcases have grillwork doors, columns, pilasters (12). Sofas of classic outline (10), occasionally with dog or lion paw feet. Beds very elaborate with curved headboards or fretwork inserts (7,8). Writing desks on high legs are very popular (6). Molding is used on tables and cabinet pieces (6,12).

SUGGESTIONS FOR USE. This style goes well with Chinese Chippendale, Hepplewhite, French Empire, Directoire, Biedermeier, Adam, Sheraton, Duncan Phyfe.

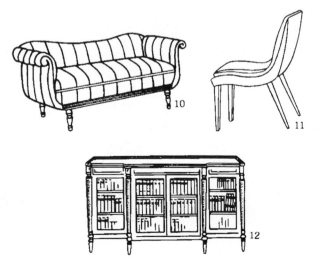

BIEDERMEIER 1800-1850

HISTORICAL. In the early nineteenth century the middle-class German burghers rejected the baroque and rococo styles formerly popular on the continent. German designers and craftsmen began producing simplified, sturdy and somewhat stolid furniture which represented the Teutonic version of Directoire and French Empire pieces. It received its name from "Papa Biedermeier," a fictitious, humorous character who supposedly typified the middle class German.

GENERAL ATTRIBUTES. Since this represents the work of many designers and craftsmen, original pieces are subject to much variation. Current replicas consist of occasional chairs, tables, secretary desks, dining room suites and occasional bedroom pieces. All pieces are functional in design, and virtually without ornamental carving, brass mountings or elaborate inlaid decoration. Desks and cabinets (1) have square lines and are designed for simplicity and efficiency. Chairs (3,4) are scaled for comfort and are sturdy and substantial with thickly cushioned seats. Legs of chairs are straight and tapered (3,4), occasionally slightly curved (6). Table legs are generally round, straight (2,5), and often connected by heavy bases (2,7). While decorations may consist of native fruits or flowers, domestic animals, painted details, the beauty is in the highlighted wood grains often offset with black finished trim. Woods are maple, birch, ash, mahogany and fruitwoods.

SUGGESTIONS FOR USE. Biedermeier occasional pieces go well with both provincial French and American pieces and with eighteenth century formal styles. Because of its simplicity of line and scale it is highly desirable for contemporary settings.

HARDWARE THROUGH THE AGES.

Drop Handle 1675-1720   Early Willow Pattern 1720-1760

 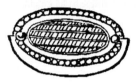

Bail Handle
1760-1785

Pressed Brass Oval
1780-1810

Rosette and Ring   Inset Ring   Rosette
1790-1820   1800-1820

VICTORIAN 1830-1890

HISTORICAL. Victoria mounted the English throne in 1837 and reigned until 1901. During her reign a style of furniture developed in England and then was enthusiastically copied in America. This American version of Victorian is still found in some older homes.

GENERAL ATTRIBUTES. The Victorian era was one of romantic sentimentality, dignified respectability. All of these characteristics are reflected in the furniture of the time. Developed from American and English Empire designs, it resulted in a large, heavy and substantially built style. Rich, deep shades of upholstery and dark finishes with restrained curves and straight lines are skillfully combined. Victorian pieces have a quaint charm. Mahogany, primarily, but also black walnut and rosewood were favored woods. Carving, turning, inlay of brass, wood and mother of pearl are typical. Favorite motifs are scrolls, flowers, leaves (8), classical figures and such nautical emblems as dolphins, anchors, tridents.

In all fairness, much of the criticism of Victorian "stuffiness" is due more to the decorative ideas of the time than to the actual furniture. Rooms were often decorated with incidental pieces and bric-a-brac.

CHAIRS. Characteristic chairs of the time have oval (1) or horseshoe-shaped (4,5) backs. These are invariably solid and upholstered. Some are button-tufted in regular designs. Seats are

upholstered, usually round or oval (1,4,5) and crowned in the center. Side rails are usually simple moldings with occasional carved ornaments in the center of the front rail. Arms are curved and low (1,7) often joining the seat rail near the back (7). Rockers are popular. Their seats are low and backs usually high (5,7). Dining chairs (4) have rounded, open backs with one horizontal splat as a rule. Feet are often simple scroll curves (1,4).

OTHER PIECES. Occasional tables are usually round (3), oblong (9) or oval. Many have marble tops (9). Central pedestals are the rule, even on larger, round dining tables. Occasionally, in early models, the central pedestal is made up of several carved or turned columns (6). Wash stands and dressers have marble tops. Beds are large with high head and footboards. Spool turnings are popular. Dressers often reach almost to the ceiling and have long beveled edge mirrors. Sofas have sweeping curved backs with carved ornaments on top rail of the back (2).

Victorian furniture reproductions range in quality and price. But, lines are pleasing. Gayer colors have replaced much of the darker horsehair upholstering. Softer seats and backs have brought new comfort. Proportions have been scaled down. The atmosphere of charm has been retained.

SUGGESTIONS FOR USE. Victorian goes well with Queen Anne, William and Mary and Colonial walnut pieces.

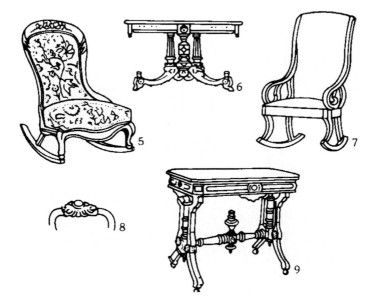

FRENCH PROVINCIAL 1650-1900

HISTORICAL. Early French Provincial furniture was peasant furniture, created by craftsmen in the provinces of France. During the 16th and 17th centuries, pieces were primarily practical and functional, built to fit the needs of the peasant farmer. During the 18th century, however, craftsmen began copying the styles popular in the court at Paris, simplifying the ornamentation and using local rather than imported woods. As a result, though all pieces have the local characteristics of their province of origin, they achieve a basic unity through common inspiration. Craftsmen of Normandy and Limousin generally copied Louis XVI; in Lorraine, Gascony and Burgundy, Louis XIII; in Provence, Louis XV; Louis XIV, elsewhere. Most of the current reproductions are simplified versions of Louis XIV and Louis XV styles.

GENERAL ATTRIBUTES. French Provincial pieces are comfortable, useful and unpretentious with a peculiarly timeless quality that makes the American reproductions popular today. Early French Provincial pieces were confined largely to functional pieces such as bunk beds, stools, benches, commodes, wardrobes and trestle tables. The 18th century pieces (those principally reproduced today) offer a wide variety of styles in chairs, tables, desks, buffets, chests, wardrobes and clocks. Local cabinet makers produced comfortable, unpretentious pieces, simply decorated, that maintain a remarkably continuing popularity.

CHAIRS. Ladderback chairs were developed in Normandy and Burgundy. Ladderback settees (10) were made in Provence. Straw seated chairs were common in Poitou, Vendee and other provinces. Solid top rails were characteristic of Breton workmen. Chairs have flat, curved arms, resting on turned supports, sometimes upholstered (4,5). Armoires (linen cabinets) are common to all sections. Beds have high posts and canopies (12), usually with enclosing draperies.

OTHER PIECES. Nearly all of the early pieces have straight legs (5,10,11,12). On later ones, simple cabriole legs are found (2,3,4,7,8). Bun feet are also characteristic of both chairs and chests. Stretchers, some straight, some turned, some curved, appear on many pieces (5,6,10). Bench arms are frequently arcaded. Upholstered loveseats appear in later versions. Upholstered pieces followed the general design of the court furniture they copied; decoration was simplified (4,5,7). Tables, chests and cupboards often have shaped aprons (1,2,7,8). Many chests and buffets have curved fronts (9). Early tables were of the trestle type but later ones have cabriole legs (2,3,7,8). Decoration is chiefly of a carved nature.

Depth of carving varied but was generally deep in Burgundy, shallow in Provence. Paneling and carving in geometric and conventional designs replaced the inlay of the court pieces. Brass, copper and steel hardware predominated. Large locks, oversize hinges and key plates served as decorative details. Native woods like oak, walnut, chestnut, ash, poplar and fruitwoods, were widely employed.

SUGGESTIONS FOR USE. Because of its informality and its simplicity of line and decoration, French Provincial furniture goes well in colonial homes. It can be mixed with American Colonial, Biedermeier and the simpler pieces of 18th century styles. Many decorators also recommend its use with Victorian and Contemporary.

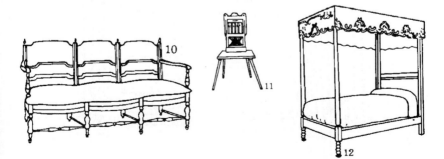

ITALIAN PROVINCIAL 1700-1850

HISTORICAL.   This is a rather loose style designation applied to the furniture turned out by craftsmen in the Italian provinces of the 18th and 19th centuries. These rustic craftsmen copied the elaborate furniture of Rome, Milan, Venice and Florence. In the process, they simplified the lines and eliminated ornate decoration.

GENERAL ATTRIBUTES.   As in the case of French Provincial, characteristics of these furniture pieces vary according to the individual provinces and also according to the date of the original pieces. Early Italian Provincial shows strong influences of the Italian baroque style. Local craftsmen retained the rather large, bulky scale, but eliminated the lavish decoration.

Late Italian Provincial is of neoclassical inspiration and was strongly influenced by the French styles of the late 18th and early 19th centuries. Modern replicas are great improvements over the originals since they have been scaled down and reproportioned. Only the most graceful pieces have been revived.

Lines of cabinets (7), sideboards (2), desks (3) and chests (6) are predominantly rectangular with straight, square, tapered legs (4). Where curves appear in tables and dining chairs (1) and occasional pieces (5), they are smooth, graceful and unbroken by ornament. Wood is walnut, mahogany, fruitwoods, often painted or enameled. Brass hardware is common and molding often follows the outline of drawer or door (6,7).

SUGGESTIONS FOR USE. Italian Provincial can be used with French Provincial, American Colonial and other informal styles. Many occasional pieces can be used with formal 18th century and modern pieces because of the simplicity of design and the graceful proportions.

AMERICAN COLONIAL 1620-1790

HISTORICAL. "American Colonial" is a term applied rather loosely to all American furniture produced or used in the colonies prior to the Revolution. Actually it is a composite of several types of furniture including the rough, homemade pieces of the frontier, the New England versions of Jacobean and Cromwellian (Puritan) styles, the furniture imported from Europe by settlers and the Americanized versions of formal English and European periods. There is no clear line of demarcation but most authorities agree this era may be divided into Early Colonial and Late Colonial.

EARLY COLONIAL. The first New England settlers were Puritans and favored severely plain, utilitarian furniture. Consequently the furniture of the early colonies was an undecorated version of Jacobean styles supplemented by crude but efficient frontier pieces made on the spot from whatever wood was available. Sturdiness, simplicity and serviceability were prime requisites. Chests were of prime importance; these serving for both storage and seating in the early years. Tables (6) were generally of the trestle type. Benches, stools, cradles, cupboards (7) were other favored pieces.

As the colonies prospered, they attracted craftsmen who introduced better styling and a wider variety of pieces. Many were patterned after European models but usually the American versions were simplified. Popular chairs were bannister backs (1), ladder backs, rockers (5), butterfly and gate leg tables (3), high chests (4), cupboards (7) and settees. Chairs had seats of solid wood, leather, woven rushes (1,2,5). Upholstered pieces were scarce and usually imported. Early legs were rough-hewn and square; later ones show simple turning and shaping. Pine, birch, maple, walnut and other native woods were used.

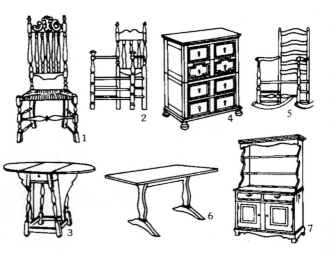

PENNSYLVANIA DUTCH 1680-1850

HISTORICAL. Eastern Pennsylvania, New Jersey and southern New York were settled principally by families of German (miscalled "Dutch" for Deutsch) and Swiss origin. They brought their own ideas of furniture-solid Germanic pieces suitable to the needs of a rural people. Because they retained their native speech and customs, they continued to produce furniture with distinctive characteristics for more than a century and a half.

GENERAL ATTRIBUTES. These furniture makers were excellent craftsmen who produced sturdy, plain pieces. Most famous contribution was the Kaz-the bride's dower chest (4)-a colorful and highly decorated storage box for linen, clothing, silver and china. Other characteristic pieces include the chest-on-chest cupboards (7), kneading tables, hanging cabinets and settees. Cabinets and chests are generally square. Legs are basically square (3) or round (2,5)with simple shaping or turnings. Woods are native woods, walnut, maple, fruitwoods, pine. Decoration consists of painted floral, animal, fruit, human motifs, also sunbursts, medallions, geometric designs, initials and full names, usually in German script. Colors are bright and cheerful. Knobs and simple metal pulls predominate.

SUGGESTIONS FOR USE. Because of its simple forms and rustic utilitarianism, this style can be used with other provincial styles, like American Colonial, and with many contemporary modes of furniture.

AMERICAN LATE COLONIAL 1700-1790

HISTORICAL.   In the early 18th century, the American Colonies were relatively prosperous. Wealthy colonists imported Queen Anne and early Chippendale and French styles. These were promptly copied by local cabinet makers and artisans. The designs were altered in many respects to suit American tastes. American "Chippendale" chairs have higher backs and lack the ornate carvings of the originals. Back legs of cabriole chairs are straighter. Pieces such as the desk bookcase, the highboy and the wing chair were modified versions of European originals. The rocker-originally a rural piece-became popular. Windsor chairs, Hitchcock chairs, and four-poster beds with pineapple finials became popular. Later styles were variations of Georgian and Louis XV styles. Favorite woods were maples, oak and walnut.

Note: Early American furniture was subject to geographical influences. New England modeled after English styles. Virginia and the southern colonies accepted both French and English styles. Florida, California and the Southwest were influenced by Spain; New York, the Dutch; Delaware by the Swedes; Pennsylvania and New Jersey by Germans.

SUGGESTIONS FOR USE.   Early Colonial pieces have rustic, rugged simplicity and go well with French Provincial, Shaker, other cottage styles. However, most current replicas are made of maple and are best when mixed with other maple or fruitwood pieces. Late Colonial goes well with Biedermeier, Italian Provincial and 18th century styles.

WINDSOR CHAIRS 1725-1800

Windsor chairs were named for Windsor Castle, but it was in America that they attained their greatest popularity and their most graceful styling. Because they were sturdy, attractive, light and comfortable, they became the favorite chair in the average American home. Originally these chairs were made by wheelwrights rather than cabinet makers, hence the use of a bent wood back frame, supported by spindles, and legs pegged into saddle seats. Many variations in shape-comb (4), fan (6), hoop (1), and bow backs, rockers (5) and braced (3) backs were common-some models were given the names of the city of origin or of prominent users. Later, settees, beds, tables and other pieces were introduced. Woods were varied: pine and birch for the seats; hickory, ash and birch for the bent parts; and oak, maple, birch for turned parts.

SHAKER 1776-1850

HISTORICAL. The Shakers, an American religious sect deriving from the Quakers, appeared first in New York during the Revolutionary War and spread all over the east, establishing semi-monastic, communal villages. Religion dominated their daily life, simplicity was the first requirement in all their activities, and hard work was not only an economic but a moral obligation. They looked down on trade and made everything they needed with their own hands.

GENERAL ATTRIBUTES. The Shakers were good craftsmen and their pieces show excellent workmanship. The major characteristic is the complete absence of decoration. In some communities even paint or heavy stain was frowned on and light varnish was the rule. No carving, veneering, inlays or fancy turning was permitted. Chairs, tables, desks and chests were severely functional in design. Legs of chairs and tables were round or square, tapering slightly toward the foot (1,2,6). Desks and chests rested flat on the floor. Construction details include exposed dove tailing, omission of moldings, low seats on chairs and settees. Shaker craftsmen were clever innovators and produced such pieces as swivel chairs (5) and swivel stools for desks. Early chairs were usually slat back construction (1), later ones made use of spindles. Double sewing stands (4), pedestal tables, rockers (3) and tilting chairs were clever Shaker products. Favorite wood was native pine, but maple, fruitwoods and other native hardwoods were also used.

SUGGESTIONS FOR USE. Excellently proportioned with good line and symmetry, Shaker furniture is acceptable to modern tastes. It can be mixed with any variation of provincial furniture.

AMERICAN FEDERAL 1795-1830

HISTORICAL. The Federal period covers the era between Late Colonial and Victorian in America. (Some authorities divide this into two periods: the Federal, extending from 1781 to 1800, and American Empire, 1800-1830). It is dominated by the work of Duncan Phyfe who set the pace for other craftsmen. The chief sources of inspiration were French Empire styles, but 18th century and colonial influences are apparent in much of the furniture produced.

GENERAL ATTRIBUTES. American pieces of 18th century inspiration (3) are more severe than English pieces. Only the simplest turnings are used (5), and American pieces are frequently braced with stretchers. The figure of the wood supplies most of the decoration. The pineapple finial is characteristic where carving is used.

American pieces of Empire derivation are sturdier and heavier than their French originals. Reeded columns, claw feet and bracket feet are commonly used. Legs of chairs, tables and settees are straight. Sofas have rolled arms. Chests have irregular fronts and mirrors. Center tables rest on heavy pedestals. Sideboards are heavy and decorated with columns (6). Metal mounts are extensively used. Acanthus, cornucopias, glass knobs, scrolls, pineapples are favorite motifs as are patriotic themes (2,4). Mahogany is the favorite wood with occasional use of oak, ash, hickory and fruitwoods.

SUGGESTIONS FOR USE. Rrefer to the Duncan Phyfe recommendations. Empire pieces go well with French Empire pieces. Good reproductions of both 18th century and Empire pieces are currently being produced by many factories.

DUNCAN PHYFE 1790-1830

HISTORICAL. Duncan Phyfe was America's first great furniture designer. His furniture has distinctive features as a style, yet it partakes of several contemporary styles. His work can be divided into two groups: 1790-1820, 18th century inspiration (Sheraton, Adams, Hepplewhite); and 1820-1830, American Empire (Federal). Phyfe was a craftsman who conformed to prevailing preferences.

GENERAL ATTRIBUTES. Early Duncan Phyfe pieces are modeled after the furniture of Hepplewhite, Sheraton and Adam. Yet he gave even these a distinctive touch. The lyre motif was used by Sheraton and French designers, but Phyfe made it his own and it is an easily recognizable characteristic (6,7). Later furniture is strongly influenced by French Empire. His pieces are noted for fine proportion, excellent construction and careful combining of straight lines with curves. Decoration consists of turning, fluting, reeding, carving, occasional painting, of brass as terminals for legs and lyre-strings, and china and glass knobs. Motifs are acanthus, cornucopias, leaves of oak, palm and laurel, lion's heads (8), medallions, wheat (10), swags. He used mahogany almost exclusively. Upholstery fabrics favored are silks, satins, brocades, woolens, and, later, horsehair.

CHAIRS. Chairs have both straight and curved (1,7) legs, usually carved or fluted to direct the eye. Chairs with x-crossed legs show Pompeiian influence. Turned ornamentation, including parallel rings, is common. Wooden bosses hide dowel joints. Back legs are usually splayed (1, 7). Chair backs are low and have rolled-over top rails (1,3,7). Cane panels and crossed splats are often used but lyre back (7) is distinctive. Seat rails are left uncovered. Upholstery is often tacked down in front with rows of close-set nails. Horseshoe-shaped seats are found on early models. Feet are plain (1), turned or carved.

TABLES. Most Phyfe tables have single lyre or column pedestals and curule (2,6,9,13) feet-sometimes three, sometimes four being used. This is a distinctive feature of modern reproductions. Other tables have carved molding or side rails (3) and straight, reeded legs with turned feet. Curule feet are often covered with brass tips.

Phyfe also designed other pieces such as sewing tables, dressing tables (4), beds, wash stands. His sofas have classic lines and "sleigh front" arms (5,11). Some have arms of wood with lyre motif (3) and curule legs. Others have upholstered arms and carved feet (12). Phyfe made no sideboards.

SUGGESTIONS FOR USE. His dining room pieces, especially tables, blend well with other 18th century mahogany (Sheraton, Hepplewhite, especially). His later Empire pieces go well with Adam, English Regency, French Empire, other Federal pieces. Occasional pieces are harmonious with most 18th century furniture.

IMPORTANT NOTE. Duncan Phyfe, while a definite furniture style, is not a true period. His early work was done at the end of the late Colonial period and was influenced by the late Georgian styles. His later work falls into the American Federal-Empire period, which he dominated, when the inspiration was predominately French. It is suggested that the reader refer to both the Colonial and the Federal pages of this book for more information.

ART NOUVEAU 1890-1905

HISTORICAL. Art Nouveau furniture was carved and painted wood embellished with polished brass and copper, painted vellum and rich silks. The curving flowing line of this furniture gives a feeling of airy lightness and grace. Nature appears to be the source for much of the furniture design and art work of this period depicting trees, flowers and animals.

Most of the Art Nouveau furniture makers were architects anxious to extend their control within the interiors of their buildings. Many of these designs were stripped down to elegant bare curves. Others were covered with carvings, brass, gilt or ivory. Some furniture was designed for comfort and utility. Other pieces were only designed for effect and charm. The majority of this furniture was a luxury item for the elite.

Some handmade pieces, mainly by Galle', were carved in plant or insect form. Surfaces were covered with intricate inlays featuring landscapes, plants or insects. Other designers tended to avoid the overtly floral detailing and concentrated instead on the light flowing lines of this era. The brief decade and a half of this style belies its importance in the history of furniture and art. The designs of Louis Comfort Tiffany were in great demand then and now.

GENERAL ATTRIBUTES. The essence of Art Nouveau is a sinuous curve found in every design. Some of the furniture is embellished with rich ornamentation using expressions of nature in elongated stamens, stems and leaves. Twisting ironwork, entwined vines, tendrils, and symbolistic female faces are found in lamps, magazine racks and architecture.

SUGGESTIONS FOR USE. The handmade pieces of furniture in the Art Nouveau design, an art object or accessory is timeless.

ART DECO 1908-1930

HISTORICAL. The early Art Deco style of furniture had a rich emphasis on detail and intimacy. Arm chairs became longer and deeper and stood on lower legs. Cushions were made in luxurious fabrics with long silk tassels. Dining room chairs had small rounded backs and dining room tables had one pedestal instead of four to six legs. Beds were lower and built-in cupboards were being widely used for the first time.

The development of the Art Deco style brought with it not only the change of forms but of materials and finishes. The dark woods, oak and walnut, were replaced with a taste for more exotic woods with a decorative grain or pattern. As the decade progressed, the whole feeling of furniture became heavier. Legs became more solid and ornamentation began to disappear.

In 1930, Le Corbusier and a number of other architects and designers were pioneers of design as we now see it. They made extensive use of steel, aluminum, glass and plain rough leather. They were the first designers to promote stackable furniture.

Many artists identified with the Art Deco style show the influence of Modernism and Cubism. Many of the paintings and sculptures depict animals. Sculptors of the nineteenth century created so many small-scale animal sculptures they were called Animaliers. Small statuettes, the majority of which were fantasy female figures, were cast in bronze. Many were of carved ivory in a combination with gilded and patinated metal with semiprecious stones. Today these beautiful statuettes have acquired enormous period charm and are much sought after. One of the most memorable painters of this era was Georges Lepape who created the lovely languid ladies for the covers of Vogue magazine. Erté, a prolific artist of this period, designed not only clothing, costumes for revues, opera and ballet but also scenery for theatrical productions.

The classically beautiful furniture designs, painting, sculpture, jewelry and pottery from the Art Deco period were forerunners of what we term today as Modern.

GENERAL ATTRIBUTES. Art Deco is smart or elegant. Many pieces of furniture were made of palmwood, zebrawood, maple or ash. Wrought iron, metal and glass were incorporated into these designs. Deep primary colors came into favor. Fruit and flowers, mother-of-pearl, enamel, animals and nudes with flowing locks are all Art Deco motifs found on furniture, pictures and art objects.

SUGGESTIONS FOR USE. The sleek simplicity of Art Deco furniture will give a feeling of opulence to a contemporary setting. Candlesticks, often in a combination of metal and bronze, a small sculpture, an ebony armchair or a mirror rimmed with mother-of-pearl will give a touch of luxury to any decor.

Examples of furniture made during the Art Deco period.

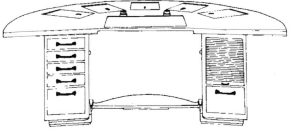

Art Deco Cabinet in White Painted Wood - Designed by Prutscher around 1910.
Art Deco Desk in Macassar Wood and Gilt-Bronze by Ruhlmann - made around 1926.
Line drawings courtesy of the publication "In The Deco Style" (Klein, McClelland, Haslam).

MODERN/CONTEMPORARY (A PERIOD IN TRANSITION.)

HISTORICAL. Until the time of the 1925 Paris Exposition, almost all American furniture consisted of reproductions of historical periods. Inspired by the "art moderne" style of the French, American designers now turned their attention to the creation of truly modern furniture. These early designers relied on geometric forms and exotic woods. They were greeted with some wonder and much ridicule but they did pave the way to today's modern furniture.

Following these early efforts, progress was rapid. The famous Bauhaus of Germany made outstanding contributions to modern furniture design. More and more American designers, like the late Gilbert Rohde, created pieces of simple design, practical utility, wide public appeal. The Chicago Exposition of 1933 gave modern furniture further impetus. Today it is by far the most popular single style.

In considering modern furniture, however, it should be remembered that modern cannot be defined and delineated as historical periods are. Styles such as Victorian, Louis XVI and Chippendale have firmly established characteristics, common lines, ornamental and decorative details. Types of legs, arms, backs and pediments, and similar identifying features are historically fixed.

Modern or Contemporary on the other hand, is a style still developing and will always remain in a state of transition. New changes occur as contemporary designers add their interpretations, ranging from simplification and adaptation of traditional designs to original creations bordering on the bizarre.

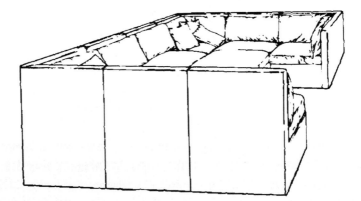

In any consideration of current modern furniture the mass production methods of present factories must be carefully weighed. Clean, simple lines and the elimination of unnecessary ornament have made modern furniture quite practical for quantity production. As long as this condition prevails, and as long as American tastes lean toward the restrained, unembellished forms, modern-by whatever name it is called-will enjoy maximum popularity.

GENERAL ATTRIBUTES. Because modern is constantly changing, definite limitations on its characteristics cannot be set. In general, however, the lines are clean, simple, restrained. Flat surfaces and straight lines are combined with graceful curves. While it is no longer severely functional, the utility of each piece is clearly indicated and greatly influences design and construction. Incidental details which do not contribute to usefulness or comfort have been reduced. Designers and manufacturers seek clean-lined contours, attractive proportion and subtle dignity to achieve unity of design. Comfort and eye appeal are major factors.

Ornament for ornament's sake has been eliminated. There is no deep carving to collect dust, no finials, urns or pediments to break off. Applied decoration is avoided. Inlay is rarely used. Knobs and pulls are functional, harmonizing with design.

Legs are smooth and undecorated. They may be square and tapered, or round and tapered or even of metal. Sofas and upholstered pieces are light in scale, with legs and graceful proportions. They are straight lined or gently curved, but are marked by deep springs and careful tailoring. End tables, coffee tables, dining tables, bookcases, serving carts, cabinets and desks are essentially functional. The bed's footboard is very low, or more likely, has been eliminated. Bookcase and cabinet headboards or platform beds are popular.

Virtually all types of cabinet woods are used. Veneer is employed on a broad scale. Matched grains and wood patterns furnish ornamentation. Employment of light and bleached woods is common. Metals, plastics and glass are sometimes used. Fabrics on the modern furniture of the 1930's were predominately in solid colors. Now, stripes, floral designs and overall patterns are common. Where solid colors are employed, interest is supplied by texture or by novelty weaves. Colors range from bright to pastel. Plastic and plastic coated fabrics are popular.

SUGGESTIONS FOR USE. Although modern pieces can be used with traditional period pieces, and many decorators recommend it, modern is at its best when used alone. It goes well with Chinese Chippendale and the simple Sheraton pieces but tends to look out of place with Victorian and other ornately curved types.

CONTÉMPORARY AND FUNCTIONAL. Both of these terms have been widely used in describing modern furniture but confusion exists over their true meanings. Actually "functional" truly refers only to those pieces where mechanical action influences design. "Contemporary," by dictionary definition, means the current designs of the day, but this term describes also furniture in a modernized form of classic design. Much of the "modern" furniture being sold today falls into the "Contemporary" classification. Simple, graceful of line, it depends on beauty of good finish and design rather than on artificial decoration.

SECTIONAL MODERN. The "sectional assembly" type of furniture in this style category is highly in demand. Cases, chests, bed headboards and night stands are of uniform height and varieties of groupings may be assembled to fit varying architectural backgrounds and individual needs.

GLOBAL MODERN. The descriptions in this section apply to modern furniture of American origin. Other nations are also creating furniture representing a complete break with traditional styles. Many show evidence of being strongly influenced by American designers.

Since "modern" is an influence rather than a rigid style or period, it is constantly changing. It will pay the reader to study the trade papers and home planning magazines to know and recognize current trends.

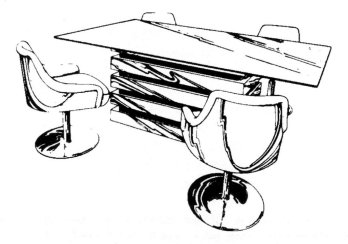

Two avant-garde contemporary designs from the Ligne Roset "style de vie" collection: "Fugue" a part of their modular upholstery system is shown above and "Paraphe" a low table in brown beech veneer, below. Ligne Roset, U.S. and Canada, http://www.ligne-roset-usa.com.

ORIENTAL MODERN

HISTORICAL. The Far East-China, Japan, India and neighboring nations-has contributed minimally to the development of furniture, even though their cultures are old. However, the oriental countries have historically had a great tradition in art and design and their influence, while remote, goes back to the 15th and 16th centuries. In recent years, their designers have made a strong and sometimes a resounding impact on furniture styling.

GENERAL ATTRIBUTES. The crisp lines of Chinese and Japanese chests, tables and chairs are to be seen in modern furniture everywhere. Leg terminations (1,4) still hint of the early Chinese culture as do geometric treatment of both upholstery and frames (2,3). Teak, koa and sometimes bamboo are favorite woods, with simple oil stains widely used. Walnut with a light filler is used for greyish or honey-toned effects. Oversize hardware (4) and accents, (beads, gold and silver with lacquer) are popular.

SUGGESTIONS FOR USE. Oriental furniture blends well into unstylized settings and is useful with formal styles for its accent value. Increasing world travel and instantaneous communications have shrunk the disparities between Orient and Occident, permitting each to adopt the best features of the other's culture and mode of living.

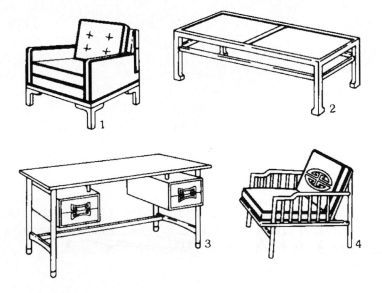

SCANDINAVIAN MODERN

HISTORICAL. During the 1930's Swedish and Danish designers produced outstanding modern pieces that were successfully marketed under the names "Swedish Modern" and "Danish Modern." Most of them were simplifications of more traditional Empire styles with plain, unadorned surfaces, graceful curves and smooth, tapered legs. The sculptured feeling emerges as their most distinctive characteristic. This style reached its peak of popularity in the 1950's but its influence is to be found in contemporary European and U.S. and Canadian furniture designs of today.

GENERAL ATTRIBUTES. Scandinavian is fundamentally decorative, its renditions running to chaste, even severe, silhouettes and an almost total absence of ornamental flourishes. This style's designers confine themselves to light, plain woods (walnut, teak) in simple curves and roundings, with tapered feet and flat turnings. Legs are square-tapered (4,5) or round-tapered (3). Woven fibers are used widely in chair seats (4) and modern plastics are evident in upholstery (1,2).

SUGGESTIONS FOR USE. Modern Scandinavian stylings are still in heavy demand for formal and informal living areas.

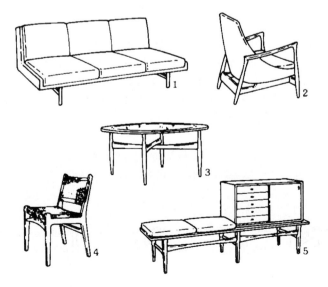

FRENCH COUNTRY

HISTORICAL. French Country is a classic style that combines beauty and charm with function. It is not a delicate look but one of substance. This style has evolved since the 13th century in the many provinces in the south of France where local craftsmen used native woods and materials to create furniture. This furniture reflects the warm, earthy, unpretentious and comfortable way of life in this region.

The design, ornamentation and refinement of this furniture vary in each province. Painted cupboards with simple lines are deep with drawers the right size for utensils and jars of jams and jellies. There are wide shelves for linens and clothing. In contrast, massive armoires made of beautiful woods are embellished with carvings of vines, wheat, ribbons, flowers or animals. The interior of these storage pieces was often lined with bright fabric.

Long kitchen tables, usually in a rectangular shape, were made of solid wood to withstand hard usage. These tables often had drawers or breadboards in each end. Chairs for the most part were simple, sturdy and rustic. Rush seated banquettes, seating three or four people, looked like chairs combined with an arm on either end. Seat backs were a curved slat type. These were painted in earth colors.

Beds were simple with arched or scalloped headboards and had plain posts and low footboards.

GENERAL ATTRIBUTES. French Country furniture is noted for its beautiful native woods-the soft patina of walnut, olive wood, pearwood, and cherry. Wrought iron work, ferrures, enhance the finer pieces. The ferrures are found on cabinet doors and drawers. Painted pieces are charming in colors of soft blue, faded red, olive or worn yellow. Metal park chairs, tables and benches have become popular pieces.

SUGGESTIONS FOR USE. French Country styles blend well in contemporary, country, and French settings. The classic armoires of this era would be a welcome addition to any decor.

Illustration page 61: Pine French Armoire with great molded doors, c. 1830, from Normandy. From the French Country Collection - Boones Antiques, Lexiton, Kentucky.

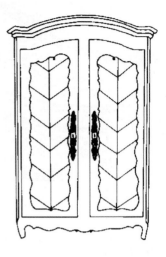

Early French Vasselier in oak, c. 1830, from Normandy

Large Cherry Armoire, 19th century - Typical of LeBerry area with carved cornice. Doors are crotch cherry in herringbone pattern.

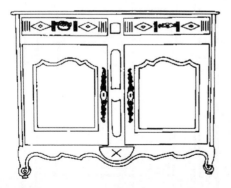

Large Cherry Buffet c. 1780, from Normandy with carved drawers and molded doors.

Ferrures

From the French Country Collection - Boones Antiques, Lexington, Kentucky

The popular armoire, shown here in bedroom setting, is at home in any room today--and certainly a beautiful addition. The buffet is also from the French Country Collection of Thomasville Furniture Industries, Thomasville, North Carolina. Reprinted from Furniture Facts© 27th Edition.

AMERICAN COUNTRY

HISTORICAL.   The earliest settlers in America were far from home and family and tried to create a setting that was similar to the lifestyle they left behind. Many brought family pieces with them and these were copied by local craftsmen for homes in their area. In the 17th and 18th centuries, most colonists were still using styles and fashions from their home countries. As the population increased and people moved inland and to other coastal areas the new styles the settlers brought with them were copied by country carpenters who followed the general design but added their own interpretation to the piece. This was the start of the true country look. Wood was plentiful and pieces were made of cherry, pine and maple. Different nationalities added their special touches to the needed furniture and many painted pieces in the form of cupboards, tables, chairs and chests became a part of this style of furniture. These primitive pieces, simple and sturdy and of fine woods were not considered collectibles until the 1920's when they began to gain some popularity.

GENERAL ATTRIBUTES.   The common denominator of American Country is a mood rather than just actual furniture. It is a harmonious mix of many textures, materials and colors. American Country is a homey style where comfort and ease reign. The furniture is often unique, incorporating design features of other periods, the wood made mellow by years of wear and love. This vigorous, glowing furniture is combined with quilts, hanging on the wall or as coverlets on the beds, handmade baskets to hold wood, magazines, the cat or your knitting, rag rugs, stoneware crocks and pillows and curtains made of a homespun type fabric. The colors are from nature -- yellow, blue-gray, persimmon, natural and woodsy green. Upholstered pieces are plump-often without exposed wood with slipcovers for a seasonal change.

Stepback cupboards, simple stools with woven seats, chairs with sturdy legs and detailed rungs, benches to pull up to the fire and low chests with hinged covers that were used for seating and to hold clothing and linens all have a country heritage. Furniture was often dual-purpose: beds with blanket rails; chairs with pull-over tables; chests with alternate table tops; etc.

SUGGESTIONS FOR USE.   The simple lines of this furniture mix well with Contemporary, American Colonial, French Provincial, and Shaker. American Country is at home in city apartments as well as rural settings.

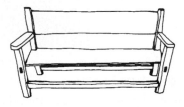

Classic American Oak dining room grouping. Thomasville Furniture Industries, Thomasville, North Carolina. Reprinted from <u>Furniture Facts</u>© 27th Edition.

THE "EARLY AMERICAN" STYLE

HISTORICAL. Furniture was built by itinerant country craftsmen using native maple, pine, cherry, birch, and other local woods. The simple designs, influenced by provincial farmhouse furniture of the English and Dutch, were made entirely of solid wood. Constructed solidly for daily use, the fact that so much of what was built in the 19th century is still in use today attests to its solid durability.

The more formal furniture built in the Colonies and later as the country evolved into the United States was made by master craftsmen who immigrated from the British Isles. This furniture was strongly influenced by English designers including many classic elements of design. It, too, was made mostly of native hardwoods.

Pennsylvania Dutch farmhouse furniture significantly influenced Early American furniture. The style accounted for over one-half of furniture sold during the two decades following World War II. Unfortunately, most of this was priced at the low end, damaging the image of the style, and causing some of the finest makers of Early American furniture to go out of business in the 60's. These included Burkey & Gay, Consider H. Willet and Cushman.

Early American with all of its design elements has continued to be important in the U.S. market. Antique Early American furniture that ranges from the crudest pieces made by itinerant cabinet builders for use in farmhouses, to those incredibly beautiful pieces showcased in the finest homes, is much in demand and are bringing record-breaking high prices.

This style is important and its influence can still be seen in much of the furniture sold in the U.S. today.

GENERAL ATTRIBUTES. Decorative flourishes such as are observed in the arms of the sofa (2) and the hutch scrolls (3) are prevalent, and ornately turned legs (1) are common. Drawer pulls and escutcheons tend toward garnished effects. Mechanical equipment is used widely to provide dual-purpose pieces such as the sofabed (2), the swivel chair (4), and the rocking chair. Maple and the fruitwoods are used extensively, with ash, hickory and pine sometimes employed. Natural finishes prevail.

SUGGESTIONS FOR USE. Casual living areas, such as dens, libraries, family and TV rooms, lend themselves to Early American furniture pieces as do the more formal rooms of the home if their themes run to the provincial. In many of our larger cities whole stores are now being devoted exclusively to Early American pieces, with the widest selection imaginable.

"AMERICAN MEDITERRANEAN" STYLE

HISTORICAL. The countries on the north shores of the Mediterranean Sea, notably Spain, Italy and Greece, have made timely contributions to the advance of European furniture styling. Like French Provincial and Italian Provincial (which was largely developed in the north of Italy), the Mediterranean influence sprang from local peasant craftsmen who used native woods and materials to build furniture for local use. The Moorish influence had a considerable effect on the decor, and on the lavish use of high color and abstract geometric patterns which the Spanish and Italian artisans adapted. While the Mediterranean spirit prospered from the 16th century on, it lost some of its appeal in the late 19th century. It has enjoyed some popularity in recent years, often called Spanish Modern.

GENERAL ATTRIBUTES. Mediterranean furniture runs the gamut from almost primitively functional to extremely formal. Spanish pieces favor the vigorous, masculine look with deep moldings. Italian interpretations are more restrained. They are "built to the floor" with comparatively short, squat, ornately turned legs and feet. Facades of chests, cupboards, cabinets and the headboards of bedsteads have a sculptural feeling with decorations of frets and guilloches (3). Hardware is heavy (2), sometimes burnished. Hip-joint chairs (4) have frames suggesting two semicircles joined together. One set forms the legs, the other the framework of the seat. Geometric interlacing (1), turned spindles (6) are common. Pecan, chestnut, walnut, red pine and mahogany are favorite woods.

Many opulent Florida estates have caused Mediterranean style to retain its popularity with its classic forms.

CAPSULE COMMENT ABOUT OTHER FURNITURE STYLES

ART MODERNE. An extreme, modernistic French style launched at the Paris Exposition of 1925, characterized by straight lines, angles and geometric decoration.

ARTS & CRAFTS 1900-1920. Artisans reaction to industrialization resulted in a resurgence of craftsmen and artists in the U.S. The period produced many designs and designers of note.

AMERICAN FRONTIER 1790-1890. Furniture of this type was created to meet the demands of the frontier. Originally derived from Jacobean and used by the early settlers in the Midwest, it persisted in rural and ranch settlements as the frontier moved westward. Characteristic pieces were wagon seat twin chairs, highback settees, sinks without plumbing, food cupboards, cobblers' benches. Woods were ash, hickory, black walnut, maple and pine. Pieces usually painted in black or primary colors.

AMERICAN RANCH. Ranch furniture of the early West was heavy, sturdy, plain and utilitarian, often showing strong influence of the native woods and craftsmen of Mexico, and on the West Coast, Spanish. Includes furniture for virtually every room of the home.

Ranch furniture is an informal, provincial style. Simple and rustic in design. Use of leather, interlaced cord or rawhide and surfaces of joined boards, with no attempt to hide junctures, help maintain the western pioneer atmosphere. Wooden seats are flat, not hollowed, and decorative cushions are frequently used. Legs are usually square-cornered and tapered, but occasionally are turned. Southwest decorative motifs and hardware with color themes and finishes suggested by the hues of desert foliage. Primary native woods are employed. Augmented by Mexico imports and designs to become a definite style factor-for both casual living and more formal homes.

BORAX. Not strictly a period style, this word came into use circa 1920. It is applied to cheaply made furniture. It has since come to be synonymous with all tacky, cheaply made furniture as well as the questionable ethics of those who deal in these products.

CAROLEAN 1660-1688. Also called Restoration and Late Jacobean. Named after Charles II, but included reign of James II. A period of reaction from Cromwellian austerity. Elaborate, deep carving, spiral turning or twirls on legs and stretchers, molded paneling are characteristics. Stretchers are elaborately carved. Scroll feet are used on chairs, tables and bed terminals. Cane seats are common. Rich tapestries used for upholstery. Oak, occasionally walnut, favored.

COMMONWEALTH 1649-1660. Also called Puritan, Cromwellian and Middle Jacobean, this was a complete departure from ornate furniture of the Stuart (Early Jacobean) period. Pieces are straight and severe with very little decoration. Proportions are square and rectangular. Bulbous legs have disappeared. Chairs have stout underbracing, the stretchers often being raised from the floor. High straight backs and low seats are found on settees. Somber-hued upholstery is the rule. Oak predominates.

DIRECTOIRE 1795-1804. Following the Revolution France was ruled by five directors. Signs of aristocracy and royalty were diminished. Furniture design was controlled by a Jury of Arts and Manufactures. Griffins, caryatides and classic ornament replaced royal decorations. Greek, Egyptian and Roman influence is strong. Pieces have grace, elegance, simplicity and purity of line.

DUTCH RENAISSANCE 1500-1600. Interesting mainly because of Dutch influence on later English styles. The furniture itself is square, solid, heavy, with straight lines predominating. Turned legs, straight stretchers, straight, low backs characterize the chairs. Carving is chief decoration with foliated ornament and scroll work. Seats are sometimes covered with leather attached by heavy brass nails. Oak predominates.

EASTLAKE. A style, designed by Charles Eastlake, which achieved popularity in England and America from about 1879 to 1895. It consisted of furniture of medieval outline with Gothic and sometimes Japanese ornamentation. Cherry wood and other fruitwoods were extensively used. Metal and tile panels, conspicuous hardware used in decoration. Original pieces have become highly sought after by collectors.

EGYPTIAN 4000-300 B.C. Important because of influence on later craftsmen and because it shows antiquity of furniture shapes, chairs, inlay, carved decoration. Pieces were highly colorful and decorative. Carving featured lotus and papyrus, animal and human forms. Frames were mortised and had cane or leather seats. Feet were elaborately carved. Loose cushions were common. Sycamore, yew, cedar and olive wood were used. Ivory, gold and jewels were inlaid.

FLEMISH 17TH CENTURY. This refers to furniture produced by the craftsmen of Flanders (Belgium) and is interesting as an influence rather than as a distinct period. Flemish furniture is generally included as part of the Dutch Renaissance. Actually it differed in many respects due to French influence. Flemish pieces are noted for elaborate and skillful carving. The Flemish foot is another contribution.

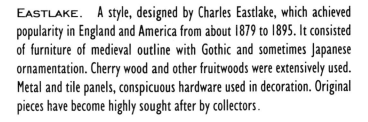

FRENCH CLASSIC 1760-1785. This furniture, an influence rather than a true style, climaxes a revolt against the curved line and was inspired by the Italian imitation of antiquity. The vertical spirit prevailed, accentuated by fluting and grooving, while curves were straightened out. All ornament was classic and symmetrical; geometric marquetry was popular. Mahogany was used freely; rosewood, tulipwood and even ebony less frequently.

FRENCH EMPIRE 1804-1815. This expressed the imperial ambitions of Napoleon and was created at his command. Of classical Greek and Roman inspiration, it is ponderous and ostentatious, but has a certain classic dignity. It is simple in construction, depending on varnish and high polish for beauty. Motifs are symbolic of empire wreaths, torches, Roman eagles, lions, sphinx and the letter "N" enclosed in the visitor's wreath. Metal feet are common, curves are few, table tops often of marble. Mahogany, rosewood and ebony were used.

FRENCH REGENCE 1715-1723. Covers the first years of the reign of Louis XV when Phillip of Orleans was regent. Departs in design and form from Louis XIV, yet retains many basic forms. It introduces rococo ornamentation. Fantastic curves and elaborate decoration are the rule. Many eccentric designs result, yet effect is sometimes pleasing. Many new pieces-commodes, secretaries and chiffoniers were used.

FRENCH RENAISSANCE 1453-1610. Covers reigns of many rulers, Francis I, Henry II, Henry IV, the most important. Inspiration came from Italy, but the furniture is smaller in scale than Italian Renaissance. Chiefly noted for elaborateness and excellence of wood carving, and for progress in textile manufacture, weaving of tapestries. Oak predominates in early pieces, walnut in later ones.

GOTHIC 1180-1509. Pieces were large, straight and heavy. Much of it was produced in monasteries, hence ornamentation consisted of canonical figures and other ecclesiastical carvings. Trestle tables, stools and cupboards were produced. The box chair with paneled fronts and sides, high paneled back and storage space beneath seat was a favorite. Oak and pine were principal woods.

GRAND RAPIDS STYLE 1900 -1950. At the turn of the century, Grand Rapids, Michigan was the center of manufacturing and marketing for furniture in the U.S. Furniture with the words "made in Grand Rapids" came to be the hallmark for quality. Names like Baker, Century, Herman, Miller, Stickley Bros., and many others were trend setters. This furniture was made in many styles and periods. One of the most popular items, still produced today, is the pedestal oak table.

HITCHCOCK STYLE 1820-1850. Created by Lambert Hitchcock, a Connecticut craftsman. His best-known pieces are chairs derived from Sheraton designs and have an oval turned (pillow back) top rail, turned legs, rush or cane seat enclosed in wooden strips. Usually of maple, painted to simulate rosewood or ebony and decorated with powdered gold stencil fruit and flowers. Hitchcock produced chairs, stools, settees, cradles, rockers, cabinets, and chairs. The chairs are a very popular design and are being reproduced today.

ITALIAN RENAISSANCE 1400-1600. Furniture shows classical inspiration. Lavishly decorated with carving, inlay, marquetry and classic figures. Chairs are straight and square, built on flat runners with heavy stretchers. Tables are large and rectangular, heavily decorated, braced with stretchers. Walnut predominates.

JACOBEAN 1603-1649. Covers the reigns of James I and Charles I. Some authorities include all furniture of 17th century in this designation. Furniture is large, square and rectangular lines are dominant. Wood is extensively carved in low relief. Chairs have flat seats and low stretchers. Tables have stretchers and rectangular shapes. Virtually all this furniture is of oak.

LOUIS XIII 1610-1643. Furniture of this period follows straight lines for the most part. Chairs and beds are square. Cabinets are divided into two parts, with square panels and broken pediments. Twisted columns, spiral legs and turned balusters are prominent. Inlay, marquetry, elaborate relief carvings and incrustation are favored decorations. Principal woods used are ebony, walnut and oak.

LOUIS XIV 1643-1715. This is also known as the Baroque period. Louis XIV, a patron of the arts, encouraged furniture designing. Pieces are constructed on a massive, formal scale. Straight lines predominate. Chairs are high-backed, carved and upholstered. Marble-topped console tables with elaborately carved understructure are typical. Legs are rather heavy with underbracing on both tables and chairs. Oak, walnut, and ebony are principal woods used. Decorative details include metal mounts, elaborate carving, painting, gilding and inlay. Cloven hoofs, fauna and nymphs, acanthus leaves are basic motifs.

MISSION 1895-1910. Mission gained greatest popularity during this era. It was a development of furniture originating in Southern California. Desks, tables and chairs are included. Pieces are of oak, simple, square and sturdy entirely without decoration. Legs are straight and joined with stretchers. Chair backs are composed of plain slats. Seats are of cane, rush or solid wood. This style was largely utilitarian. The architect Frank Lloyd Wright was influenced by this functional style. A resurgence of interest-especially to use with modern upholstered pieces has caused furniture designers to reproduce more of the Mission style furniture.

ORIENTAL 1500-1800. Japanese and especially Chinese art and furniture have influenced Western furniture styles through the years without ever being a major factor in the industry. Chinese furniture is lacquered, with much reliance on relief carving for decoration. Chairs, chests and small tables are simple in line and construction and depend on delicate decoration for beauty. Teak, sandalwood and bamboo are favorite woods. Chinese rugs and wallpaper are famous. Lattice work strongly influenced Chippendale.

SPANISH RENAISSANCE 1500-1700. Strong Moorish influence. Wood surfaces are elaborately carved with geometric moldings, inlay in Moorish patterns, ornate metal mounts and studding of large brass nails. Bright green and red leather upholstery. Pieces have elaborate wood or iron stretchers, carved feet. Writing desk or varguena, (shown here) was popular in the U.S. in 1920's. Woods: walnut, oak and cedar. It can be used with other Renaissance styles. The style is still popular in the south and west U.S.

TUDOR-ELIZABETHAN 1509-1603. Covers 16th century and is a phase of the English Renaissance. Furniture shows continental Renaissance influence in elaborate carving and decoration but furniture shapes are stiff and straight like Gothic. Underbracing on chairs, tables and cabinets. All pieces are massive. Oak predominates.

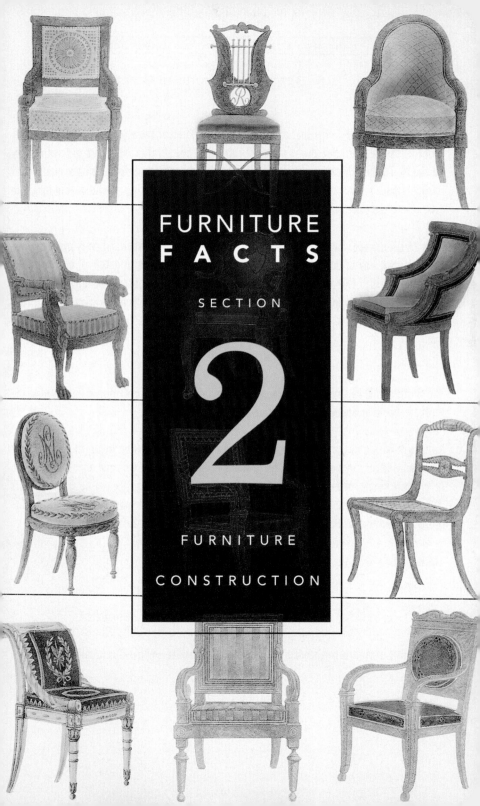

FURNITURE FACTS

SECTION

2

FURNITURE

CONSTRUCTION

HOW BETTER FURNITURE IS BUILT

Antique furniture still in use that dates back three hundred or more years is proof that better furniture can be built. Not always the most expensive, but always constructed to basic quality standards. The fact that many, if not most, of these methods feature the same basic quality and standards found in furniture built today is even more proof that investing in good quality furniture even at medium price points is a good investment.

There are a multitude of ways that furniture can be built better or cheaper and every manufacturer has their own way of doing what they do. It would be impossible to detail all of them. The objective here is to give a comprehensive outline of those features of construction and materials which are commonly found in better grades of furniture. This will include traditional and current processes and materials.

ATTRIBUTES OF QUALITY

The finish should be smooth and agreeable to the touch. If stain or varnish is employed in the finish, it should be applied evenly and to a uniform thickness.

For design and decoration reasons, most of the structural details of furniture are hidden. Most of the details and construction features of well-made furniture can't be seen and almost none of the benefits are visible. When the salesperson or Interior Designer makes the prospective customers aware of their needs for the benefits of these unseen features and demonstrate how the benefits of these features meet their needs it is persuasive and convincing reasons to buy.

The method used for the construction of all joints is proof of:

♦   strength, or
♦   an indication that shortcuts were taken and weaknesses are probable.

The detailing of construction, sanding or finishing of undersides and backs is usually a sign of high quality.

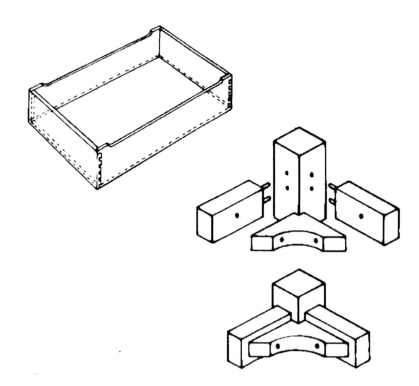

Construction features: (Above.) Good drawer construction with concealed dovetail at front, dovetail back ends and shaped sides; corner strengthened by dowels and corner blocks.

DOWEL JOINTS. The dowel joint (*above and below*) is perhaps the most common method of joining and is quite strong. The dowel is a peg of hardwood, or sometimes steel, fitted into holes in the pieces to be joined. Grooved dowels which prevent the forming of air pockets in the glue are superior to smooth ones. In better grade chairs, dowels are used in joining the side rails to the legs and this joint is further strengthened by using a corner block. Grooved dowel, glue dowel, corner dowel (below, left to right).

MORTISE AND TENON JOINTS. This type of glued joint (*right*) supplies a strong union. It is used to join stretchers to leg posts or top slats to the back post of the chair. When a good glue process is used, it is one of the most satisfactory methods. Below, left to right, other tenon joints not as prevalent today. Loose tenon or feather joint. Common mortise and tenon. Round or peg tenon. Blind housed tenon. Dovetail half-lap joint.

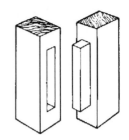

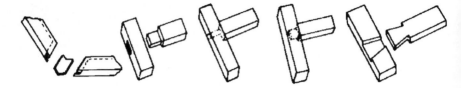

DOVETAIL JOINTS. Have traditionally been considered a benchmark for quality drawer construction. Its purpose is to stabilize drawer fronts so that years of use won't loosen them. In earlier construction, notched (and often, concealed) dovetailing was used.

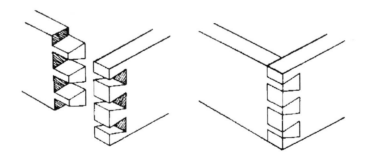

GLUE JOINTS. Plain glue or rub joint. Double-groove and loose tongue joint. Tongue and groove (A) and (B). (*Below, left to right.*)

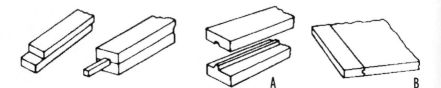

A   B

CORNER BLOCKS & JOINTS. Corner blocks (illustrated, previous page) are essential at the point of greatest strain. They are used to strengthen corners of seat frames and prevent the dowels from cracking under pressure. Corner joints: (*left to right below*) : Plain corner butt. Lap butt. Lock joint. Plain mitre joint.

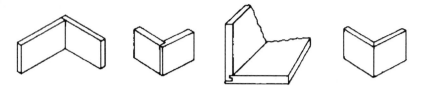

CHAIRS. Box seat chairs, such as dining room and occasional chairs, are produced in a wide variety of grades. Styling and finish account for much of the difference in price. There are certain points of construction common to these chairs which should also be considered. The diagram shows a box seat chair with its parts labeled. Assuming that good material has been used, important points to check are the joints which are subject to stress when in use and good craftsmanship is necessary.

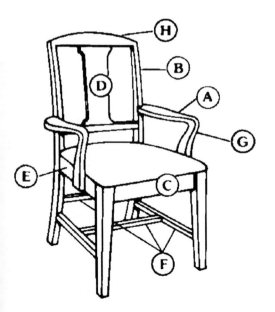

A. ARM

B. BACK POST

C. FRONT RAIL

D. SPLAT

E. SIDE RAIL

F. STRETCHERS

G. STUMP

H. TOP SLAT

SEATS. Most seats of this type of chair are simply pieces of plywood, padded and upholstered. In some types of seats, the weight is supported on webbing that is helically suspended from the frame. The helical springs supply added resilience, distribute the weight, and is more comfortable.

TABLES. So-called solid top tables are very seldom made from one solid slab of wood. Such a piece, if one could be found sufficiently free from defects and with a pattern of sufficient beauty, would be inclined to warp or split from atmospheric conditions. As a result, solid top tables are made by joining several boards together by simple glue joints or by tongue and groove joints. This can be done with superior craftsmanship so the joint is not visible. The majority of tops today are veneered. This type of construction (see veneers later in this section) gives both solid strength and firm resistance to warping and cracking; second, it permits the use of beautiful woods, the matching of grain figures to produce attractive effects, and the use of rare woods with unusual texture.

BRACING. For adequate strength, tables should be well braced at points of stress. Stretchers, if used, should be attached to the legs with mortise and tenon or with dowel joints. The corners should be braced either with corner blocks or steel braces. The latter are especially recommended in small tables which are made with KD (disassembled or knocked down for shipment) construction. Table tops should be held to frames with glue blocks, dowels or steel slips.

DRAWERS. Historically, the quality of wood furniture with drawers was based on the wood used, its joints, and slides. Center-guided drawers with dovetail corner joints were the standards of quality in case goods. Dust-proof panels between each set of drawers and at the base of the case were also indications of quality construction, their function was to stop air circulation that carried dust particles, thus protecting the contents of the drawers. Drawer pulls might be knobs, recessed finger grooves, hinged bales or fixed grips. Sticky, hard to open drawers was a problem with most case goods as humidity and other atmospheric conditions affected the wood.

CASE GOODS BUILT IN THE 21ST CENTURY "NEW AND IMPROVED."

DRAWERS.
♦ Drawer side guides with nylon wheels are commonly used.
♦ Wood or metal center guides allow smooth opening and closing of drawers.

♦ A variety of other drawer guide systems are in use. Comparing them is the easy way to see that the quality of these are still an important indicator of the quality of the furniture.

♦ Solid hardwood or premium plywood is still used in the construction of high quality furniture. Drawers of molded plastic are sometimes found in inexpensive furniture, but high grades of plastic are in use among high grades of furniture--especially in office furniture and contemporary style furniture.

THE CASE.

♦ The interior and back of case goods are still the best indicators of quality. The back panel on a case is an indicator of quality and usually means more attention was given to details. A recessed back panel cannot be seen from the side of the case. The method of attachment of the back panel to the case might include tacks, staples, screws, or be grooved vertically so the back panel slides into a frame.

♦ Dust proof panels, before air conditioning became prevalent in homes, were necessary to keep dust and air contaminates from discoloring garments in the drawers. They are still commonly found in case goods manufactured today, but are no longer essential.

♦ Drawer interiors should be sanded smooth to the touch and finished or waxed with no snags, burrs, or splits.

♦ Drawers with hardwood or quality plywood sides and backs with dovetail joints on all four corners are still the best indication of quality case goods. However, new methods, composite materials and successful developments in bonding materials permit good quality as well.

The quality of case goods is most evident when carefully examining the interior of the furniture.

RETURN MOLDINGS.
These are base moldings, or those under the top of the case and between the drawers on the outside of the case that are mitered and continue to the back of the case on both sides. These are quality details in some designs and styles.

LEGS.
The legs of case pieces are a crucial consideration for two reasons:

♦ When the drawers are full, the case is heavier. Poorly installed legs will break off when the case is moved. If you can see under the case, it is an area that must be cleaned and in all probability will be moved.

♦ Quality construction will reveal properly scaled and properly installed legs.

FURNITURE WOODS AND THEIR USE

Wood is an inherited part of the American Culture. Americans, as a whole, blessed with vast varieties of forests have, always preferred the warmth of wood grain to other materials of pattern or finish for their home furnishings. The more one knows about the unique characteristics of wood and its source, the better they understand how deeply rooted it is in the American culture.

Dendrology, the study of trees and wood, is fascinating to those interested in furniture. Like a fingerprint, each piece of wood is unique. Furniture made of wood is one of few things in the world that all people can own and know that they are the only person in the world who owns that particular grain pattern and its inherent beauty. Each grain pattern is a unique masterpiece of design, texture, and splendor. Even defects in graining and knots can add even more beauty. Extended use gives wood even more character.

CLASSIFICATION OF WOOD. Historically all wood is classified as being either:

◆ **hard** if it was a leaf bearing tree. (Even though some leaf bearing woods are very soft and some coniferous very hard.) Hardwood (leaf bearing) trees start bearing leaves in the spring as the sap starts to flow carrying moisture and nutrients that cause it to grow. In the fall it sheds its leaves as colder weather causes the sap to stop flowing. Or,

◆ **soft** if it was a coniferous or evergreen. Coniferous trees are the oldest known form of tree and preceded leaf bearing trees by eons and eons.

Technically, the grain of wood is determined by the arrangement of the wood's "pores" and "rays." "Pores" are a form of tubes bearing moisture and minerals from the roots. Rays, sometimes called pith or "medullary" rays. These run in thin layers at right angles to the pores. In lay terms wood structure is easily understood.

FURNITURE HARDWOODS. When the tree is sawed down its age is determined by the number of rings formed by the hardened almost non-porous sap of what is called winter growth and the softer more porous wood called summer growth.

Trees will not grow above the timberline. This line circles the earth to the north and south where the temperature is so cold year round it prevents growth or it is most easily seen on the side of very high mountains that remain snow capped year round. For this reason the same genus hard wood tree grown in the deep south would have far more softer summer growth and less hard resinous winter growth, while the closer the tree grew to the timberline the less summer growth and the more hard resinous winter growth, causing it to be extremely hard.

There are literally thousands of different genus of trees in the world. For example, there are about one thousand trees classed as mahogany although only a very few of these are widely used as cabinet woods.

CABINET WOODS. Woods used in making case goods, tables and chairs require grain structures that make them strong in post strength and beam strength. Beam strength is determined by how far it will bow before breaking while post strength is determined by how much weight its end-to-end will bear. The most commonly used cabinet hardwoods are walnut, mahogany, oak, maple, birch, beech, ash, cherry, fruit woods, elm and pecan. Historically, walnut has been considered to be the best furniture wood because of its hardness, grain structure, post and beam strength. It was so popular that the U.S. government restricts the use of American walnut to veneer and further restricts the thickness of the walnut veneer. The most commonly used cabinet soft woods are red cedar, redwood, and several different varieties of pine. Most of these cabinet woods are used for solid wood construction and veneer.

CONCEALED WOODS. Woods most commonly used for interiors, backs of cases, drawer sides, and other concealed areas include gum, basswood, cottonwood.

FURNITURE FRAMES. Woods used for frames do not require a finish, but they must be free of structural defects with strong post and beam strengths. For this reason, plywood is being used more and more often with solid hardwood frames still dominating. The hardwoods used most often are oak, elm, poplar, gum, birch and ash.

VENEERS. Veneers are largely used because of the beauty of the grain patterns. Many of the most valuable antiques use some form of veneer. Commonly used cabinet woods are used for veneer as well as solid wood construction. Veneers often employ rare and exotic wood because of its inherent beauty of wood grains and coloration. (More about veneers on following pages.)

PREPARATION OF LUMBER

The tree is felled, stripped of branches and limbs and taken to the sawmill where it is rough cut into boards. The thickness of these boards is stated by the quarter inch: A rough cut board one inch thick is four quarters, 1¼" thickness is five quarters and so on.

This lumber is graded at the mill based on knots and other imperfections. These grades determine for what purpose the lumber can be used.

KILN DRIED. The lumber is placed in stacks over heat radiators in the kiln (oven). The heat is circulated up from the bottom through the rack of lumber. Great care is taken to keep the exterior of the wood from drying before the interior moisture has evaporated. Cold air enters from above and the warm moist air is removed through exhaust stacks. When the moisture is gradually removed and the lumber properly dried expansion and contraction are held to a minimum.

UNIQUE CHARACTERISTICS OF WOOD

(A) When trees are felled, cut into logs, then sawed into boards the wood is still green and has a high water content. When rough cut into lumber/boards it is usually air dried in stacks outside for a minimum of 60 days (and not too long ago, up to two years). The lumber is then put in huge ovens called kilns where the moisture content is reduced to about four percent.

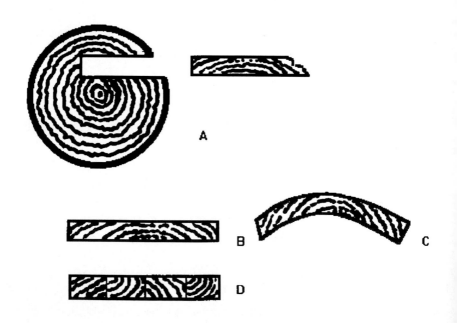

A

B

C

D

(B) Since the moisture content of solid wood boards goes up and down as the humidity level rises or falls, the size of bulk of the summer growth is increased, causing the board

(C) to widen and warp. This tendency is greatly reduced by the drying process and eliminated in veneers.

(D) For solid wood construction, the board is sawed into narrow lengths and the grain pattern is reversed. It is then glued back together to form whatever width and length is needed. Random widths are the rule in solid wood construction. The wood shades and grains are matched during this process, called "quarter sawed and matching."

Even then, a solid wood table top, cabinet top or end used in a southern coastal area with very high humidity year round will cause solid wood furniture to expand significantly. For this reason, fine solid wood cabinets start with a well made inner frame. The tops and ends are attached from the inside with screws. The screw holes are slightly larger than the screw which permits the top and ends to expand or contract without effecting the integrity of the case.

The grade and quality of woods used for interiors, drawer sides and backs tells a lot about the overall quality of the furniture.

This is an overview of basic wood and cabinet construction. The variables are endless. These variables coupled with design, workmanship and details is what causes wood furniture to be one of the best investments a person can make. Its function and beauty make it a great investment. Its durability, when well cared for, can make it a valued inheritance for generations.

Starburst veneer shows the beauty of the wood's grain, below.

IMPORTANT FACTS ABOUT VENEERS AND PLYWOODS

HISTORICALLY. Over 2,000 years ago, Pliny, the great Roman historian wrote: "The Romans used chiefly cedar and veneered their furniture with olive, box, ebony, Syrian terebinth, maple, palm, holly, elm, ash and cherry." Veneers used in fine furniture date back hundreds of years in the West and even farther back in the Orient. While plywood as used today is a relatively modern product. Structurally, plywood and veneers are built the same way. The primary difference is in the surface layers.

PLYWOOD. Logs (4 or 8 feet long) are put on a wood lathe with a blade the length of the log. As the log is slowly rotated, a continuous thin layer of wood is peeled off. The four foot widths are cut into eight foot lengths. The eight foot widths are cut into four foot lengths.

If it is to be three-ply, one 4' x 8' is put between two 8' x 4' sheets, then glued together. This is called "cross banding," an effective method to strengthen and stabilize the wood.

For five-ply, five cross banded sheets of wood (layers) are glued together. These are still the most commonly used sizes, but seven-and nine-ply are still made--mostly for construction purposes.

The quality and price of plywood varies due to the core wood, glue (waterproof or not) and surface layers of wood. One or both sides may be suitable or not suitable for finishing.

Even in early times the waterproof glue process made the board stronger than wood in its solid form. The computer and modern machinery has transformed the making of plywood and veneers into a far more precise process that has eliminated almost all of the problems that were historically experienced with plywood and veneers when used in the construction of furniture.

WOOD BY-PRODUCTS. Modern technology has developed a wood product called particle board or chip core. One is composed of sawdust, the other uses wood chips. Both are made by being mixed with binding materials and then compressed into sheets. Usually these types of boards are made to be ¼, ½, ⅝ or ¾ inches thick. When tempered, particle board can be as hard as a rock. Put under less pressure, it will be lighter and easily broken due to its lesser density. Much of the wood veneers used in furniture today have a particle board core.

VENEER. The advantages of quality veneer on solid hardwood furniture are numerous. Since a veneer log produces thousands of feet of beautiful surface wood, veneered effects offer the most efficient and economical means of using a scarce natural resource.

Veneer is a very stable product not subject to the expansion and contraction of solid hard woods. Solid woods tend to split with the grain, but the veneers of today eliminate splitting, warping or cracking. As good as veneers have proven to be over the past several centuries new glues and machinery have greatly improved them.

Here are a few of these improvements:

♦ Precision cutting. Veneer sheets can now be cut by both rotary and slicing methods in thicknesses from 1/26th of an inch to 1/100th of an inch with very close tolerance.

♦ American hardwood veneers are currently cut 1/26" to 1/36"; European, 1/48" to 1/50"; Japanese (Orient) 1/88" to 1/100", but could change.

♦ Improved machine edges now can glue sheets of veneer without tape. This enables veneer splicing mills to make single sheets of veneer of unlimited sizes with glue joints that are stronger than the wood itself. Hot plate presses can handle single flat panels up to 220" long and 60" wide.

♦ Synthetic resins (phenol and urea) used in adhesives that produce the waterproof bond essential to marine construction were introduced in 1940. Today, they are produced in such volume that costs have been lowered drastically, therefore putting an end to the use of inefficient glues once used in the construction of cheap veneer furniture. (This is important information because the mass market--the majority of people in the U.S. -- associated the word veneer with earlier cheap furniture. It is their children and grandchildren who are buying furniture today.)

♦ Compregnated or impregnated plywood. This process impregnates thin sheets of wood veneer with phenol resins. When heat and pressure are applied to the veneer sheet, it becomes stronger than steel and must be machined like metal. It is non-corrosive, a non-conductor of electricity and impervious to moisture, heat and acids.

♦ Compreg is the term used when the veneer sheet is soaked to satiety.

♦ Impreg is the term used with less impregnated veneer.

Certainly the most beautiful wood grain patterns found on furniture at all price levels are achieved using veneers and the qualities--even at medium price levels--are excellent.

TRADITIONAL METHODS OF CUTTING VENEERS

The pattern of any wood depends partly on the wood grain, partly on the way it is cut. The most common methods of cutting have been:

♦ **Rotary cut.** The log is revolved against knife which pares off veneer in thin, continuous sheets;

♦ **Flat cut.** A half section of a log is sliced directly through heart producing combination of straight grain and heart figure;

♦ **Quartered.** Small segments of a log (quarters, eights) cut at approximately right angles to the annual growth rings for a striped effect;

♦ **Half round.** The log or a portion of it mounted to an eccentric and cut off center so that adjacent sheets yield a symmetrical pattern when matched for veneer;

♦ **Hack cut.** The log is fastened to the stay log on the bark side so that first sheets come from tree heart;

♦ **Rift cut.** Knife cuts at a 45° angle to both rings and medullary rays to produce a striped effect called a "comb-grain" or "rift";

♦ **Sawn.** The log is cut straight and quartered. This method is used mostly for oak, to reveal its flake pattern.

VENEER FIGURES AND PATTERNS

Beautiful figures in decorative veneers are achieved by cutting methods, by the part of the tree from which the log is cut, by the pattern resulting from annual growth rings, pith rays, pigmentation and color distribution, and by growth accidents like burls, crotches and other grain irregularities. The following figures have been the most popular:

DIFFERENT FIGURED TYPES. **Bee's wing:** mottle figure appearing in narrow-stripe wood; **Bird's eye:** a pattern, usually found in maple, due to buds unable to force their way through the bark to the tree surface; **Blister:** figures produced by irregularities under annual rings; **Black Mottle:** Diverse figure from straight or broken stripe interrupted by short waves or curls; **Curly:** wavy grain usually round in outside sections of trees; **Peanut:** a mottled figure of distinctive character; **Quilted:** a large blister figure; **Roll Figure:** a wide, wavy grain.

SPECIAL TYPES. **Burl:** unusual figure obtained from cutting wood with large wart-like growth resulting from injury to the tree; **Butt:** synonym for "stump wood" described below; **Crotch:** striking effect from slicing confused, irregular patterns often formed where tree trunk divides into two large branches, twisting the fibers; **Feather Crotch:** crotch cut with feather or plume effect near the heart of the log; **Moon Swirl:** irregular line pattern cut from a crotch near the bark; **Stump Wood:** attractive pattern cut from trees whose stump grain is wrinkled and irregular due to branching off of roots.

REGULAR GRAIN TYPES. **Broken Stripe:** a stripe broken at irregular intervals by twisted or spiral grain resulting from quarter-cut of interwoven grain; **False Swirls:** half round cutting of certain tree trunks causes swirling appearance in annual rings when bent; **Fiddleback:** result of a fine, wavy figure in grain; **Flake:** quarter-cut of enlarged pith rays in trees like oak and red cedar; **Knotty:** typical figure on wood near surface caused by branches, buds, knots; **Oyster Shell:** pattern produced by angle cutting across sections of limbs and small trees; **Pin Knotty:** a fine, faint figure on surface of wood; **Ribbon Stripe:** a wide-stripe figure; **Rope Figure:** mahogany pattern resulting when stripe breaks in a single direction; **Shell:** (also known as Leaf) bias cut of a log section producing shell-like figure whose lace angularly crosses the growth rings; **Stripe:** a distinctive band produced by quartering some species of trees.

METHODS OF MATCHED VENEER

The art of matching veneers to form an overall pattern is so highly developed that almost any desired effect can be produced.

BOOK MATCHING. Two adjacent sheets of veneer are opened like a book and glued side by side. This produces a symmetrical pattern.

END MATCHING. This is similar to book matching except the sheets are joined end to end. It produces a continuous pattern. Four-way match is produced by combining book and end matches.

SLIP MATCH COMBINATION. This is produced by slipping top sheets into a side-by-side position. Various grains and cuts can be combined to obtain such variations as diamond, reverse diamond (shown below left to right), herringbone or checkerboard.

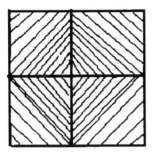 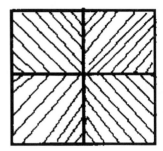

INLAY, MARQUETRY AND INTARSIA

INLAY. Designs in the surface of furniture formed by inserting woods, ivory, metal (usually brass), mother-of-pearl or other materials of contrasting color. This is accomplished by routing the pattern out of the solid wood and inserting woods of different grains and shades. Borders, ornamental patterns, flowers, medallions and other decorative effects are also often obtained by this means.

MARQUETRY. Marquetry is the term applied when an entire surface, such as a table top, is covered with veneers or inlays in a closefitting pattern. This is usually done by fitting the pattern into a thin sheet of wood/veneer and then gluing it to the furniture. Other materials as with inlay may also be used to form a pattern.

INTARSIA. Intarsia is an Italian type of decoration, similar to marquetry and inlay. The design is formed using a variety of woods with varied grains and shade to form patterns and scenes. Italy is still the primary source for furniture with intarsia patterns.

Inlay, marquetry and intarsia are used for decorative purposes only and is usually a part of well-made cabinetry. Even small touches of these crafts indicate quality. While these methods are usually associated with traditional furniture, there are master craftsmen who do fine work of this type for contemporary styles.

WOOD CARVING, SHAPING AND TURNING

HISTORICALLY. From earliest times, craftsmen have added character and beauty to furniture by shaping wood. This dates all the way back to the Stone Age when chips of flint were used to shape wooden bowls or weapons. Hand carving remained the only way to shape wood until the wood lathe and shaping machinery was developed. Most carving found on wood furniture produced today is done with machinery, but even so, the considerable detailing and finishing work which must be done by skilled craftsmen is a costly process.

UNFINISHED OR RAW WOOD FURNITURE

There has been a resurgence of companies who offer "raw wood" or "unfinished" furniture in recent years. Normally, quality furniture of this type will be well made of aspen, oak or pine and have a light in color appearance. It is often the same price as finished furniture. The pieces may be finished in various ways and it behooves the purchaser to research the processes and consult experts before attempting the project.

FINISHING PROCESSES

HISTORICALLY. The objective of most finishes on wood furniture is to enhance the beauty of the grain patterns. Because this pattern is formed by winter and summer growth, some of the grain is soft and pithy while the other is hard and almost non-porous. When stain of any type is applied to the raw wood and the surplus has been wiped off it highlights the pattern and beauty of the grain.

When clear coat finishes are applied over the stained wood it gives a hard durable surface that when properly cared for will give years and years of beauty and use.

Whatever the finish applied to quality furniture the shade must be consistent as most pieces will be used together. As a finish ages it will change shades ever so slightly. Most wood furniture is made in groups of tables, case pieces and so on, and most of it gets purchased as a dining or bedroom suite. For this reason, the factory production finish must be consistent on every piece being made-- and the next production run must match the finish on the first even though slight variations occur. Each production run is matched to the original sample.

For the best uniform application most stain is sprayed on. The stain has a binder ingredient for the pigment to hold it in place when dry and to supply the proper adhesion of the finish.

◆   Stains with lacquer type binders can be sponged dry quickly.

◆   Oil or varnish binders allows a wiping stain which may be sprayed or can be dipped or brushed on, then wiped off.

FILLERS . Open grain woods like oak, ash and elm require filling if a smooth finish is desired. To avoid excess filler buildup a wash coat of highly reduced lacquer or shellac may be applied over the stain. When dry it is scuff sanded to remove any raised wood fibers. The filler is then sprayed on or applied with a brush and packed into the pores by rubbing across the grain with a cloth thus removing the excess.

SEALER.   When sprayed on, dried, and sanded it provides a smooth base for the finish coat.

GLAZES.   Finely dispersed pigments in a slow drying solution. It is either applied by brush or spraying. Highlighting effects are achieved by removing the glaze with a soft cloth.

TOP COATS.   Here is where modern technology excels. Synthetics and polyesters can produce very durable finishes that are impervious to many things that in the past damaged wood finishes. This can produce hard high gloss finishes without the old labor intensive hand rubbing and polishing.

OIL FINISH.   Walnut, pecan and other hard woods with rich natural colors can be finished by applying several coats of a 50/50 mixture of boiled and raw linseed oil two or three days apart. The oil is brushed on and wiped after setting 30 minutes. This finish may be renewed with another coat when desired.

MODERN OIL FINISH.   The oil finish is duplicated in appearance using a penetrating oil stain sealer followed by a low solids lacquer to acquire the stain resistance achieved with several coats of oil.

POLYESTER FINISHES. This finish coat is being used more often because of its resilient durability, depth and ease of maintenance. Primarily, it is used for black and or white finishes, but is also available in a wide selection of colors. For a high-luster clear coat finish on wood or wood veneers, it is unparalleled in brilliance as well as in resistance to mars and scratches. High-gloss finishes of this type can produce a mirror-like finish. There has been an untold number of improvements in fine furniture finishes (making most of the old processes obsolete) that simplifies the process while improving appearance and durability.

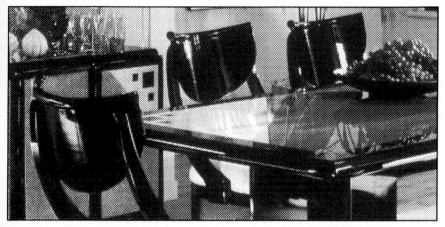

Above, close-up of Ashley Furniture Company's 17.5 mils high-gloss deep polyester finish with Tiger wood veneers from Ashley Millennium™ Collection.

[Editor's note: Because finishes are in a constant state of development and refinement, the furniture salesperson and Interior Designer must be sure to keep themselves up-to-date through manufacturers and trade journals.]

TRADITIONAL DECORATIVE FINISHES

ANTIQUING. The process of making new furniture look old. A bright surface that has been toned down by an application of a thinned or colored oil glaze. The surface can then be rubbed down with fine steel wool to reveal the color underneath. Using crackle varnishes can aid in the aging process. When used in the manufacture of new furniture its objective is to give the furniture the look of age and patina that is currently desirable. (It is important to know that antiques must be 100 years or older in order to <u>be</u> genuine. Interior Designers should be well-versed in the tell-tale marks of a reproduction or fake.)

COLOR WASHING. Using a thinned paint or glaze, the color is applied over a dry surface. The color is then wiped off using a cloth, feathers or a brush. Each of these will give a different feel and texture to the overall look. The surface looks best if only a thin layer of the glaze remains.

COMBING. Using a cloth, cardboard, or decorators' comb, (this comb can be plastic, steel or rubber), run the object thru a wet surface, paint, glaze or a light plaster. This produces a checkered or parallel effect.

DISTRESSING. This begins with glazing to conform to normal use of the piece. Then it is flyspecked with black-brown, ink-like material by splattering with a stiff brush. It is completed with brown crayon streaking to duplicate worm holes or normal use marks. A medium rub instead of a high-gloss finish is more effective. (Distressing may also be accomplished by beating the wood with a chain before it is finished to inflict dents and marks, or shaving or sanding corners and edges to give the appearance of years of use.)

DRAGGING. The use of a dragging brush to a wet painted or glazed surface to give a distressed or uneven look. This method works best on a large area.

GILDING. Water-gilding: Wafer thin leaves of gold are applied with a gilder-tip to a gesso-layered surface. Oil-gilding: A smooth painted surface is first painted with gold size. When the size is almost dry, the transfer gold is pressed on with cotton.

HIGHLIGHTING. This is a positive not a negative effect designed to obtain certain color values which accentuate the design of the furniture.

LACQUER. A form of resinous varnish capable of taking on a high polish. Oriental craftsmen first perfected the process of coating wood with many layers of varnish. Each coat must dry and be lightly sanded before the next coat of varnish is applied to the surface. The art of lacquering was first imitated by the French and spread to craftsmen in other countries.

MARBLING. A glaze is wiped over a white or eggshell oil-based undercoat. The veining is then applied using flat brushes in a stippling and dabbing action.

RAGGING. Remove an oil glaze from an eggshell base coat with a crumpled lint-free rag, a piece of paper or plastic, heavy linen or a chamois. Depending upon the texture of the rag or paper, the color can range from a soft delicate look to a more defined design.

SCUMBLING. Dried surface paint is modified by applying a semi-opaque layer of another color over it with loose circular strokes to create subtle color effects, surface texture and/or the appearance of age.

SPATTERING. Paint is flecked onto a dry surface from a wet brush using a variety of finger and hand movements.

SPONGING. A sponge, man-made or natural, is used in applying a glaze to any flat surface. This will produce an irregular marbled or cloudscape effect.

STIPPLING. A stippling brush is used to remove small quantities of wet paint or an oil glaze from the surface of furniture, a wall or floor onto the brush.

TORTOISE SHELLING. A beautiful decorative practice of projecting the mottled shells of sea turtles on small tables, boxes, bases or chairs. Wet varnish is applied to a base coat and then worked into broken bands. Lines of a darker color are painted on top and then softened with a soft brush.

TRADITIONAL LIGHT AND BLONDE FINISHES: "Blonde" wood is a term which has been applied indiscriminately both to bleached and light colored woods. Actually, it technically refers only to darker woods which have been artificially lightened. It runs the gamut of shades and colors from white through eggshell, cream, straw, sand, beige, yellow and light brown. Woods that are bleached and unbleached vary according to suitability. Blonde walnut, blonde mahogany, maple, light oak and birch plus the wide variety of exotic, unusual woods (satinwood, myrtle burl, holly, avoidure) being used so extensively for veneering and decoration are employed. Method of finishing "blonde" furniture is a treatment which employs a transparent rubbed finish most effective in bringing out the natural grain pattern. English harewood, one of the most distinctive, owes its beautiful silver grey to a dye which is used on the natural light yellow color of harewood (sycamore). Some of the most striking and beautiful effects in today's furniture are achieved by using blonde woods in combination with trimming of dark woods.

Refer to <u>Furniture Facts</u>© Dictionary and Glossary, Section V,
for more information and enlightenment.

HOW TO CARE FOR FURNITURE
MADE OF WOOD & WOOD VENEERS

Know how it is finished. Since 1980, there have been many new developments in furniture finishes. Older furniture with traditional finishes may use one or all of the care suggestions below (and even so, try these methods in an inconspicuous area to test first.) Most manufacturers of new furniture will supply a description of suggested care. It is in the best interest of salespeople and Designers to know and inform prospective customers of these facts.

Below, are some care tips from earlier editions of Furniture Facts©.

CLEANING. Soap and water are not advisable for wood surfaces. Saturate a cloth with cleaning wax (many products available, but always read the directions and/or seek professional aid) and wet the surface thoroughly, a square foot at a time. Wipe area dry with a clean cloth.

CLOUDY APPEARANCE. If a polished surface grows foggy, rub it with a cloth dipped in solution of a tablespoon of vinegar to a quart of water. Rub, with the grain, until surface is completely dry.

WHITE MARKS. Restore a finish whitened by water or heat by rubbing lightly with flannel cloth dampened with spirits of camphor or peppermint essence. Let dry thoroughly, then apply a wax furniture polish. To remove white spots in a wax finish, sponge with turpentine. When dry, apply fresh coat of wax. Or, wet the surface with cleaning wax, wipe dry and apply coat of fresh wax.

SCRATCHES AND BLEMISHES. Clean the area with naphtha. Using linseed oil, coloring crayons, paste shoe polish or iodine (depending on color of finish) touch up and then apply polish or wax. Deep scratches require filling. Clean area as above, after removing loose splinters, and work stain into scratch with a brush or swab. Let dry 12 hours. Fill the scratch with white or orange shellac using a small art brush. Let dry four hours and repeat if necessary. Smooth the surface by sanding very lightly. Sometimes you can repair a scratch by rubbing it with a paste made of rottenstone (pumice) and linseed oil or other vegetable oil.

BURNS. Clean the area with a sharp knife or razor blade. Smooth it with 3/0 steel wool. Clean again and rub, with grain of wood, using 6/0 or 7/0 sandpaper. When dry, fill area with color-matching stick shellac applied with a warm blade. Sand and rub down the area after it is dry.

DENTS. Best advice is to seek professional aid.

REGLUING. If joints are loose, carefully and painstakingly scrape away all traces of old glue. Using a good commercial glue or epoxy, coat the affected surfaces, let them grow tacky, and fit them together again. Clamp the joint until glue is thoroughly dry and hard.

MARBLE. Genuine marble, even though surface-treated, is an item that requires care in use. Liquor and other beverages--even water can stain or mar the marble surface. Having a marble cleaner/care kit on hand will help if the stain is treated immediately. (Many strong cleaners made today can cause an irretrievable scum on marble.) Marble experts should be called to re-surface and polish and bring marble back to its original lustre.

TIPS ON MOVING FURNITURE

"New and Improved" packing materials and shipping expertise have practically eliminated the problems of furniture damaged in transit. Furniture shipped or delivered by truck should be padded to protect the surface. Special care should be taken in handling any furniture on legs. Furniture should never be shoved or dragged any distance, but lifted, carried and placed. There are products on the market--pads to be placed under the furniture in the home that allow smooth moving without lifting--but care should always be taken not to weaken the points of stress in any furniture.

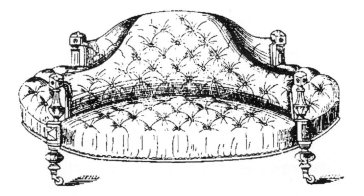

Button upholstered circular ottoman divided with four seats, ca. 1840-1845.

UPHOLSTERED FURNITURE

There are three basic classifications of upholstered furniture:

♦ FULLY UPHOLSTERED FURNITURE: This is generally considered to be upholstered seating pieces where wood is not visible except perhaps the feet and decorative touches.

♦ PARTIALLY UPHOLSTERED FURNITURE: Seating areas are upholstered with exposed wood, metal, or plastic frames.

♦ DUAL PURPOSE UPHOLSTERED FURNITURE: Concealed motion mechanisms within upholstered furniture. Advanced technology, modern construction methods and manufacturers attuned to customer's needs have produced added features with much needed and most desirable benefits without reduction of beauty, quality, or durability, when built to basic quality standards. Sectionals, love seats, chairs, ottomans and sofas may feature these mechanisms.

> The most prominent of these features are bed units within sofas or love seats. These may be made up and ready for use, then folded up without anyone being able to detect the hidden unit nor feel a difference in seating comfort. The buyer may have a beautiful sofa and the benefits of an extra bedroom. Like all products, some are cheaply made, but most found in medium-priced and expensive furniture have quality units and are available with a quality mattress (See Sleep Equipment - Section IV.)

> Reclining seat and back mechanisms are often built into sofas, love seats and chairs. When quality mechanisms and construction are used, this furniture offers added benefits without giving up any of looks and comfort benefits.

SECTIONAL. This term is used to describe two or more pieces of furniture to be used stacking or abutting. (May apply to upholstered goods and/or case goods.)

HISTORICAL. Most of what is commonly referred to as sectional furniture has been developed in the 20th century.

UPHOLSTERED SECTIONS. Earliest and most common was a sofa cut in half with the armless ends finished. These were made to be used with a large corner table. Armless single double and three-cushioned sections were developed. Upholstered corner sections were developed. Upholstered corner sections both curved and square came into use and from there the development of section upholstered furniture is practically limitless.

♦ Sections with twin full and queen size concealed beds are commonly available.
♦ Sections with reclining mechanisms are commonly available.
♦ Sections with built-in storage and/or electronics are readily available.

BENEFITS. Sectionals offer unlimited seating arrangement and permit the maximum number of seating units in a given amount of space. Even an efficiency apartment can be made comfortable with plenty of seating if a sectional with corner seating, queen size bed, and one or two units with tilting mechanism or reclining mechanism are used. The sectional is usually considered casual in style, but offers many extra benefits.

UPHOLSTERED CHAIRS that rock, recline, swivel, and/or massage (with or without deep, thermal heat) built-in audio systems and so on, are now available in almost every style.

♦ The first consideration must be quality as a chair. A chair with reclining mechanism, used in its reclined position, will only be as good as it was as a chair. Seating will be its primary function.
♦ The second consideration is comfort and that means the body must fit the chair.
♦ The third consideration must be safety--as well as ease of operation. Crawling infants and toddlers are curious about thermostats, controls, handles and under- construction and parents should be aware of the potential danger.

Wide variances in price and quality exist in seemingly identical fully and partially upholstered furniture due to the differences in the materials and workmanship, much of which is not visible. Before 1950, most fully upholstered furniture was built with similar component parts. The difference in price and quality was determined by the quality of the component parts and the workmanship. The following description of terms show and tell how most upholstered furniture was constructed in the first half of the 20th Century. This history has been retained in Furniture Facts© because (A) there are many master craftsmen in the world who still build very fine upholstered furniture to the highest standards of yesteryear and (B) classic upholstered pieces that date back one hundred years or more are being restored and have become sought after and very valuable. Radical changes started to take place in the 1950s and have not stopped.

PLYWOOD FRAMES. More and more plywood is being used for the main part of upholstered furniture framing. When built to quality standards it has proven to be very durable.

KILN-DRIED HARDWOOD FRAMES. This frame is still the basis of most upholstered furniture but since most wood or other materials used in the frame are unseen, often the quality and durability of the piece depends on three factors:

1. Engineering. This determines the strength of the frame when the upholstered piece is a finished product. It requires the proper wood types.

2. Proper proportions and scale. This determines the seat pitch and depth whether deep comfort is desired, shallower more upright pitch (that makes it easier to get in and out of) and all variances in between. This feature will often make the sale for the knowledgeable salesperson and lose the sale for those who are not.

3. Types of joints and fasteners. The best known joint is double-doweled, and glued with a corner block that has been glued and screwed into place. It's still the best for most frames. It is also one of the most expensive.

Modern technology permits a variety of joints. A good frame will rack (flex) a little bit. This permits it to adjust itself and set level on the floor even though there may be slight variances.

SEAT AND BACK CUSHIONS FOR UPHOLSTERED FURNITURE

HISTORICALLY. The most expensive cushions were filled with imported white goose down, but the qualities and prices of down range from junk to priceless. It is a good source for the allergens that affect those with respiratory problems and it is no longer much in use. However, high grade down cushions are still considered the most luxurious.

Innerspring cushions dominated until foams were introduced. High grade cushions today may have pocketed coil springs encased in urethane foam wrapped in synthetic fibers that are commonly called fibre-down.

[Editorial Comment: The word "stuffing" has been a word which commonly has described all

forms of padding, cushioning and fillings used in upholstered furniture--even the most expensive white European goose down! Today, quality furnishings don't have "stuffing" -- that word should be reserved for a Thanksgiving turkey.]

MATERIALS USED IN CUSHIONS

♦ LATEX FOAM RUBBER. Latex is a milky complex emulsion secreted by the cells of certain plants, namely the rubber tree. Latex foam rubber was first used in cushions about 1950. By 1960, it was used in over one-fourth of all upholstered furniture. By 1980, latex foam rubber had been replaced almost entirely by urethane foam. Latex foam rubber proved to rot with age and develop an odor as it deteriorated. And even though new processes have eliminated these effects, it has not regained its wide acceptance among upholstered furniture manufacturers.

♦ POLYURETHANE FOAM. Urethane is a derivation of a chemical compound. The prefix "poly" simply adds "various" to the type. Urethane foam was first used in furniture cushioning about 1950. As they improved on the chemical compounds and methods of production, it gained an increasingly large share of market. By 1990, more than two-thirds of the cushions or padding materials used in upholstered furniture manufacture was polyurethane foam.

♦ FIBER DOWN. Polyester batting was first used for padding in upholstered furniture in the early 60s, while cotton synthetic blends came into use about 1975. Today, these two forms of padding account for about one-fourth of all padding and cushioning used for upholstered furniture and almost always used in conjunction with urethane foam.

These man-made materials are constantly being improved and salespeople and/or Interior Designers should make a point of staying up to date on types of cushioning used. (In the interest of history, other types of upholstery cushion materials were in use but steadily decreasing during the last half of the 20th Century: hair and hair pads (including horse main, leg, and tail and hog hair) as well as loose natural fibers (including cocoa fiber, tula fiber, palm fiber, Spanish moss, kapok, wood wool or excelsior and down.)

Visiting factories who manufacture low-, medium- and high-end upholstered furniture will serve to enlighten one's comprehension of the methods, materials, and comparative values. The Interior Designer or salesperson will be better prepared to aid the prospective customer in selecting the best for its intended use.

FOAM. Modern technology constantly improves foams. Foam is one of those products used in furniture construction that can be made cheaper and sold for less or made better to be sold for more. Quality upholstered furniture selling in the medium price range will most often have some form of foam cushions wrapped in a synthetic fiber down. The fiber down gives it the plush softness while the foam offers support and retains the shape of the cushions. Back cushions often have the same filling as the seats but will use a softer foam. This is a simple overview. The more you learn from the individual upholstered furniture maker, the better prepared you are to choose the best for its intended use.

Loose, reversible seat and back cushions are one of the important developments in furniture. The addition of scatter pillows is another. These features increase comfort, make the furniture look better and last longer. The covers on seat and back cushions often have zippers or Velcro closures. These are used to close the cushions covers in production and should never be used to remove the cover from the cushion for cleaning or other reasons.

When buying upholstered furniture those pieces with reversible, interchangeable seat and back cushions permit the owner to reverse and shift all cushions on a sofa, love seat and chair once a week which distributes the wear evenly. This rotation keeps the furniture looking better and wearing longer while retaining its comfort, important when furniture is used often, because inevitably only a few of the cushions get most of the use.

SPRINGS. Most seating pieces will have some form of springs installed in the seat and back of the frame. These are the four types most commonly used:

◆ HAND-TIED COIL SPRINGS. Used in the seat and back, are still considered by many to be the best. They are one of the most expensive spring systems. But, when cheaply done with poor materials they are not as good as other spring systems.

◆ DROP-IN COIL SPRING UNITS. This is a pre-built coil spring that is dropped into the frame and affixed to it. More costly than zigger or sinuous springs, the quality tends to be better.

◆ SINUOUS SPRINGS. (Also knows as "zigger wire.") In its simplest form the "zigger" wire is attached to the front and back rail of the seat. They are attached to the top and center rail on the back using a metal clip with Teflon™ or nylon bushing. This type of spring is currently the most widely used and is found in all price ranges of furniture. The price can be increased or lowered with the use of more or fewer rows per seat and usually varies from four to six rows under each seat cushion and three to four in the back. When the proper number of springs are used to best distribute the weight applied, it makes a very good spring base and back that is durable, resilient, and one of the most quiet.

♦ STRAP SPRINGS OR WEB BASES. Historically, interwoven straps of heavy burlap were tacked to the seat and back frame. Flat bands one inch to two inches wide made of spring steel which are interwoven and attached to the frame with small helical springs were used mostly in contemporary furniture. In the last decade of 1900, as an alternative to metal springs, elastic type bands of high-grade materials became widely used in Europe. They are being used by more and more U.S. manufacturers.

SOFT RAIL. (Also known as spring edge where coil springs are used or "fish mouth" with sinuous springs.) The front edge of the seat will compress when pushed down if it has a spring edge. This is often considered a more costly feature, but not as a firm rule.

FURNITURE FABRICS

Fabric can have more to do with the style and price of a piece of upholstered furniture than any other component part. The selections today in quality, weave, fibers, patterns, and colors are endless. (See Fabric Glossary in Section V.)

As of 1999 in the U.S., about one-third of all fully upholstered furniture sold is upholstered in leather. Qualities range from cheap to priceless exotic hides. (See "Leather" later in this section.)

The computer is widely used for pattern layouts and cutting the fabric. This increases precision, reduces waste, speeds up the process and in most cases it improves the quality of the finished product.

There are four major types of upholstery fabric used on furniture, classified by origin:

♦ ANIMAL ORIGIN. Wool, silk, mohair, leather.

♦ **VEGETABLE ORIGIN.** Cotton, linen, jute.

♦ **CHEMICAL ORIGIN / MAN MADE.** Acetate, nylon, rayon, polyester, polypropylene, etc.

♦ **MIXED ORIGIN.** Combinations of any of the above as well as fabrics made of aluminum, or with silver or gold threads.

DYING. Historically, fading was a major problem. About 30 hours of direct sunlight seriously faded most fabrics and carpet, but chemical dyes and modern dying processes have greatly reduced this problem. It is the responsibility of upholstered furniture manufacturers to inform the furniture salesperson and Interior Designer as to how colorfast their fabrics are. It is essential for salespeople to know how much sunlight a fabric or hide will be exposed to and how colorfast their recommended fabric is.

In the past, most dissatisfaction with upholstered furniture could be traced to the fabric than all other things combined. The expectations of the owners were greater than the benefits of the upholstery produced. Today, the furniture buyer has a wealth of color, pattern, and surface comfort in fabrics from which to select--but still the fabric must be matched to the user's lifestyle for best results--and applied fabric protection adds to the total benefits and enjoyment of the upholstered furniture.

WOVEN & NON-WOVEN FABRICS. Almost all fine upholstery fabrics were machine woven, processes that produced over 200 different types of fabric in a wide range of qualities. The types and quality of fabrics available has grown to proportions that a study of fabric manufacturing is an area of expertise in itself. For example: polyester is often better known as Fortrel, Dacron, and Kodel--the trade names; Herculon and Vectra are made of olefin; and on and on. Non-woven fabrics or vinyls (trade names such as Naugahyde and Duran) may have a laminated fabric backing or not, depending on the quality. Vinyl resembles leather in appearance and is durable for hard use. Vinyls may be solid in color or patterned. Flocked fabrics are another example of non-woven fabric, where cut fibers are glued to a flat woven base cloth to give a raised, three-dimensional effect to the surface of the cloth.

PRINTING. Dyes and printing processes have improved so much over the past 50 years that they have overcome many of those things that had historically caused problems. The making, dying, and printing of manmade fibers makes it possible to produce fabrics that are almost impervious to the sun although some will actually decompose over a period of time. Here again this technology is being improved on an ongoing basis. Keeping up to date is essential. This information is always available from mills that make quality fabrics.

TECHNICAL TERMS. Synthetic fabrics, dying and printing processes can require a dictionary of gargantuan proportions for the technical terms. The important information remains "What are the benefits of the features of the fabric that make it best meet the needs of the buyer and users?" The professional must obtain this information from the mills' representatives.

SELF-DECK. The same fabric as that used on the upholstered furniture is used on the deck. This adds some cost to the construction. When in use the deck is sometimes visible, and self-decks are more desirable. A lesser alternative is the use of strips of the upholstery fabric on the deck between where the cushions are adjoined.

Paying visits to factories who manufacture low-, medium-, and high-end upholstered furniture will serve to enlighten one's comprehension of the methods, materials, and comparative values, for the Interior Designer and the professional salesperson.

TIPS ABOUT MOTH PROTECTION

Moths will not attack fabrics of cotton or silk. Mohair and wool fabrics should be carefully guarded. The best way to prevent damage to upholstery (or floor coverings) by moths is to keep them out of it. Frequent, thorough brushing and/or vacuuming will remove or crush all larvae and eggs. The less accessible places should receive the closest attention. Loose cushions should be removed and every seam, corner and "pocket" should be given a brisk brushing. If larvae have hatched and begun their destructive work, brush the article thoroughly and then investigate insecticide sprays used by experts in fabric treatment. Of the standard moth preventatives (such as moth balls) those containing naphthalene are most effective.

LEATHER

Leather is an animal hide or skin processed for use by man. Large animals are said to have hides (cow, horse) while smaller animals have skin (goat, sheep). In either case, the hide or skin is composed of water and proteins, and unless preserved, decays quickly. Leather is made from rawhide in three basic steps :

1.   PREPARING. Removal of undesirable flesh, hair, fat and other matters leaving a concentrated network of high protein collagen fibers greatly softened and interspersed with water.

2.   TANNING. Treating the hides with an agent called tannin, that displaces the water and then combines with and coats the collagen fibers. Tanning increases resistance to heat and decomposition caused by water and micro-organisms.

3.   FINISHING. To obtain proper thickness, moisture, lubrication, and aesthetic appeal. This leather is essentially animal skin protein combined with tannin, small amounts of oils, dyes, finishes and moisture.

By suitable choice of rawhide or skin and tanning method, the tanner obtains leather possessing such properties as the non-stretchiness in upholstery and in the drape of clothing.

HISTORICAL BACKGROUND. Ice Age man used leather to protect his body against the cold and his feet against rocks and thorns. Preserved specimens of leather date back to 5000 B.C. Leathers may have been man's earliest manufactured goods.

Development of tanning methods. Vegetable tannage is quite ancient dating back to about 400 B. C. The Chinese cured skins with mud and alum. Alum, an accidental substitution for salt, led to tanning, the first mineral tannage.

A wide assortment of vegetable tannin are used today. Synthetic tannin were introduced in 1911. In the classical method of vegetable tannage, the pelts are placed in a vat, on alternating layers with ground vegetable, tan bark, pod, leaf, wood, or root. Water is poured on to cover the pelts and left to cure for six to twelve months. Even today, the sandwich or contact tanning method is employed--with modification. Two or more processes were sometimes combined to produce finer qualities of leather i.e. nappa, patent leather, and so on.

MODERN LEATHER MANUFACTURE

Although any hide or skin can be tanned into leather, those most often used come from cattle, buffalo, sheep, goats and pigs, and sometimes horses. All animal skins vary in size, shape, texture, thickness and quality.

Quality depends on:
-     How and why the animal was reared.

♦   Whether it was slaughtered or died of old age.

♦   Its age, sex and environment.

Damages of many and varied kinds reduce the value of hides and skins. The most common defects are those produced on live animals by parasites, diseases, old age, malnutrition, brand marks and barbed wire scratches. With dead animals, damage can occur with poor stripping of the skin, or in handling and storage.

Hides and skins are divided into three layers each distinct in structure and origin:

1.   A thin outer layer called "the epidermis"
2.   A thick layer called the corium or dermis.
3.   Flesh or adipose layer.

The finest leather used in upholstery is the *epidermis* or top grain leather. Even then, the quality of the hide itself, the tanning, dying, and finishing can make an enormous difference in the beauty, durability and comfort.

MODERN TANNING METHODS. Vegetable tannage is still an important method. Over the past 100 years, many forms of tanning have been developed to achieve a wide range of leather qualities. Some to make it cheaper, most to make it better.

Better means:

◆ It lasts longer   ◆ It feels better

◆ It smells better   ◆ It looks better longer

These modern tanning methods use a variety of chemicals and minerals with a wide range of processes. Invariably combination tannage is the current practice for most leathers.

DYING. After excess water and wrinkles are removed from the tanned hides, the leather is shaved or split to uniform thickness and then dyed. Dyes may be applied to leather in many ways. Dyes are applied to leather by brushing one side, tray dying, spray dying, solvent dying, vacuum dying and dying through a tank and squeeze rollers.

♦   QUALITIES. Levelness, penetration, richness of shade and fastness to light, and rubbing.

♦   LUBRICATION. Unless lubricated, leather dries hard.

Dyed leathers are treated with oils and fats for lubrication, softness, strength and waterproofing. There are many different oils and fats used for this purpose and many processes of application.

DRYING AND FINISHING. After dying and lubricating, leather contains 45 to 60% water and is dried to about 14% moisture content. Among the most popular drying methods is air drying on racks or hung on sticks with fans or the natural flow of air. Vegetable tanned hides are air-dried. This process is cheap and gives slow drying with uniform light colored products. And for those reasons it widely used, but it is the slowest process.

MODERN DRYING. Tunnel drying is a process with controlled temperature, humidity, and counter current air circulation that provides efficient drying. Newer technology permits drying to be completed in three to ten minutes. Most of these processes are quite expensive.

MODERN FINISHING. This involves mechanical and chemical treatment. The dried leather is first conditioned with damp sawdust that raises the moisture content to 20%, then staked by hand over a steel blade or by machine to stretch and soften it. Some leathers are impregnated with synthetic resins; polyurethanes give the best scuff resistance. Impregnated leathers are usually buffed with an abrasive paper to remove surface blemishes and lift nap fibers in suedes. Leather is further finished by coating the grain surface. A good coating will adhere to the surface, is elastic and resists abrasion, cracking, pulling, rubbing and light. (Sunlight can cause fading if leather hasn't a good coating.) A wide variety of colors, pigments, resins, lacquers and waxes are used in impregnated seasoning. A simple glazing finish or seasoning may contain egg, albumin, water, and glycerin. Beeswax and casein made soluble as mild alkali will also give a glossy finish. Pigmented finishes may be aqueous or non-aqueous and usually contain pigment that is 6 to 50% protein or resin to bind and dispense pigment; 10 to 20% plasticizer; 5 to 20% to soften dye stuff; .05 to 6% preservative; and .05 to 2% water or other solvent. Finishes are applied by hand, brush, pad or spray; or by a seasoning machine on a conveyor system; or by means of a flow-coater in which the leather passes through a curtain of finish. Automatic spraying is also used. Water resistance is obtained by treating the leather with silicones and waxes. Glaze finishes may require further treatment by a glazing machine. Matt or resin finish leather is usually plated by passing it between polished heated cylinders.

UNIQUE QUALITIES OF LEATHER

Today's leathers like all other products come in a wide range of qualities. In fact, leathers may come in a wider range of characteristics, types, and qualities than any other product with the exception of those which are woven.

Currently, over 30% of the upholstered furniture bought in the U. S. is leather. This percentage is increasing. Knowing the basics of leather is important, but today a comprehensive knowledge of leather is essential expertise needed by the salesperson and Interior Designer. While it is unlikely that all of this information would ever be required throughout a lifetime, having any bit of this knowledge could be an important factor in a decision to buy or not to buy. In furniture, quality leather doesn't have to be the most expensive. But, quality leather offers the ultimate benefits on upholstered furniture, while cheap leather is a poor investment.

Food for thought: Currently, an automobile which comes from the factory with upholstered interiors, costs $2,000 more if leather upholstery is applied -- in addition to the cost of the fabric upholstery already paid for. By comparison, that makes quality leather furniture one of the best buys in the world today.

Often, an item made of leather, although every quality process has been utilized, will have a disclaimer tag attached to it. This bit of information helps the first-time consumer of leather upholstered furniture to understand the intrinsic qualities of leather. Following is an example for an item made of suede by a well-known and reputable clothing designer/manufacturer:

"Suede is leather finished by a special process originally applied to kid, whereby one side is buffed on an emery wheel to produce a napped, velvety surface. The skins used to produce this item are the best available. Occasionally color shading will appear. The shadings are evidence that several skins have been used to make the garment and the individual skins accepted the same dye differently. This is not an indication of poor dying or poor skin quality, but is a quality to be expected when purchasing a suede garment."

The salesperson or Interior Designer should be well versed on any disclaimer for the product they are presenting. These disclaimers are there to prevent expectations that cause dissatisfaction. When understood beforehand, the leather furniture customer is caused to be even more satisfied.

CARING FOR LEATHER. Quality leather is one of the easiest of all upholstery materials to maintain, but the buyer must be made aware of the maintenance needs and methods.

♦   Quality leather care programs made available by retailers are the best protection.

◆ There is a wide range of leather cleaners and conditioners on the market today. It is a good idea for sellers of leather to know and recommend the products best used on the products sold. This added service gives the consumer added confidence when purchasing leather furniture.

◆ Much of the leather used today is washable, but only with a mild and <u>pure</u> soap (Pear's, Ivory, Neutragena to name only a few.)

◆ Pencil and ball point marks can often be removed with a clean art gum eraser.

◆ The oily ink used by newspaper producers can stain leather. Call an expert, as there is no satisfactory home remedy.

◆ The sun's ultra-violet rays can fade leather, especially the darker shades.

◆ Leather furniture should be placed at least a foot or more from heat vents and radiators to reduce the effects of drying.

◆ Rips and tears in quality leather, although rare, can be repaired without visible evidence by a specialist.

◆ It is in the best interest of Interior Designers and salespeople to gather in-depth information made available to them by leather companies and upholstered furniture makers. When well-informed, the buyer of quality leather furniture has made not only an excellent investment in comfort, durability and natural beauty, but can take great pride in having leather furniture in his or her home.

THE CARE OF UPHOLSTERED FURNITURE

HISTORICALLY. North American families used their living room and its furniture only when company came to visit. Occasions when everyone wore their best clothes and were on their best behavior. Furniture was traditionally covered with doilies and throws to protect their investment. The following "Spots and Stains Removal" section in <u>Furniture Facts©</u> has been retained from earlier editions primarily to show all of the things that could happen to permanently damage upholstery fabrics--and for students, salespeople, and Interior Designers, it should be required reading. At best, these recommended cleaning methods will remove only part of a stain. Close your eyes and imagine these things happening to your own new furniture!

Today, we can enjoy the full benefits of upholstered furniture due to the benefits available from two products--a revolutionary factor in the way we can now actually live in and enjoy our homes and our furnishings. These two products offer the most wanted benefits ever available to upholstered furniture buyers.

FABRIC AND LEATHER PROTECTION

When a fabric protection or leather protection of quality is properly applied, it offers the most desirable benefits available for upholstered furniture.

Once the customer has decided on what upholstered furniture to buy, then made aware of his/her desire to keep their new furniture looking new longer and to protect it from many of those mishaps that might permanently damage the fabric, they have become a fully qualified prospective customer for fabric or leather protection. When the salesperson makes the simplest of demonstrations to show how the furniture could be permanently damaged by a spilled liquid, but saved from harm if it has had an application of fabric or leather protection, customers will opt to take this added feature to get those benefits. And consumer's guides tell us the customer wants the best protection they can buy. Salespeople have a responsibility to their customers to make them consciously aware of the potential permanent damage and demonstrate the benefits of the protection. Having fabric and leather protection on upholstered furniture is a wise investment.

It is advised that all retailers considering a source for fabric and/or leather protection select the best they can obtain. The Better Business Bureau or consumers groups and other satisfied retailers should be consulted before making this decision. Fabric protection components have been improved in the last decade to make it environmentally safe and the same is true of leather protection and maintenance products.

Some fabrics are treated with fabric protection at the mill. Furniture with treated fabrics usually bear a tag stating its use of the process.

[*Editorial Note: Furniture Facts© and its publishing company does not endorse any brand names nor companies that market Fabric and/or Leather Protection, nor is income or renumeration of any sort derived from those companies.*]

FABRIC SPOTS AND STAINS REMOVAL

Spots and stains on delicate fabrics should be treated by an experienced dry cleaner. The following methods are effective on wool, cotton, linen or mixed fabrics. If two items are recommended as removers, they must be applied separately, in the order named, and not mixed.

MILDEW. Rub vigorously with a soft cloth soaked in warm soap suds. Rinse by rubbing with cloth which has been immersed in cold water.

GREASE SPOTS AND LIPSTICK. See "Important Update" next page.

PAINT AND MACHINE OIL. See "Important Update" next page.

INK. Use a five percent vinegar solution or a 20 percent oxalic acid solution to loosen up the spot, permit it to dry and then brush gently. Talcum powder mixed to a paste, then rubbed on and removed, also eradicates ink.

CANDY. Scrape residue gently with the back edge of a kitchen knife. Chocolate should be sponged with clean warm water and allowed to dry. Follow with cleaning fluid, if necessary. Sugar candy may be sponged with lukewarm water.

MEDICINE. Dissolve with alcohol, follow with damp cold water rubbing and let it dry completely.

RUST. See "Important Update" next page.

COFFEE OR FRUIT. See "Important Update" next page.

BLOOD STAINS. Soak spot with hydrogen peroxide. Use a paste of thick starch and tepid water on thick goods. Spread freely and remove when dry. Use borax water (10% solution) on silk.

IODINE. Use alcohol and a 10 percent potassium iodide solution. After it has dried, brush gently with a soft brush.

TAR , CHEWING GUM, SOOT, ICE CREAM, SHOE POLISH. See "Important Update" next page. (Earlier Furniture Facts© editions recommended use of carbon tetrachloride.)

ALCOHOLIC BEVERAGES. Blot up excess liquid. Add a teaspoon each of neutral detergent and white vinegar to a quart of warm water. Apply solution to affected area with a clean sponge or cloth. Let dry, then brush gently. Repeat process of necessary.

IMPORTANT UPDATE!

Carbon tetrachloride is out! New products are in! Historically, carbon tetrachloride has been the best known chemical solution for removal of grease, gum, lipstick, make-up, coffee, juice, ice cream, shoe polish, and so on. But it has proven to be ecologically dangerous and is no longer produced. U. S. companies have manufactured products to solve problems once solved with carbon tetrachloride. Here are three good examples of those products: Capture by Milliken Corp. (a major supplier of upholstered furniture products); Spot Shot by Spot Shot Products; Shawnee Mission, Kansas; Instant Spot Remover by Folex Co., Spring Valley, California. *Always follow manufacturer's instructions.*

SHAMPOOING FABRICS. *The best advice? Call a professional!*
Dissolve a neutral soap in boiling water, add cold water to resulting paste and stir until a thick suds results. Working in a circular motion, scrub a small area of fabric with the suds and a stiff brush. Use lots of suds to assure even cleaning. Scrape off suds and rinse with a weak salt water solution applied with a soft cloth. Always wipe a deep pile fabric with the nap. When cleaning mohair, wash with warm water and soap suds, using a sponge squeezed almost dry. Then rub with a damp cloth followed by a dry one. Do not saturate the fabric and be sure to rub with the pile. If spot grows shiny, spread hot damp cloth over affected area, then dry with a warm iron. Follow with a light brushing to raise the pile again.

VINYL UPHOLSTERY. Clean with a damp cloth lightly soaped; wipe with a clean damp cloth. Let dry and apply a medium-lustre vinyl care product as directed on product. See professional vinyl product for ball point marks.

WICKER. CANE. WILLOW.

Historical. These types of material have been used in some form for furniture and accessories for the home as far back as history is recorded.

Baskets evolved into chairs, cradles, and tables as early civilizations found more and more methods of using these materials. Readily available worldwide, these materials were plentiful and inexpensive. Expert craftsmen learned to develop processes and hone their skills to produce some of the world's most beautiful and functional furniture.

During the 1800s, frames, chair and sofas made of willow were delivered in wagon loads to farmhouses where the whole family wove the arms, backs and seats during the winter months for extra income. When inexpensive seat cushions were added, these became the most durable, comfortable and most economical seating furniture in America (and offered in the earliest catalogues of Montgomery Ward and Sears-Roebuck.) During this era, summer homes were being built on lakes, rivers and coastal areas in great numbers and there was a great desire for easy-care, cool, but good quality wicker, willow, and cane furniture that might be used indoors or out. Porches or verandas were an important part of architecture in those days as families gathered to enjoy the cool of the evening. Victorians, especially, enjoyed the elaborately designed rocking chairs and plant stands for their porches and solariums. Some of the best of this furniture is still made today by the same manufacturers.

Before the Second World War, its popularity waned, but a revival begun in the late 1950s continues to this day. Inexpensive imports during the 50s of peel cane chairs gained momentum and into the 60s as specialty retailers began springing up around the U. S. Today, it is an important segment of the home furnishings market with products for every room of the home and in a wide range of styles, qualities, and price. Much of this category of furniture currently falls in the contemporary style vein, but it blends well and often is considered for "eclectic" use ranging from primitive abodes to palaces.

UNDERSTANDING WHAT "WICKER" FURNITURE IS ALL ABOUT

Wicker, by strict definition, means "small, pliant twig." It is derived from the Swedish words *wida* (to bend) and *vikker* (willow). Practically speaking, however, wicker refers not to the material itself, but to a construction technique.

CANE. Technically cane grass. Any of various grass plants with slender, flexible stems. They are usually jointed as in bamboo and rattan. This is the outer layer of rattan that has been peeled off, cut into strips and woven into matts to be used for seats, backs and outer surface material for tables, chests, etc. There are hundreds of species of reed and grass plants which are used in he making of baskets, accessories, and furniture items.

BAMBOO. A cane grass that is sometimes used in furniture. It resembles rattan, but is hollow and tends to split so its primary use is for frames.

RATTAN. This is a long, very tough stem of a palm. There are a great many varieties of rattan that grow throughout southeast Asia, the South Pacific Islands and Australia. Although they are technically palms, they grow like vines clinging to trees. They reach lengths of several hundred feet. Whole rattan is very strong. Unlike bamboo it has a solid core. Using steam, it can be bent into almost any shape without cracking or breaking. When used as the exterior frame for furniture, it is both durable and beautiful.

RUSH. The stems of cattail or Timothy grass are woven into a very strong coarse cord or rope. These are handwoven onto the frame for seats and backs. It is a costly process, but its rugged beauty and durability make it worth the cost.

FIBRE RUSH. This is a coarse, twisted manufactured paper made to resemble rush. It has been in use since the early 1900s. It greatly reduced both materials and production costs, and it does resemble natural rush. Fibre rush is not by nature water-resistant, but may be coated with a man-made finish or protectorate by the furniture manufacturer.

WILLOW. There are many species of willow trees (over 100 in the United States alone.) Branches (or osiers) from willow trees are stripped of their leaves, then dried and later produce the long flexible shoots used to make bent willow furniture sometimes called wicker. Unlike wicker furniture, bent willow furniture isn't woven, but constructed from taller, sturdier trees used for sofas, etc., and from whips--slimmer trees used for chair arms and backs, etc.

[Editorial Note: It would serve the salesperson and Interior Designer well to study this subject. In-depth knowledge of the history, materials, and methods of construction are available in colorfully illustrated and authoritative books. Unsolicited, we found Wicker, Cane and Willow by Beth Franks, Grove Weidenfeld, New York, ©1990 especially easy to read, colorfully illustrated and interesting.]

METAL FURNITURE

HISTORICAL. Before 1800, cast iron was primarily used for ornamental iron work, railings, window guards, lamp irons, gates and fences and other outdoor uses. The Industrial Revolution brought many changes to the properties of iron. It could be poured more easily and sharper definition could be made in the castings. Modern methods of manufacturing iron, cast aluminum and other metals have allowed furniture of this type to be lighter in weight.

Today, many elements make up metals used in furniture manufacture, the subject too vast to approach here. Generally, metal furniture may be identified in being in one of the following categories:

CAST IRON. Commercial iron produced in a blast furnace and containing a large proportion of carbon. Cast iron may be made hard and brittle or soft and strong. The term "cast iron" is commonly used to describe iron that has been cast into a mold to achieve the desired shape, while wrought iron is beaten or hammered, extruded, or bent into shape. While most popular for garden seating, deck and balcony furniture, occasional tables, metal furniture has found its way into living areas--particularly in sun rooms and dens. The Bistro set, a small table with two chairs, is a common sight among restaurants and sidewalk cafes. Ornamental iron is now available in many different finishes--often verdigris which emulates the patina of an aged piece.

WROUGHT IRON. Brings to mind the blacksmiths of old who with extreme heat, an anvil and hammering fashioned horseshoes. The process is much the same today, but brings modern machinery to the task. Wrought iron is iron which has been shaped with tools--either by extrusion, bending, beating or hammering. Wrought iron, being a malleable steel, is used by furniture designers today for interesting and beautiful effects in furniture--especially bedroom furniture, accessories and occasional pieces.

CHROMIUM. A lustrous, hard, brittle, metallic element used in alloy steels for hardness and corrosion resistance, as in stainless steel, and for plating other metals. Chrome steel is another name for metals containing chromium steel. There are many applications of chromium: chromium acetate, for example, used in the manufacture of many fabrics; chromium elements are sometimes used in processing leather for furniture use. Most furniture designs which use chromium are made of steel that has been chrome plated and is widely used in contemporary designs.

Office furniture today--both modular and free-form arrangements as well as furniture for traditional office settings--often employ metals as its primary design element. The look is one of clean lines and with its ease of maintenance, strength and durability, it must definitely be a consideration for high-traffic business environments.

MODERN METAL AND MOLDED PLASTIC FURNITURE

HISTORICAL. Since World War II the use of metal and plastics in home furniture has steadily increased. Prior to this time it was confined to pieces for the kitchen, porch or patio. Later, the use of chrome-plated tubing on dinette sets paved the way for further experimentation. Machines were developed to mold plastics that produced fairly durable and lightweight chairs and other items.

GENERAL ATTRIBUTES. Metal and part-metal furniture is extremely functional today. Lines, are simple, straight or smoothly curved--or even free form. Form and finish take the place of decoration. Upholstered cushions are often tufted. Many metals are used, including brass, stainless steel, chrome-plated tubing, aluminum, copper and wrought iron. These are combined with cloth, glass, wood (plastic coated as well as grained), plywood and various synthetic (molded plastic) substances.

Chairs are formed and shaped with thin legs that are predominantly straight lined, although frequently v-type or hairpin shaped. Legs often terminate in glides or casters. Metal ferrules or sleeves are quite popular. Plain surfaces are smooth, highly polished, brightly colored, often of anodized metals. Novelty fabrics, coarse weaves, washable vinyls or leathers predominate.

Metal furniture is attractive and easy to maintain. The variety of styles and prices are now full range. Look for sturdy construction. Quality pieces will be well built and strong.

THE BUSINESS ENVIRONMENT

HISTORICAL. Desks were usually box-like affairs until the early 1900s with most furnished as strictly utilitarian--a standard knee-hole desk, a desk chair, a file cabinet, and a visitor's chair--with very few embellishments. In 1936, the distinguished architect, Frank Lloyd Wright, built a new home office building for the S. C. Johnson Company, makers of Johnson's Wax. Wright called these offices "the great workroom" and it was the first office to incorporate what we now know as open office planning. Wright related the furniture he designed to what people were doing and what they needed to accomplish their work quickly and efficiently. He designed the first workstations and brought vertical storage to a general office desk by cleverly utilizing the area above and below the work surface.

In the 1950s, industry began to expand with advanced technology in the manufacturing plants and the advent of the computer--and along with it as many people in offices as in factories. Computers brought an onslaught of paper, cluttered workplaces as well as frustrations and low productivity. In 1960, a German group of management consultants, called Quickborner Team, experimented with office organization in terms of work flow instead of organization charts. Like Frank Lloyd Wright, the Quickborner group started with need and arranged the office to solve it. By discarding interior walls, they described an easier more economical way for the office to change and grow and called it the "office landscape."

As more and more electronic equipment appeared on the scene, it was necessary to find an efficient way to handle the wiring. This contributed to the rise of the privacy panel concept. The panels accepted hang-on units ranging from storage bins to work surfaces. Flexibility was greater and the wiring could be hidden inside the panels, or inside accessory posts.

In modern offices, where people in related occupations must be grouped together for efficient communication, the trend is toward the vertical workstation with incoming work sorted and held at eye level and the work surface used for one job at a time. Compact work stations make possible substantial savings of floor space and can be moved easily to meet changing office needs. The private office, like the home, is a place where personal taste should reign and the type of furniture and decorations may be strictly utilitarian or a showcase. Both metal and wooden desks have many options for filing and storage--along with coordinated cradenzas, book cases, desk accessories, and so on.

Perpetually working in front of a computer or at a desk can be tiring and has caused the manufacture of a great variety of office chairs with a multitude of features. Today's office chair, often with a molded body, upholstered in a variety of fabrics and leather, is adjustable to the height and weight of the person, and with swivel-tilt mechanisms of all sorts, and casters for mobility. Modern office furniture of quality is built for people, yet it is durable and combines good looks with versatility. The selections are wide and so are the price ranges and qualities. See Section III of <u>Furniture Facts</u>© for more about the home office.

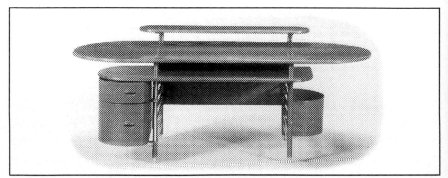

Art Deco office desk by Frank Lloyd Wright for the Johnson Wax Building (1939)

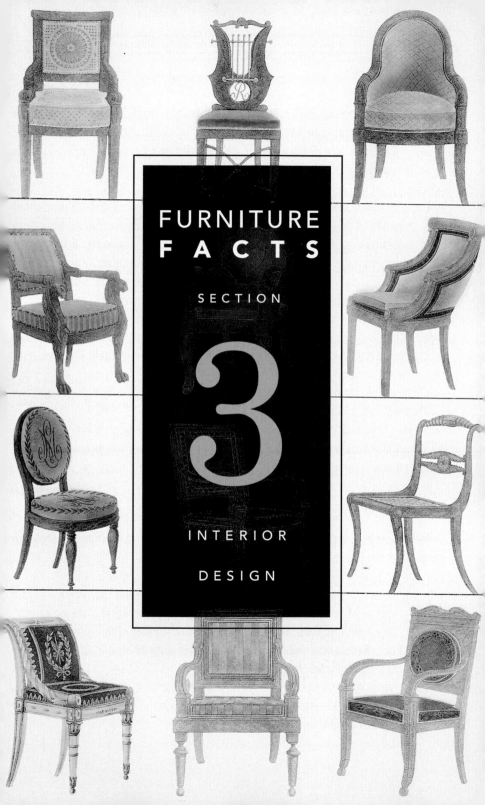

FURNITURE
F A C T S

SECTION

3

INTERIOR

DESIGN

INTERIOR DESIGN

DESIGN. A synonym for design is "plan." Interior design is simply planning the inside space of the home or business as an architect plans the structure of a building by developing a blueprint or plan. A plan is developed for the interior of a home or business by careful consideration of its occupants and their lifestyle.

PROFESSIONAL INTERIOR DESIGNERS learn history along with the principles of good design and planning. They make it their business to know what resources are available to them in furniture, accessories, fabrics, floor coverings, window treatments, lighting, color coordination, and all of the other aspects of decoration. They are imaginative and appreciate beauty in many forms. They make it their business to know prices because an inherent part of a successful design and happy conclusion is the challenge to stay within the budget allotted for the project. They know that good design is timeless, and transcends fads. They know how to communicate abstract as well as concrete ideas. Capable professionals will never force their own preferences on a client, but will guide them to an atmosphere that will reflect the owner's interests, personality and functional requirements. The only legitimate objective of the Interior Designer and retail salesperson is to turn prospective customers into satisfied customers. Satisfied customers are those who take pride in and are comfortable with their purchases.

All successful interior decorating starts with a plan and whether or not a professional Interior Designer is to be a part of it, there is pre-planning to be done.

FUNCTION PRECEDES STYLE

Begin with a simple floor plan of a room (or entire house) that is slated for change. Using graph paper makes this easy: one square on the graph paper equals a foot.

I.   Measure the walls and mark where the windows and doors are. Add an arrow at each door which tells you whether the door opens into the room or out of the room.
2.   Note North, East, South, and West as you would on any map. This is your natural light plot. Western-faced windows will give warm light in the afternoons, for example. (See following Color & Light sections.)
3.   Sketch in any permanent structures or built-ins that are a part of the room: fireplace, wall niches, alcoves, bay windows, etc. Put a star by anything you would like to consider eliminating or drastically modifying.

4.   Now, visualize the room as an empty white room (a blank canvas, so to speak) while answering (honestly and being realistic) these questions:

♦   Who will live and use the space in this room?

♦   What will be the primary activity of each of these people in this room?

♦   What time(s) of the day or night do these activities take place?

♦   What is the traffic pattern for the room? (Use dotted lines to show on the floor plan.) If there is only one entry, you can build a traffic pattern for the room. Is there one major "trail" from one door to the next? This requires some thought. (Putting a favorite sofa or chair in the day-to-day path of children carrying peanut butter and jelly sandwiches from kitchen to outside doors is asking for stress!) Traffic patterns can be altered by furniture placement, but it is unrealistic to erect barriers for inevitable family traffic. So, consider whether you should "go with the flow" or alter the habits of the rooms inhabitants.

♦   What would the people like to do in the room that is not possible now? Read? Have a cozy conversation? Watch TV? Computer work or play? Entertain guests? Gather with the entire family? Relax? Play board games? Think in terms of activity groupings when arranging furniture.

♦   Does the room need to serve more than one function? Perhaps the room could double as a guest bedroom, when need arises? As a library with books (to some, an important part of their lives) to be accessible? Collectibles artfully arranged and displayed for people to admire? A home office? A craft and game room? More storage needed? Here is an area where thinking of possibilities needs to be unlimited. For example, the room that is named "the dining room" in your home might not serve as a dining room except on major holidays. How could the room be used and enjoyed year 'round? As a library with bookcases lining the walls? As a showcase for a crystal collection? As a home office?

Re-thinking how and how often a room is used can be enlightening. There are many wonderful solutions in the marketplace today. For example, the Murphy bed, a handsome built-in cabinet by day, a pull-down bed unit by night, has been in use, manufactured by the same company since the early 1900s. Sofas, love seats, and chairs are manufactured with hidden fold-out mattresses. Beautiful armoires hide computers and/or TV sets. Modular wall units give the appearance of built-in libraries and/or showcases. Multi-purpose game tables are great for both crafts and entertaining. Sectional seating arrangements get maximum use of space and provide seating for the entire family at one time--with built-ins for everything from telephones to throws--and other options including reclining portions. There is a world of possibilities out there with perfect solutions in every category of furniture for every lifestyle. Just keeping an open mind, along with a realistic idea of what is needed to achieve the living goals of its occupants, will lead the home decorator to a successful conclusion.

5. Make a list with three columns: one for "definite items to include"; one for "to make use of somewhere else"; and one for "replacements wish list." Jot down each item in the room. With the answers to the questions (above) in mind, judiciously (mentally) put only the items that the family must have -- or can't live without -- back into the "blank" room. Perhaps it is an antique table, a leather chair passed down from a beloved grandfather, or a valuable painting, etc. Under the heading of "replacement wish list" might be two comfortable chairs for conversation near the fireplace--with a reading light on a table between them. Under the heading of "to make use of somewhere else" might be an antique dower trunk that would be perfect in the bedroom for storing quilts and to double as a bedside chest. By doing this planning, you will soon have a clear idea of what your decorating goals are -- and what you will need to implement your plan.

6. Again, with the answers to the questions in mind, decide whether it is to be a "formal" room or an "informal" room. There are many interpretations and degrees of "informal" nowadays, but "formal" rooms will probably follow most of the traditional criteria as shown in the two charts headed "Correlating Decorative Elements." "Informal" and "formal" can be interpreted as period and style or function or the overall style of the room. There are no strict rules, but combining a formal Louis XVI settee with a vinyl recliner obviously won't work. What will work is keeping everything in the room in scale, which simply means a huge, heavy canopy bed will overpower a dainty dressing table and stool, for instance. The room must be balanced -- or in scale. And furniture must be scaled to its occupants. It's really just common sense--an extreme example being an Olympic wrestler won't look or feel comfortable in a dainty pull-up chair. Manufacturers offer every weight and size and scale of furniture and usually in "collections" or groupings which reassure the buyer. But actually sitting in chairs, sofas and love seats as well as dining chairs is essential before purchasing, because the furniture must be scaled to its users to be comfortable.

7. A few more questions to ask yourself, before moving on to color schemes:

What is my budget for my decorating project? Short-term? Long-term?

What are the expectations of other family members for my project?

What weather factors will influence my decorating?

What are the favored colors within members of my family?

What textures suit me and my family best? (Silk? Cotton? Vinyl? Others?)

Are there elderly or handicapped family members who have special needs? The furniture industry has kept pace with these people's needs--no longer is the "hospital look" the only option.

♦ What one word would describe my hopes for this room? Crisp? Mellow? Dramatic? Comfortable? Beautiful? Elegant? Interesting? Striving to answer this question will bring to mind visual pictures of how you would like it to be. Now, draw a picture of the room as you've visualized it--even if crayons are all that is at hand--and arrange the furniture to do what you would like in order of importance. For example, the conversation center, or chairs that recline before the television, or a home office in an armoire, or a sitting-room-by-day-guest-room-by-night room, or a circle of hexagon-shaped lighted curio cabinets in the center of a large room to dramatically present treasured collectibles.

The arrangement of a room must satisfy real people in real situations. Think in terms of activity groupings. Actually, your plan will solidify upon doing a little soul and personality searching-- and your decorating confidence grows because you are making the room(s) work for you. It achieves what you need it to. That is function and dictates the style preferred.

UNDERSTANDING COLOR

Homemakers and interior decorators often find color a difficult and bewildering area. This lack of confidence is largely the result of unenlightenment of the basic principles of color.

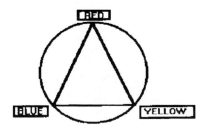

The color wheel is a rainbow bent into a circle--a simplified version of the spectrum.

Color Wheel — Note the difference between the Warm Colors with their yellow undertones and the Cool Colors with a blue undertone.

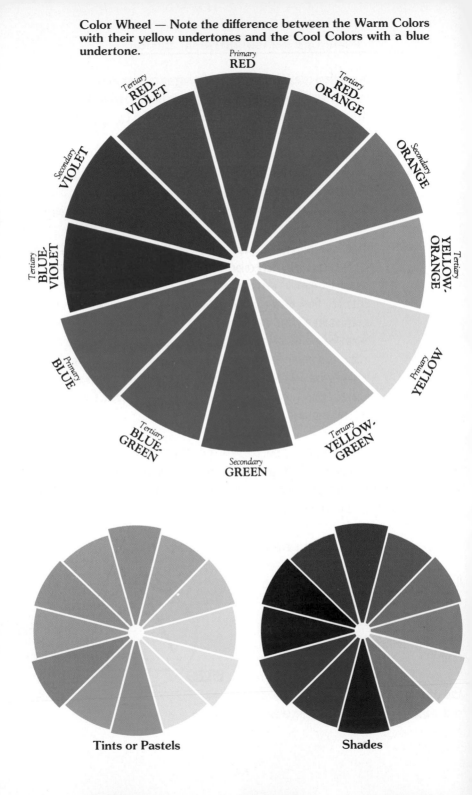

Tints or Pastels

Shades

PRIMARY COLORS. **RED; BLUE; YELLOW.** The primary colors are equidistant on the color wheel. Why are they called "primary"? Because they cannot be made by mixing other colors.

SECONDARY COLORS. **VIOLET; GREEN; ORANGE.** The secondary colors are obtained by mixing equal amounts of any two primary colors. Red + Blue = Violet; Blue + Yellow = Green; Yellow + Red = Orange.

TERTIARY COLORS. **RED-VIOLET; RED-ORANGE. BLUE-VIOLET; BLUE-GREEN. YELLOW-GREEN; YELLOW-ORANGE.** The tertiary colors are made by mixing an equal quantity of a primary color with a secondary color.

Of course, further intermediate colors can be made by repeatedly mixing varying amounts of each neighboring pair until you have an almost continuous transition of color.

DEFINING COLOR TERMS

HUE. Hue is another word for color. The word is used when generalizing to describe similar colors. For example, apple red, scarlet, rose, vermillion are all reds close in hue.

INTENSITY. Intensity refers to how bright or strong a color is. Vivid, pure colors are strong in intensity. Pastel or greyed colors are low in intensity. The intensity of pure color can also be reduced by mixing it with its complementary (the color opposite on the wheel) to achieve grey or muted colors.

TONE. Tone, or value, refers to the relative lightness or darkness of a color. Obviously, the yellow of a lemon is by nature lighter than a banana yellow; the cloudless sky on a summer day is a blue lighter in tone or value than the blue of the sky just before dark; the forest hue is green, but some trees are lit by the sun others obscured in shadow and gives each green a chromatic tone--from light to dark.

In home decorating, tonal values are vital if you wish to successfully express mood and atmosphere. The effect of light causes the tone of a color to change. The more a surface faces away from the light, the darker it becomes. Bright morning sunlight streaming in from a window onto a lemon yellow of high intensity, will make it appear to be white in tone. The same intense lemon yellow in an unlit corner of a room will appear darker in value.

TINT. When white is added to a color to lighten it, the color becomes a tint of that color. Example: White added to red becomes pink depending on how much white is added.

SHADE. When black is added to a color to darken it, the color becomes a shade of that color. Example: Black added to red may become a burgundy.

COLOR SCHEMES

There are two basic ways in which colors react with each other. They contrast or harmonize.

◆ **Harmonious Color Scheme.** Colors adjacent to one another on the color wheel form a related, harmonious sequence with a calming effect because the eye is allowed to slide from one to the next.

Harmony is accord or agreement of things (or parts of a whole) to each other. What a wonderful way to describe a room, home, or office! A well arranged and decorated interior brings harmony to the inhabitants. The harmonious color schemes seem to make people feel more comfortable and at one with their surroundings. There may be a wide variety of tints and shades, patterns and textures, but the result is harmonious.

◆ **Monochromatic Color Scheme.** Variations of the same color; or one color with white or black added to form many tints or shades of that color. This color scheme can be beautiful (and perhaps easiest to use) with its many patterns and textures of one dominate color. A focal point furniture grouping or a cheerful accessory or a structural bonus (as a marvelous garden viewed from French doors) become more interesting and important in the room with this color scheme as a handsome background.

◆ **Analogous Color Scheme.** Usually one main color and three next to it on the color wheel. Even if the colors are intense it produces a harmoniously pleasing effect. Example: a cool analogous color scheme can use blue to yellow-green on the wheel.

A WORD ABOUT NEUTRAL COLOR SCHEMES. Mark Hampton, noted Interior Designer, *House & Garden* contributor and author, in his book Mark Hampton on Decorating (Random House, New York, © 1989), presents a fresh and engaging approach to color and color schemes. Here is a snippet from his chapter called "The Quality of White": "For something most people do not count as a color, white and all the tones of off-white provide a variety of rich decorative effects that no bona fide pigmented hue does.... ...white along with the pale neutral range that I call no-color has developed into a real point of view which still exists as a bold, stylish way to decorate a room.... The extraordinary aspect of these rooms is that they are all so different..... ...(predominate neutrals) allow a host of elements to come into play. As a background for art and antiques, a no-color scheme is both subtle and dramatic. For the lovers of gardens and landscape views, it provides a non-interfering middle ground through which the details of the outdoors are seen with special clarity. In the hectic and dirty confusion of city life, it offers a surprise combination of extravagant luxury and quietude. Architectural details, both modern and traditional, stand out in marvelous relief against an airy color-free backdrop. And if there's family controversy over which colors to use, why not settle it by opting for no color at all? It would be a lot more satisfactory than tossing a coin and ending up with a color you don't like."

♦ **Contrasting Color Scheme.** Colors opposite one another on the wheel are contrasting colors. If two colors of the same tone and intensity are juxtaposed, they intensify one another. The eye is caused to rapidly jump back and forth, causing an optical vibration that makes the colors shimmer. When using complementary colors as the basis of your color scheme, white or neutral areas act as a foil for the vibrant hues, pulling it together for the eye.

TONE = LIGHT AND COLOR

TONE AND DESIGN. The framework of light and dark areas that make up a room -- the broad tonal pattern -- is what first attracts attention and provides an immediate introduction to the mood and content of the room. If the tonal pattern is strong, it encourages a closer and more focused examination, and invites the person into the room.

Tone can easily be understood when it deals with black, grey and white as in a charcoal sketch. But tones and colors are modified by adjoining colors, and a color that appears dark when alone in a white room may well seem to have a lighter tone when surrounded by other colors and vice-versa. Look at a wall of pictures in an art gallery -- the pictures with a well-designed tonal pattern will make the most impact on the viewer. In fact, a favorite good painting can provide (or be your starting point) for a successful color scheme, because if you analyze the colors and tones and how the artist has treated light and shadows, you will have a clear picture of just what your basic decorating color tools are.

THE GOOD NEWS. Do-it-yourself decorating has never been easier! Quality furniture designers and manufacturers do a lot of research and studying of projected color trends before any group of furniture is presented to the public. Upholstery materials are carefully selected from a world (literally) of colors, textures, weaves, and fibers and applied to furniture giving the consumer built-in color schemes to take the worry out of developing a successful overall color scheme for the home. And this is true of furniture, wallpaper, paint, fabrics, and accessories for every room in the home--from the living room to the bathroom--in almost all price ranges.

Paint stores have vast displays of color chips which you may select from and take home to look at in all the natural light and dark conditions of your home. Many of them have color resource books, as well. Artists' supply stores have all sorts of inexpensive color wheels with which you may study color schemes. One in particular is made by M. Grumbacher, Inc. and called Color Computer ™. Although it is primarily for painters of art, it graphically shows many color scheme possibilities (and can greatly ease the fears involved when choosing colors of greater intensity or tone).

The Color Association of the United States has an Interior Color Committee, a group of selected interior designers and decorating item manufacturers, who formulate color trend forecasts. The salesperson, student, and consumer may see these trends in shelter magazines as soon as they are announced. Interior Designers may subscribe to this association and its literature; choose from many trade journals; or investigate one of the many web sites online which provide current information of all types for interior design professionals.

USING LIGHT AS A DECORATIVE TOOL

Taking advantage of light is a key factor in decorating a home. Good lighting is crucial to the successful room. The type of light and its source are also important in protecting eyes from strain during all hours of day and night.

♦ First, natural light is an integral and important part of the basic room or house plan. Morning light is cooler and less intense. Afternoon and evening sunlight is stronger, warmer. Artists want a studio with north light (south-facing in the southern hemisphere) because it is ideal in that it offers indirect light, largely reflected from the sky, that remains constant during the whole day. North light is also neutral in hue, since it has none of the yellow cast of direct sunlight. Color intensity changes with light. That is why it is wise to see paint chips or drapery material swatches in the exact place where they might be placed, and viewed at all hours (and do not discount the importance of clean windows!). Of course, harsh light can be cooled and subdued by utilizing draperies, shades and/or curtains. (See Window Coverings later in this section.)

A cautionary word about direct sunlight. Direct sunlight can harm, not only skin, but furniture and accessories. Valuable artwork and other collectibles must be guarded from devastation by direct sunlight. Galleries and museums are designed to eliminate this problem. Man-made fibers, as well as leathers and other natural materials used on upholstered pieces can simply deteriorate over time when exposed to direct sunlight. Floor coverings, too.

◆ Second, where is light needed that isn't there naturally? Artificial light tends to cast shadows, which can be a terrific added decorating element or a blight. Firelight might be a synonym for cozy--or with its dancing shadows cast on a wall a synonym for sinister. Here is where an analysis of how the room will be used by its inhabitants becomes a game plan for not just lighting, but furniture arrangement. Chronic eye strain is a health consideration that must be addressed in the decorating plan.

Artificial lighting can also be warm or cool. Often, just the selection of the light bulb for a lamp can change the character of the area it illuminates. For example, many rooms in homes built in the 20th century featured a fixture in the center of the ceiling-- often with a single bulb--producing a bleak effect. Today, there are hundreds of better solutions as innovative manufacturers and designers listen to the needs and desires of consumers--from elaborate chandeliers to simple clip-on shades--and in all price ranges and styles. The same is true from table lamps to com- puterized lighting systems--for indoor and outdoor use.

The wise decorator will visit lighting specialty centers regularly to become knowledgeable about lighting; to remain current; and to just be made aware of all of the options available to them. The American Lighting Association is also a good source for information regarding the lighting industry for professional designers.

While you are working out your floor plan, make a light plot by answering the following questions:

Mark the windows (and doors if applicable) and what kind of light comes in. How far into the room does the light travel when at its peak? When it isn't at its peak, what kind of light do you need in that area to illuminate your activities there? At night? (Perhaps, this is where you will opt to put your writing desk to enjoy the morning sun with a cup of coffee and a croissant. But, what if you want to write a letter at night? What kind of artificial light do you need there? A floor lamp or a desk lamp? If so, how much light does it cast over the writing surface? Enough not to cause eye strain?)

Is the fireplace a source of light or primarily a structural element? What family activity takes place around the fireplace? Reading? Playing board games? Conversation? Each of these activities requires more or less light to be comfortable and inviting.

When you enter the room at night, what general lighting do you need?

A bedside light, for example, can be switched on at the door (if wired that way or with a remote or even a hand-clap!) to give enough light for entering the room and dually, a reading light upon retiring. Measuring the height and distance area for in-bed readers' best light is a good idea before selecting the lamp or lamps for this purpose as beds and bedside tables can differ in height.

Bedrooms and closets are often neglected when it comes to lighting, but these are rooms where the right light is essential for selecting clothing (eliminates one brown sock and one black sock syndrome) and grooming. Psychologically, the quality of time spent in personal rooms of the home are very important. Getting off to a good start in the mornings is difficult when you begin the day in a dingy, dark, bath or bedroom.

Entryways should be inviting at all times of the day and night.

Halls and stairways require light for the sake of safety.

The home office requires special lighting attention. Computer monitors must be placed where light isn't annoyingly reflected onto its surface. Are there other distracting glares? There must be enough light to read the fine print of documents; filing requires light and so on.

Game rooms require attention, as well. From pool tables to television viewing, there is much to be considered, including reflections onto the viewing screen itself.

Successful lighting plots should start with a practical and objective examination of what light is there already, what is needed for the lifestyle of the occupants and why, and then (and only then) should style be a consideration.

FLOORS AND WALLS

When considering textures, floor and wall treatments come into play. These are the canvas upon which you "paint" your total room design. A room plan may begin with a wallpaper or a floor treatment. They can be a striking bold splash of color that speaks for itself, or a pleasant background for furnishings and accessories. And a word for the wise: Always shop with your measurements in hand.

HISTORICALLY. Floor materials could be anything from raked dirt to concrete to luxurious terrazzo or exotic wood. The earliest known woven floor coverings were made in the Far East and Egypt as early as 3000 B. C. Over the centuries, wool has been the most accepted fiber for carpeting. Other materials, such as flax, cotton and rush have also been used. During World War II wool was scarce, so many synthetic fibers were developed.

◆For all woven floor coverings, the type of yarn, the quantity, and the construction determine the quality.
◆The determining factors in carpet manufacturing are the pitch (the number of face yarns per inch) and the pile (height of the yarn above the backing), the ply of the yarn (the number of individual ends of yarn twisted together) and the method of weaving or tufting. All of these factors are reflected in the cost of the carpet. (See Floor Covering glossary in Section V.)
◆The most expensive rugs are the hand-knotted Oriental rugs--both new and old--and is a field of study and expertise in itself. (See illustrations of methods plus a glossary of types of carpets and rugs in Section V.)

FLOORS. Modern man-made miracles have widened the scope of flooring. Refer to the Floor Covering Terms section at the back of Furniture Facts©. Select a reputable dealer to work with. Do some research. This is a field that is changing daily--and the choice is really only limited by budget and/or personal taste.

SOFT FLOOR COVERINGS. Whether you choose wall-to-wall carpeting, room-size cut-to-fit rugs or area rugs depends upon your needs and your lifestyle. Cleaning becomes a factor. (A plush carpet is very difficult to keep pristine in a beach house.) Budget is a factor. (Antique rugs can be an investment that pays great dividends in beauty and value, yet there are many options in every price range.) Longevity is a factor. (You may know you will be moving soon and you can take rugs with you; or choose less expensive wall-to-wall carpet in a "serviceable" color now with plans to change it to white once your children are raised.) You may have wonderful wood floors and select rugs to warm certain areas. You may want wall-to-wall carpeting because it is quieter, softer to guard against breakage, more permanent in appearance, warmer on bare feet, easier to maintain, or because there are so many colors to choose from. You may want rugs on top of your carpet to define a grouping in a room.

The padding laid under carpet is usually decided by A) the amount of traffic expected, B) the make-up of the carpet, and C) what flooring will be under it. There are other considerations and a professional carpet dealer should be sought for the answers to padding questions.

HARD FLOOR COVERINGS. These would be hardwood floors, resilient flooring, brick, terrazzo, marble, stone or slate. All are long-wearing and vary in ease of maintenance. Resilient flooring materials are light years ahead in easy-care. The selection is vast. It is the consumer's responsibility to read the manufacturer's warranties and descriptions of products. Not every product will be the same, clean the same, react to elements the same, or be made of the same materials. Refer to the Floor Covering Terms section at the back of <u>Furniture Facts</u>© for clarification and enlightenment. This is another area where professional designers and salespeople need to update their knowledge constantly, because of new developments in this industry.

"Doves" Art Deco wallpaper design by Edwards Benedictus: Relais-1. Crescent Books, NY, 1988.

WALLS & COVERINGS

Wall paint comes in literally hundreds of colors and textures, as does wallpaper. (For example, a wall can be painted/textured with a paint to look like an adobe wall or there is wallpaper available which looks like a textured adobe wall.) Many paint and/or wallpaper manufacturers have completely coordinated paints, fabrics, and wallpapers from which to select. A type of turn-key decorating. It will serve the decorator well to spend time looking at wallpaper books and paint stores' wares. Constant innovation makes this a rapidly changing element of design, offering the most options for the least amount of money.

HISTORICAL. In ancient times, stone walls were covered with skins and heavy fabric to keep out the cold and give a decorative appearance. Wallpaper originated in China about 200 B. C. The earliest Chinese wallpapers, hand-painted on rice paper by craftsmen, depicted birds, flowers and landscapes. In the latter part of the 16th century, wallpapers were made in square sheets for wall use. These came to Europe via Persia. The earliest of these papers were marbleized designs made by "floating off" oily colors from a bath of water onto sheets of paper. Later, Europeans hand-printed their papers from wood blocks, putting the desired color on the block and then pressing it onto the paper. Around 1700, a Frenchman named Jean Pipillon was the first person to make wallpaper designs in repeating patterns. Today we have not only paper to hang on the wall but paper with a vinyl coating that is washable. There are papers that reproduce the warm color of wood, the cool look of marble or leather, the roughness of stone, the crispness of brick and the richness of silk and damask. Scenic wallpaper can create an illusion of space and depth. Flocked paper simulates the look and feel of cut velvet. Grass cloth is a textured paper. Wallpaper can also be dramatic when used to camouflage bad architecture or hide irregularities in your walls and ceilings.

Other wall covering options are: *Trompe d'oeil* scenes on walls painted by artists; fabrics glued or stapled to walls with decorative braid or trim for finishing; wood paneling -- or simulated wood paneling; floor to ceiling draperies; wood or metal moldings, mirrored walls (see "Accessories and Room Enhancements."), tiles, and on and on. Tiles can cover a wall--not only in kitchens and bathrooms, but plain, patterned or glazed tiles (machine or hand-made) can be applied to dry, smooth walls and floors for a long-lasting, hard-wearing, easy-to-care-for and beautiful effect. A huge selection is available. These optional wall coverings are usually selected as a solution to a particular decorating goal or to overcome a room's inherent problem as perceived by its inhabitants.

Especially fun and notable are the developments and designs of wall coverings for children's rooms -- from birth to 'teens. Bright colors, themes, chalk or bulletin board walls, and even removable whimsical decals can be economically changed as the children grow and with perpetually delightful results.

WINDOW TREATMENTS

While decorating can be a lot of fun, it is also a pretty serious business. Window treatments are very important to the final result. Windows and window/doors are structural and difficult to change, so making the most of them in decorating is a key factor. Bookstores and libraries are full of guides to focus on any particular period or style for authentic window treatments. There are craft books which demonstrate how to construct window treatments of all types. Fabric showrooms will have practical suggestions. Professional drapers are available. The Window Treatment "terms" (Section V) of this book with its illustrations will expose the reader to many options and includes complete measuring procedures.

There are a few initial, if general, basics that should be factored into window covering plans....

♦ The first consideration must always be the view from the window: Do you want to hide it? Or enjoy the view? The second must be a question of privacy. These considerations can dictate whether windows or doors should be covered in stationary arrangements, not covered at all, or flexible to open and close as needed.

♦ Curtains, draperies, shades of fiber, wood or metal, and shutters--installed or portable, are the basic choices. From these basics, there are many possibilities. Again, what is needed to function comfortably in the room is the question and imagining the furnished room in all seasons with its particular inhabitants in harmony will dictate the choices.

♦ A room with extremely low ceilings requires discipline. If the height isn't there, big valances and swooping swags will overpower.

♦ Think vertical in selecting patterns for a low ceiling room and it will increase the visual height.

♦ Good scale is the decorator's best friend. It is often easier to leave the window covering decision to the last in planning--after the major elements of the room are in place.

♦ Study the effect of curtain styles in books and magazines. Some treatments (like criss-crossed curtains) make the window seem wider while others (like panel curtains) seem taller. (See Window Treatments, Section V.)

- Unstructured valances or looped fabric will soften visual impact. Structured valances are more formal as a rule.
- Bay windows should be treated as an entity unto itself, it is a wonderful opportunity for a room "picture" or focus grouping.
- French doors are also a stunning structural asset--and often the view should not be tampered with. But, privacy might dictate the need for unobtrusive pull-down shades, shirred curtains, or shutters. French doors should be considered windows in planning, of course.
- The texture, design and care of fabric selected for window treatments should be taken into consideration. Kitchens are messy places and curtains that can be washed frequently are desirable and ease of taking them down and replacing after washing is something to consider. Rooms with less daily traffic can afford silks and other elegant fabrics. Treated fabrics are best for high-traffic areas so that accidents don't cause stress. A professional dry cleaning regimen will keep fine drapery fabrics looking new. Always ask the make-up of the fabric and how best to clean it when purchasing.
- Prints are a matter of personal taste and can be delightfully personal--whether with a big, splashy bold pattern or an airy small-dotted sheer. Just keeping the overall scale of the rooms' furnishings in mind will produce harmony.

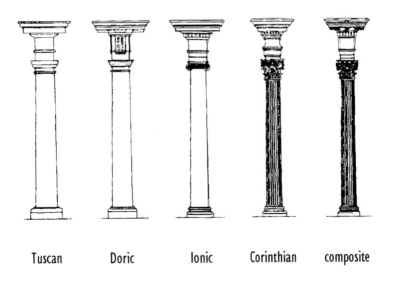

Tuscan   Doric   Ionic   Corinthian   composite

ACCESSORIES & ROOM ENHANCEMENTS

Sherlock Holmes, Arthur Conan Doyle's fictional master sleuth, got many of his clues to the personalities of the characters upon entering and observing their habitats. A room speaks volumes about those who live there. Accessorizing a room should do just that--reflect and enhance the interests and lifestyle of those who live in it without interfering with day-to-day harmony and comfort.

Function must be considered first. When selecting accessories, the first consideration is what needed useful objects must be readily available in the room. List, then mark these on your floor plan. Practical accessories or items might include some of the following, but the inhabitants of the room dictate what is needed there, not only to keep the room tidy looking, but attractive. Every home will have a different list of "must have accessories."

Clocks. Ranging from high-tech alarm clocks on the bedside chest to attractive Grandfather clocks in an entry way, the variety is endless as is the price range. For example, a centrally placed big battery operated kitchen wall clock is handy for a busy family. A porcelain mantle clock may be a useful and decorative item. (Winding keys are precious items and should be kept with the clock.)

Ashtrays & Wastebaskets. If your home is a non-smoking home, then eliminating all ashtrays will relay that message. If smoking is allowed in the home, then ashtrays should be deep and rimmed so that burning cigars or cigarettes or pipe bowls are in the bowl at all times, eliminating burns and fall-out. Of course, ashtrays can be attractive--a light-catching crystal-- or purely functional and portable. Wastebaskets can be a handsome leather one near a desk or novelty brights for a kitchen--with lids or without-- as unobtrusive or bold as you choose. Well-placed trash receptacles outside the home or the workplace can prevent needless litter.

Key Keepers. Perhaps a bowl near the door to the garage, a graceful wrought iron tree, a hand carved key rack hung where people come in and out. If car keys, out building keys, etc. are always in the same area of your home, it reduces frustration.

Fireplace Tools & Fire Screens. The variety has never been greater.

Baskets. These containers have been a part of life since the beginning of time. They blend well with any decor and are useful and valued for their hand-made beauty. A large open basket can house magazines next to a reading chair; a wicker storage trunk can, with a slab of glass, become a coffee table; a lidded basket can keep sewing supplies handy. Baskets also can be hard workers as clothes hampers, laundry baskets, or for garden gatherings. Antique baskets have great stories behind their use and can simply be objects of interest.

Trunks, Steamers, and Luggage. Storage/dual purpose accessories. These are versatile beauties that can serve several purposes at once and are popular storage decorating enhancements -- especially in family rooms where there are items that are not in use at all times such as games, cards, warm throws, movie video collections, even out-of-season clothing, and on and on.

Family Message Centers come in all materials, a handy item for busy families.

Bathrooms & Kitchens require much thought when organizing the many staples deemed necessary today especially when used by more than one person in the family.

Thinking through the daily routines of family members will bring to mind useful, logical solutions as to which basic accessories are required.

Carefully selected and arranged accessories can also bring fun and beauty to the interior. The words "carefully selected" mean several things, if the overall tone of the room is to be successful as planned. Here are a few tips and suggestions when accessorizing.

Before rushing to the stores to purchase accessories, take an inventory of what is already there in the home (including the attic and basement). Make an effort to group these items by category. For example, if you discover that you've collected an interesting array of candles and candle-holders, get them all out and see if they would look more important clustered together in varying heights on a mantle or a hall table. Often, a central theme for a room becomes evident and exciting upon rediscovering once-treasured items. A table landscaped with mementoes, souvenirs, and personally meaningful objects begs to be looked at and savored. The repetitive use of materials--such as gold, gilt, or pewter--ties disparate elements together, just as a "theme" color does. Using what you have in accessories can also allow more budget for needed furnishings.

Collectibles. It seems a collector cannot stop collecting once the interest is there. But, there is an art to displaying collectibles without creating an overwhelming cluttered look. Again, selection for display is the key. Enclosed furniture cabinetry with lighted interiors are handsome additions to any style decor. They come in all sizes, all shapes, all prices, and all finishes. Most have adjustable shelving. Books require greater depth than Hummel figurines. (Know the measurements of your tallest and smallest items before you shop.) Wall units (sectional or modular) utilize (often wasted) wall space to maximum advantage. And if the wall units don't reach the ceiling, the tops may be used as open shelving display. Enclosed china cabinets or curio cabinets mean that small items are protected from daily dusting--as well as breakage. Hanging or table-top cases can attractively house small collectible groupings. Special collections require special planning if they are to be an enjoyable asset, rather than a liability. There are many books with suggestions on decorating with collectibles at book stores and libraries and well worth investigation.

Portable Items. Tables/Trays. For casual, impromptu meals or entertaining, small tables or collapsible tray sets are handy and no longer unsightly! Often, nested tables are the perfect solution for busy households. **Pull-up Chairs.** Light in weight and portable, a chair that can be pulled into a conversation group or near a fireplace in cold weather. These versatile chairs come in every style.

Flowers & Plants. **Flowers** give a room a jewel-like quality--it comes alive and glows. Flowers help lift spirits and signal new seasons. Take an inventory of containers which might be used as interesting vases. Baskets, china teapots, earthenware pitchers, wine coolers, etc. Be imaginative. Use flower arrangements in crystal vases to add color and to attract the eye with natural or artificial light. Keeping flowers and container in proportion and to scale--first with each other and then with its surroundings when placed, will come to the most successful conclusion. Dried flowers are lovely but should be kept dust-free. Kitchen herb bouquets are fun and useful. **Plants** add a breath of fresh air to any room design. Literally, green plants give off oxygen and are healthy additions. From small violets tucked next to a treasured picture of a favorite grandmother, to an orange tree in a beautiful pot, plants are dramatic additions and pleasurable. Researching what plants do best under various conditions is wise. A flowering hibiscus, for example, flourishes in direct sunlight and vented heat, while other plants do not. Some plants are poisonous to pets. Artificial flowers and silk or beaded flower arrangements can be attractive also, it is a matter of taste.

Antiques. Antique pieces can be focal points for rooms and are the starting point for many interior designs. Scale and a sense of history are all-important when using antiques.

Wall Hangings. Again, a scaled drawing of the walls of a room with furniture in place will lead the way to good decisions when selecting wall hangings. A good rule-of-thumb for grouping pictures and objects is to use the "rectangle measure."

Construct an imaginary rectangle on the floor or table large enough to accommodate the pictures and objects you wish to include in the arrangement. First, establish the four corners. (See diagram: 1, 2, 3, and 4.)

Then, place the items until you have a pleasant arrangement, evenly spacing each item horizontally and vertically between the pictures or items within the rectangle.

Once arranged to your satisfaction, measure all elements and using a pencil, make dots on your wall to guide you. (Remember to measure the distance between the top of the frame and the hanger on the backs, also.)

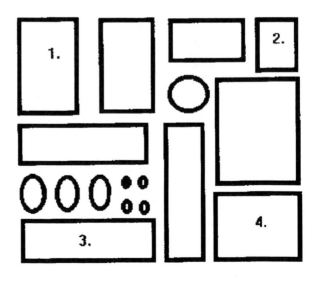

To group pictures above a table, follow the same procedure. If desired, leave enough space for any objects, architectural pieces or other irregularly shaped items which will rest on the table itself, measuring carefully as you go.

As a rule, this system works best if at least three sides of the configuration are squared.

Surface shelves and wall-mounted moldings can add depth to an open-top arrangement. Just be sure walls are structurally supportive!

Many people prefer to group pictures that form a theme, as a collection of botanical prints, for example. But many times, the interests of the person or persons who own the room tie the grouping together. Again scale is important for frames. If not identical, they should be more or less the same visual weight, so that all group harmoniously. Mixing metallics can be tricky and requires an extra dose of thought in planning because other metals used throughout the room must be considered.

The balanced large painting with wall sconces equally spaced on either side (or any two similar objects) is also an eye-pleasing arrangement of accessories. However, these are only general rule-of-thumb suggestions for wall and table groups. Shelter magazines and books on the subject abound, packed with varied and interesting suggestions for grouping accessories successfully.

Another hint or two for large paintings (and framed mirrors): keep the subject matter in the painting at eye-level if possible, and consider a gallery light attached to the frame or the wall to draw attention to the importance of the painting. These are especially beautiful at night. Large paintings or portraits are (as a rule) considered "formal" but, of course, it depends on the framing and subject matter. Framed family photographs used in a wall or table-top grouping are (as a rule) considered "informal" and most often used in family or game rooms. But, rules were made to be broken as the old saying goes and an array of interesting family photographs framed in gleaming silver and grouped on a piano or sofa table can appear formal also--the personality and lifestyle of the inhabitants is the all-important rule.

Quilts, rugs, tapestries or other fabric wall hangings are beautiful, but usually require an interesting rod arrangement and careful mounting on the wall. Vertical or horizontal plate racks are also available. "Measure before hanging" is always the best advice, along with using a level and a stud-finder, inexpensive tools but extremely helpful for wall projects.

The Magic of Mirrors. Mirrors are illusions. They can make a room seem more spacious. A mirrored wall can double the size of an area or room. Mirrors also can increase the light of a room--both natural and artificial. The eye reads a mirror like a window and when structural changes aren't feasible, a beautifully framed mirror can seem to open up a room. Mirrors can make an art object, an antique, or plants and flowers three dimensional by showing all sides. Using mirrors (intermixed with or in place of paintings) in a collage type arrangement can give a wall depth, sparkle and elegance. Mirrors have traditionally been a necessity in entryways for thoughtful hosts' guests to check their appearance before proceeding into the home. Mirrors can also be a focal point of a room--or to direct the eye to a focal grouping. Full length door mirrors or mirrored closet doors help to unify bed and bathroom space by reflecting light and creating a sense of expansiveness. Mirrored tiles or mosaics are sometimes an interesting design option. The flexibility of cheval mirrors have made them popular for centuries. Always consider what the mirror reflects as an element of the room's design.

TRADITIONAL DECORATIVE ELEMENTS

PERIOD STYLE	ASSOCIATED STYLES	WALLS & CEILINGS	FLOORS	FLOOR COVERINGS
EARLY ENGLISH TUDOR JACOBEAN CHARLES II	Italian Renaissance. Spanish Renaissance. William & Mary. Larger pieces of Queen Anne.	Oak panels. Rough plaster with oak trim. Pargetry ceilings.	Hardwood stained dark, may be planks or flooring. Stones. Tiles.	Oriental and large pattern Domestic Rugs. Plain rug.
ANGLO-DUTCH WILLIAM & MARY QUEEN ANNE	Chippendale. Early Georgian. Louis XVI. Smaller pieces of Jacobean such as gate leg table or Windsor chair.	Papered. Painted (in light tones). Hung with fabrics. Paneled.	Hardwood flooring. Parquetry.	Oriental and large pattern Domestic Rugs. Plain rug.
EARLY GEORGIAN CHIPPENDALE	Chippendale. Late Georgian. Louis XVI. Smaller pieces of Jacobean such as gate leg table or Windsor chair.	Painted Dado. Painted. Paneled. Papered upper section in Chinese motifs.	Hardwood flooring. Parquetry.	Plain or small patterned rugs or carpets. Oriental rugs.
LATE GEORGIAN ADAM HEPPLEWHITE SHERATON REGENCY	Chippendale (in Chinese manner). Louis XVI. Duncan Phyfe. Directoire.	Plain plaster. Painted. Papered. Large wood panels, painted. Gesso ceilings.	Hardwood flooring. Parquetry.	Plain or small patterned rugs or carpets. Oriental rugs.
LOUIS XVI	All late Georgian styles. 1 or 2 pieces of Louis XV and Directoire.	Large wood panels painted and decorated. Wallpaper in Chinese motifs.	Hardwood flooring. Parquetry.	Plain or small patterned rugs or carpets. Oriental rugs
SPANISH RENAISSANCE	Italian Renaissance. Early English. Louis XIV.	Rough plaster. Painted. Ceilings same or beamed	Hardwood. Tiles.	Spanish or Oriental rugs.
EARLY COLONIAL	All Early English styles. William & Mary. Queen Anne wing chair.	Oak panels. Rough plaster with oak trim. Pargetry ceilings.	Hardwood flooring or planks.	Braided or Hooked rugs.
LATE COLONIAL	Late Georgian. Chippendale. Queen Anne. Duncan Phyfe. French Provincial.	Smooth plaster light trim. Wallpaper, scenic and Chinese designs. Paneling. Ceiling, plaster.	Dark hardwood flooring.	Hooked, braided, Oriental rugs. Domestic rugs or carpet, plain, two-toned or patterned.
MODERN	Swedish Modern. Chinese Chippendale.	Painted solid colors. Stripe, figured, plain papers. Combinations of above.	Hardwood. Parquetry.	Carpeting. Rugs in solid colors. Geometric patterns.
FRENCH PROVINCIAL	18th Century American Colonial. Federal Biedermeier.	Smooth plaster. Wallpaper in scenic or Geometric designs.	Hardwood. Parquetry.	Aubussons. Homespun carpet. Small pattern Orientals.
VICTORIAN	Colonial. Queen Anne. Wm. & Mary.	Large pattern paper.	Hardwood.	Carpeting in large patterns. Orientals.

TRADITIONAL DECORATIVE ELEMENTS

PERIOD STYLE	DRAPERY FABRIC	DRAPERY COLORS	DRAPERY DESIGN	UPHOLSTERY FABRICS
EARLY ENGLISH TUDOR JACOBEAN CHARLES II	Crewel embroideries. Hand blocked linen. Silk & worsted damask. Velvet. Brocade.	Full bodied crimson, green and yellow.	Large bold patterns: tree branch, fruits, flowers, oak leaf, animals, heraldic designs.	Tapestry. Leather. Needlework. Velvet. Brocade.
ANGLO-DUTCH WILLIAM & MARY QUEEN ANNE	Crewel embroideries. Hand blocked linen. Silk & worsted damask. Velvet. Brocade. India prints.	Full bodied crimson, green and yellow.	Large bold patterns: tree branch, fruits, flowers, oak leaf, animals, heraldic designs.	Tapestry. Leather. Needlework. Velvet. Brocade.
EARLY GEORGIAN CHIPPENDALE	Crewel embroideries. Hand blocked linen. Silk & worsted damask. Velvet. Brocade. India prints.	Full bodied crimson, green and yellow.	Jacobean motifs. Also classic medallions and garlands.	Tapestry. Leather. Needlework. Velvet. Brocade.
LATE GEORGIAN ADAM HEPPLEWHITE SHERATON REGENCY	Brocades. Damask. Chintz. Taffeta. Toile de Jouy. Satins.	Delicate subdued hues of rose, yellow, mauve, green and gray.	Classic designs, small in scale: garlands, urns, floral, animals, etc.	Damask. Velour. Brocade. Satin. Petit Point. Leather in libraries.
LOUIS XVI	Silks. Satin. Damask. Taffeta. Muslins. Brocade. Toile de Jouy.	Delicate powder blue, oyster white, pearl, rose, pale greens, mauve, yellow.	Stripes sprinkled with ribbons, flowers, medallions, lyres and other classic motifs.	Petit Point. Satin Moire. Velours. Chintz. Damask. Brocade. Tapestry.
SPANISH RENAISSANCE	Velvet. Damask. Crewel work. India prints. Printed and emb. linen.	Rich, vigorous colors: red, green and gold.	Bold patterns in classic and heraldic designs, also arabesques.	Leather. Tapestry. Velvet. Linen. Brocatelle.
EARLY COLONIAL	Crewel embroideries. Hand blocked linen. Silk & worsted damask. Velvet. Brocade.	Full bodied crimson, green and yellow.	Large bold patterns: tree branch, fruits, flowers, oak leaf, animals, heraldic.	Tapestry. Leather. Needlework. Velvet. Brocade.
LATE COLONIAL	Toile de Jouy. Damask. Chintz. Organdy. Cretonne.	All colors, but more subdued than in early period.	Scenic. Birds. Animals. Floral.	Haircloth. Mohair. Rep. Linen. Chintz. Velours.
MODERN	Textured and novelty weaves. All fabrics. Leathers.	All colors. Bright to pastel.	Solid colors. Modern designs. Stripes.	All fabrics. Novelty weaves. Plastics. Leathers.
FRENCH PROVINCIAL	Chintz. Cretonne. Blocked linen. Velvet.	Subdued colors. Pastel shades.	Screen prints. Block prints.	Solid colors. Textured weaves. Tapestry.
VICTORIAN	Velvet. Brocades. Damask.	Turkey red. Other rich colors.	Solid colors. Formal patterns.	Haircloth. Needlework. Velvets.

This elegant Oriental rug, from the Royal Collection of Nourison Carpets, is woven of 100 percent pure wool pile on looms especially designed for the centuries old Persian knotting technique - about 26,000 hand-tied knots to the square foot - makes it durable and handsome. Reprinted from Furniture Facts © 27th edition.

FURNITURE
FACTS

SECTION

4

SLEEP

EQUIPMENT

INVESTING IN A QUALITY NIGHT'S SLEEP

HEALTH experts have agreed that the basis of a human's physical well being is being able to get a good night's sleep. The restorative power of sleep is amazing. Selecting the proper sleeping equipment for you and your prospective customers should be of primary concern.

WHAT SIZE SLEEP SET?

Sleep sets come in five standard sizes:

- Crib Size   27" wide x 52" long
- Twin Size   39" wide x 74" long
  - Twin Extra Long   39" wide x 80" long
- Full Size   54" wide x 74" long
- Queen Size   60" wide x 80" long
- King Size   78" wide x 80" long
  - California King Size   72" wide x 80" long

When selecting a mattress and a foundation, there are many aspects to consider. National statistics reveal that an average buyer will keep their next sleep set about fifteen years and spend over 40,000 hours on it, whether it affords a good night's sleep or not. The need for a restful night's sleep increases with age. It is a purchase well worth giving a good deal of consideration. One-third of a person's life will be spent on a sleep set.

HOW IMPORTANT IS SIZE?

- Plan on a crib mattress being outgrown by the time the child is three years old.
- Pediatricians can pretty well project how tall a child will be when grown. Select twin size length accordingly.
- Note that a full size bed at 54" wide, gives two adults the same sleeping width they had in their crib mattress: 27" each.
- Note that a king size bed requires only nine more inches on either side of the bed than a queen size. Most master bedrooms will easily accommodate a king size bed.
- Note that 74" is six feet + two inches. If the person sleeping on the sleep set is near or over six feet tall, the extra inches will be vital to his or her getting a proper night's sleep.

♦ Most people change body positions about seven times a night with up to two full body turns. Current research shows that the body movement of two adults during sleep reduces their effective sleep about twenty-five percent. King size affords each person 39" of sleeping width allowing for body movement without interfering with the other person's quality sleep; queen size allows 30" for each person.

There are four basic types of support systems used in sleep sets:

INNERSPRING. There is a wide variety of spring support systems utilized in building mattresses. Most will fall into one or two types:

♦ Pocketed coils. Also known as "Marshall Spring Units" named after the man who first developed mattresses with individually pocketed coil springs. The spring unit is composed of coiled springs individually encased in fabric pockets.

♦ Coil spring units. Also known as "Bonnell Coil Springs". The spring system is held together by small continuous coil springs called helical springs. Offset Bonnell units are characterized by when the top and bottom turn of each coil is flat on two sides, the helical spring that holds the system together makes one more turn.

THE SPRING SYSTEM. Support needed for a good night's sleep is supplied by the spring system.

THE INSULATOR. A pad, netting or wire arrangement. Almost all innerspring mattresses have some form of insulation over the spring unit to prevent breakdown in the padding.

THE PADDING. The comfort factor, which is needed for a good night's sleep, is supplied by the padding overlaying the insulator. This cushioning material is usually made of cotton, felt, foam or a synthetic fiber.

THE OUTER COVERING. The "tick" or ticking is the cover used for the exterior of the sleep set. The grades of fabric used for the outer covering greatly vary.

The quality of an innerspring mattress is determined by:

- ♦ The spring support system
- ♦ The insulator and padding used
- ♦ The ticking
- ♦ The quality of workmanship.

Every manufacturer of sleep sets offers cutaway demonstration models to retailers for demonstration use in their bedding showrooms. Each brand will differ. The salesperson or factory representative can explain each component and its function, as well as how it compares to other brands. It would be well worth the time for students and retail salespeople to visit a bedding factory to observe the sequence of production.

FOAM. There are several types of foam used in the manufacture of sleep sets. Foam is produced in a wide range of qualities. The better the quality, the more support and comfort, the higher the cost. Cheap foam is usually thin, unyielding and uncomfortable. Laminated foam cores are produced by combining two or more types of foam. The shape and construction of these cores increases air circulation in a foam mattress. A slab type of mattress will be made of a single piece of foam cut the correct bed size. Premium quality foam, thick enough to give excellent bodyweight distribution and comfort, will often have added surface comfort obtained by overlaid fibre down. Foam does tend to be warmer.

Foam and fiber down contain no allergens and are often recommended for those who suffer asthma or other respiratory problems. These people should select sleep sets based on contents with a doctor's advice.

WATERBEDS. The first waterbed was invented by William Cooper in 1851 and was described as a "new invention to aid in the practice of medicine and surgery." (However, legend has it, that the Greeks and Romans slept on "skins filled with water.") Over the next century, many flotation systems designed to alleviate the problems of bedsores failed because of the materials available at that time.

It wasn't until 1969, that the waterbed developed into a successful consumer-oriented product. Waterbeds marketed for general use in the late sixties were usually nothing more than water-filled vinyl bags placed directly on the floor. In the seventies, the waterbed mattress was refined, and the new waveless or reduced motion bed reduced objections to the concept. Interior baffles, foam cells and individual water-filled cylinders are among the internal construction techniques employed by various manufacturers to rechannel and inhibit water movement. More or less water can be added to give more or less support. Understand that the buyer or the installer will fill the unit with water after it is in the home. Waterbeds are very heavy and a second floor bedroom flooring must be able to bear the weight. Also, the thermostat which regulates the temperature of the water in the waterbed is a key concern. A reputable dealer will be able to advise you.

While to some people waterbeds have a sexy reputation, their benefits are derived from the basic principle that the body support system of waterbeds offers better circulation and more restful sleep. Studies indicate that waterbeds are effective in fighting bedsores, assisting in the recovery of burn victims, and in the care of premature infants.

The softside waterbed is so-called because a high-quality, high-density polyurethane foam frame instead of a wooden frame is used. The softsides are covered with padding and ticking that makes them look like a conventional innerspring mattress and they use conventional sheets and mattress pads.

AIR. The air mattress is an inflatable bladder of man-made materials. Because they can be deflated and rolled up or folded when not in use, they are presently conceived as a temporary bedding solution. To a great extent they have replaced the roll-away bed in homes. More sophisticated air mattresses with electric pumps which are supposed to maintain the same air pressure have been developed. There is no long-term data available regarding the use of air beds nor customer satisfaction statistics at this time.

ESSENTIAL FACTORS IN SELECTING THE RIGHT SLEEP SET

Before a new sleep set is shown or demonstrated, the salesperson must learn as much as possible about the prospective customers, their sleeping habits, and what they are currently sleeping on:

◆ What size is their sleep set?
◆ How long have they been using their current sleep set?
◆ Do they tend to roll together while sleeping?
◆ Do they find themselves coming fully awake when changing sleeping positions?
◆ Have the sides of their bed weakened?
◆ Do bones or joints or their backs sometimes ache during the night or upon arising?
◆ Can they feel equal support in the small of their backs or at their waists and hips?
◆ Do they feel the springs pressing the surface of their mattress?
◆ Does their sleep set squeak or make noises when they change body positions?

◆   Do their feet hang over the end?

◆   Does each person have enough sleeping width so as not to disturb the other when changing body positions? (The average person will change body positions seven times a night--with two full body turns.)

These are the reasons (and probably there are a few more) that people want and need a new sleep set. The better the new sleep set meets their needs, the more satisfied they will be. It is then up to the salesperson with a demonstration of a quality sleep set to have the prospective customer experience for themselves how the benefits of the features meet those needs.

HOW IMPORTANT IS A MATCHING FOUNDATION?

The foundation performs the same function as do shock absorbers in an automobile. When a mattress is worn out, so is the foundation. A new mattress on an old foundation will soon develop the same faults as the old mattress.

Manufacturers who build quality sleep sets will engineer the foundation to give proper and maximum support to the mattress. The elements which make up sleep sets often work against one another when the mattress and box spring are mismatched. Remember, a low-quality sleep set, although perhaps better than what you sleep on now, won't increase comfort with use, but will deteriorate.

About one-fifth of the U. S. population currently suffers from respiratory problems. Old bedding is now considered the prime source of contact with the asthma allergen.

WHAT ABOUT METAL BED FRAMES? Most are standard in construction. When buying a metal bed frame for a queen size sleep set, however, it is very important that it have a center support.

HOW TO CARE FOR YOUR INVESTMENT

Innerspring mattresses should be turned over and turned end-to-end monthly. This distributes the body's impact, stabilizes the interior padding, and creates longevity. This, along with allowing the mattress and foundation to air out on the days you change bedding will allow it to "breathe" and feel fresher.

A quality mattress will have handles that are strong enough to be used when turning and rotating, as well as carrying the mattress. An innerspring mattress should never be bent or folded as it could permanently damage the spring system.

Over-stuffed mattresses tend to compact with use, resulting in deep body impressions that require much more frequent turnings of the mattress. The extra weight of this excess padding makes this a physical challenge. Too, these deep impressions restrict body movement and may soon reduce the quality of sleep.

ADJUSTABLE BEDS

Long considered "hospital" beds, the modern adjustable bed can add comfort and extra benefits when manufactured with a quality mechanism. These added benefits include:
- The ability to raise the upper part of the body preventing reflux and heartburn.
- In some cases, slightly elevating the feet and legs has improved circulation.
- When quality mechanisms, spring systems and mattresses are purchased, it can make reading, eating, writing, and TV viewing in bed more enjoyable.

PLATFORM BEDS

Platform beds are basically a plywood base, with wood veneer surface. When quality plywood (thick enough for proper support) is used, it makes an almost indestructible base for a mattress. And when extra thick, high grade foam is used, it can be a fine piece of sleeping equipment. Innerspring mattresses built to be paired with a box spring unit, will not give the same degree of comfort when used on a wooden platform base.

DUAL PURPOSE BEDS

DAY BED. Historically, this is a single bed with a coverlet and bolsters or throw pillows to be used as a sofa during the day and a bed at night. Through the 20th century, the day bed evolved into a pair of ends/arms attached to a flat metal spring unit and back frame to be used with a twin size mattress. The styles, materials used, qualities and prices are unlimited.

TRUNDLE AND/OR POP-UP TRUNDLE BED. A flat spring unit with wheels that can be raised to the day bed level or lowered and rolled under it. Usually twin size, this option permits the owner to have two twin size beds in the space of one. Ideal for children's, guest and dual-purpose rooms as well as efficiency or studio apartments.

FUTON. Historically, the futon was used in the Japanese home which had limited space. The bed, in most homes, was a pad on a reed mat. It could be rolled up and stored when not in use or the pad could be placed on a wood frame for seating during the day. When introduced to the United States after World War II, it was for the most part presented as an inexpensive chair or sofa with a wooden frame and a pad to be used over it. Futons were sold mostly in waterbed stores in the 70s. Today, the quality of construction of futons runs the gamut from a minimal back frame with pad to be lowered for sleeping to those with frames made of wicker, teak and other expensive woods with fine fabrics and construction available in fine stores.

YOUTH BEDDING AND FURNITURE

BUNK BED. One bed over the other. Historically, built into barns, stables, and other outhouses for servants or hired hands to conserve space. Today, most often used in second home cabins, lofts, and children's rooms.

Two important factors must be considered when selecting bunk bed units:

♦ **Safety.** U. S. government safety standards have been established for the design and construction of bunk beds. When these safety standards are complied with these have reduced injuries, but not eliminated them. Two components are essential to safety: The ladder should be solid and firmly attached. Getting in and out of the top bunk should be easy; The guard rails should be substantial and firmly installed.

♦ **Changing the bedding** and making up bunk beds when placed against a wall can be a difficult procedure.

LOFT BED. Similar to bunk beds, these may be combined with other furniture to take on varied configurations, i.e. desks or bookcases along the end of the unit, built-in storage chests, etc. Again, safety features and ease of cleaning and making up the bed must be considered.

The types of sleep units above are usually installed in youth rooms. Because this is the time when children's bodies are growing and posture developed, one must consider a quality mattress with adjustable support a key factor when selecting children's beds.

BABY BED/CRIB. Safety, not design, must be the first consideration. Federal safety standards have been established for the manufacturers of baby beds. These include the distance between the side uprights which must allow air to circulate, but must be built close enough vertically so that an infant's head cannot wedge through. Finishes must be non-toxic as teething babies will chew on practically anything.

Features to be considered when selecting the baby bed/crib:

♦ **Drop sides.** Can the release be operated with the knee as well as one hand? Does only one -- or both sides drop? (This is important depending on crib placement in the room.) Does the top rail have a non-toxic plastic cap firmly attached? Does the side rise and fall easily and evenly?

♦ **Spring unit base.** Can it be raised for the new-born and lowered as the baby grows? As infants become toddlers, their ability to scale new heights makes this an important feature.

♦ **Crib Mattress.** Like all mattresses, crib mattresses come in all price levels and qualities from best to "junk" which is usually with cardboard insulators over the springs, low quality foam or padding, and cheap covers.

♦ **Antique or used cribs.** Family cribs handed down are common. Many lack needed safety features. If paint is original remember that toxic lead-based paints were used well into the 20th century. New finishes and other modifications for safety's sake should be considered.

QUALITY. QUALITY. QUALITY. The old adage, "You get what you pay for..." certainly holds true when buying bedding. Since the purchase of a sleep set is such a personal choice, it is best to buy from a reliable local retailer where you are free to see, feel, test and learn which one is best for you. If you are new in an area, a call to your local Better Business Bureau is often wise.

WHAT ABOUT MATTRESS SURFACE PROTECTORS?

When buying a new sleep set, it is a good idea to have it treated with a fabric protection of quality. The best protection is a high-quality fitted mattress pad that has been treated with fabric protection. Check cleaning and care instructions upon purchase.

THE COVER STORY

SHEETS AND PILLOWCASES: *When buying sheets for your bed know the exact size and depth of your mattress and take along a measuring tape.* Fitted bottom sheets give a smooth finished look to the bed and add to sleeping comfort. The top sheet should have at least a 12" edge for tucking in on all sides.

Sheets are manufactured of many cloths and qualities to fit personal preferences and budgets:

*   **Linen.** Expensive, but long-wearing, wash well, and resist dirt. Linen has a crisp feel to its texture and is often used in the world's finest hotels.

*   **Percale.** "The finest cotton sheeting available, made of combed yarn. Has a soft, silk like feel. Made of single 40s or better, the pick count ranges from 180 up for total number of ends and picks combined, per inch. This smooth, luxuriant sheeting was first made by Wamsutta Mills, New Bedford, Massachusetts." *Modern Textile Dictionary.*

*   **Pima & Egyptian** are cottons of high-quality due to long stape and are very smooth to the touch developing a softer feel with laundering. Pima is the longest U. S. grown stape; Egyptian is longer than Pima.

*   **Cotton** sheets can range from a fine percale to a loosely woven coarse fiber. Read and compare manufacturer's labels.

*   **Cotton/Polyester** sheets' no need for ironing is its main benefit. They are strong and easily washed and dried.

*   **Cotton flannel or flannelette** sheets are long-wearing and toasty warm in winter.

*   **Cotton knit** sheets have a "tee-shirt" feel and are also machine washable.

*   **Satin sheets** are glamorous. Also, slippery and cold to the touch.

There are many well-designed sheets on the market today. The large range of colors and motifs have made sheets popular as a fabric to upholster furniture, make slip covers or draperies as well as bedspreads and duvets. Some designs also have matching or coordinating fabrics, bedspreads, table cloths, pillow shams, wallpaper, rugs and even bathroom accessories, towels and shower curtains.

Blankets are primarily made of cotton, wool or synthetics. The natural fibers of wool and cotton breathe and provide the most sleeping comfort year round. Synthetics are easy to care for but trap heat and therefore are often not as satisfactory year round. There are many, many weights from which to select. Electric blankets are lightweight and durable--and should have a thermostat for safety and comfort. These are manufactured with single and/or dual controls, depending on the size.

Quilts, bedspreads, duvets should be functional as well as decorative in the bedroom. The choices are unlimited, but should be dictated by personal preferences and needs. Again, measure before shopping and check the labels for sizes.

PILLOWS: Pillows and pillowcases come in various sizes e.i. standard, king, etc. The function of a pillow is to support your head so that your neck and back are in alignment. A well-made pillow will hold its shape and the type of filling determines its price range. Down pillows are resilient, lightweight and expensive. (Down pillows and comforters may be aired outdoors in the sunshine for several hours to help restore resiliency.) Polyester fillings are non-allergenic and often machine washable. Again, the price is the indicator of quality. Always lie down on a pillow before buying.

There are many specific-purpose pillows on the market filled with everything from beans or dried corn to freezable/microwaveable pellets to alleviate various pain zones. Your doctor may be able to advise whether these would be of aid to you. Bolster pillows are usually made to be fairly hard to retain their visual "plump effect" and once the decorative pillow shams are on them, are not normally used for actual sleeping, but may be.

Ashley Furniture, Inc. bedroom groups: Above, youth bedroom with storage and style from Ashley's "Sunny Brook" collection. Below, Ashley's moderately-priced "Jamestown" oak Collection designed in the true spirit of Colonial America.

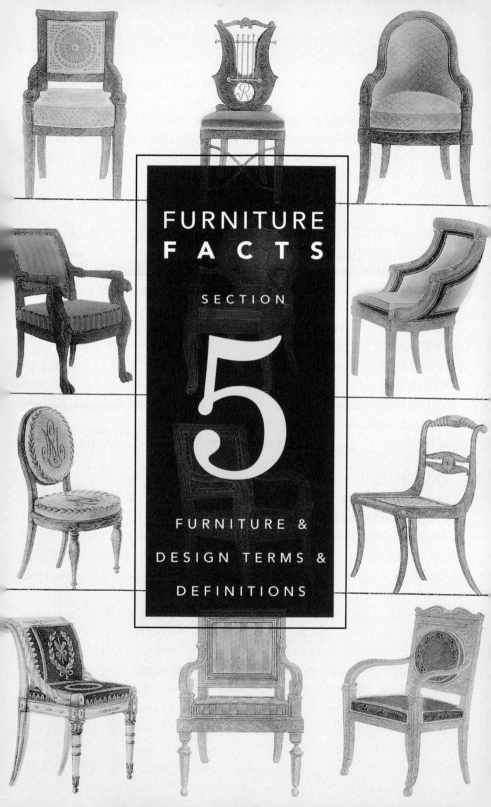

FURNITURE
FACTS

SECTION

5

FURNITURE &
DESIGN TERMS &
DEFINITIONS

DICTIONARY OF FURNITURE TERMS

This dictionary alphabetically arranged for easy reference, names and describes popular furniture terms in use from medieval to modern times. In some cases, the word or phrase has virtually passed out of use but it is still listed for reasons of historical interest. Cross references are noted for related terms listed under varying names.

A

ACANTHUS LEAF: Popular Greek decorative motif adapted from the acanthus plant. Found in almost all classic design, notably the capital of the Corinthian column.

ACORN TURNING: Knob, pendant or foot shaped like an acorn. Popular in Jacobean period.

ADELPHI (Greek brother): Trademark of the three brothers Adam 18th century furniture designers.

ALMERY: A cupboard for doles of pensioners, family retainers.

AMBULANTES: A small portable table.

AMORINI: Cupid ornaments on Italian Renaissance furniture.

ANGEL BED : A bed with a canopy but no front support.

ANTHEMION: Conventionalized honeysuckle design from a classic Greek decorative motif. (Any conventional flower or leaf design.)

APRON: Strip of wood adjoining the base of cabinets, seats and table tops extending between tops of legs or bracket feet.

ARABESQUE: Decorative scroll work or other rather intricate ornament employing foliage, vases, leaves and fruits, or fantastic animal and human figures. Arabesque won its highest triumph in the Loggia of the Vatican.

ARCADE: A series of arches, with supporting columns or piers.

ARCHITRAVE: In a classical building, the beam resting directly on the tops of the columns.

ARMOIRE: A large movable cupboard or wardrobe, with doors and shelves for storing clothes (or other large items). Also called wardrobes.

ASTRAGAL: A small convex beaded molding usually placed at the junction of a pair of doors.

B

BAGUETTE: A small, convex molding with semicircular contours.

BAG TABLE: Eighteenth century serving table with drawers and a cloth bag attached.

BAIL: Half-loop metal pull, hanging from metal bolts. First used in America about 1700.

BALLOON BACK: Chair style developed by Hepplewhite early in his career.

BALL FOOT: End of a turned leg, shaped round and with a hooded effect.

BALUSTER: A turned, supporting column, generally slender, used as a pillar.

BANDING: Inlay or marquetry which produces a color or grain contrasting with the surface it decorates.

BANDY LEG: American colonial term for the cabriole, or curved leg.

BANISTER-BACK CHAIR: Generally maple, often ebonized with vertical split-banisters in the back. Widely used in rural America from 1700 until the end of the century.

BANQUETTE: An upholstered bench or settee. Also the ledge at the back of a buffet.

BAROQUE: (Italian equivalent of French rococo.) Irregularly shaped, overly fantastic design. Used as a general term to denote a style of furniture common in the early 18th century. The word comes from a 15th century Italian architect who was called Barrochio.

BARREL CHAIR: A chair shaped like rustic chairs which were originally made from half of a wine barrel. The back is usually upholstered in vertical ribs. Seat has loose cushion.

BAS-RELIEF: Sculpture or carving whose figures project only slightly from the background.

BEAD: A small, convex molding of a nearly semicircular section.

BEAU BRUMMEL: Georgian dressing table for men, named after an English fashion arbiter.

BEDSIDE CHEST: A small bed-high chest with drawers.

BELL FLOWER: Conventionalized hanging flower-bud of three, sometimes five, petals carved or, more often inlaid one below the other in strings. Used down the legs of a table, chair or sometimes a chair splat.

BERGERE: Comfortable French arm chair with upholstered back and sides and squab cushions. Popular in Louis XIV and Louis XV periods.

BIBLIOTHEQUE-BASSE: A low cupboard fitted with shelves for books and doors often of glass but sometimes fitted with grilles.

BIRD'S-EYE: A marking of small spots often found in the wood of the sugar maple. Used and much prized from the earliest to present times.

BLANKET CHEST: Colonial storage chest often used as a bench.

BLOCK FOOT: Square, vertical foot at base of any straight, untapered leg.

BLOCK FRONT: A chest composed of a concave center panel flanked by two convex panels.

BOISERIE: Carved panels used on French pieces of the 17th century.

BOMBE: (French) An outward swelling. Applies to commodes, bureaus, armoires.

BONHEUR-DU-JOUR: A small writing table usually on tall legs and sometimes fitted to hold toilet accessories and bibelots.

BONNET TOP: When the broken-arch pediment of tall case-furniture covers the entire top from front to back, this hood is called a bonnet top.

BOSS: A circular or oval protuberance for a surface ornament. It also applies to work in relief.

BOSTON ROCKER: An American rocker (19th century) with curved seat, spindle back, and a wide top rail.

BOULLE: Celebrated designer of the Louis XIV period noted for his inlay of metals and tortoise shell. "Boullework" is a descriptive phrase.

BOWBACK: One of the types of Windsor chairs popular in America in the 18th century.

BOWFRONT: A front that curves outward to appear convex.

BOYS AND CROWNS: An old term for a type of carved ornament on the cresting of chairs, daybeds, etc.

BRACKET FOOT: Low foot on case goods. Runs both ways from corner, forming a right angle.

BREAK FRONT: A bookcase or china cabinet made of three sections, the center one projecting forward beyond the two end sections. In bookcases, the lower part of the center section sometimes has a desk.

BREWSTER CHAIR: Wooden chair with large turned posts and spindles. First made in American colonies and named for Governor Brewster of Massachusetts.

BUFFET: The French definition of the word is "a sideboard, a place for keeping dishes." Today, more often the chest which supports a china cabinet of the same width.

BUN FOOT: A flattened ball, or bun shape, with a slender ankle above. Popular in William and Mary period.

BUREAU: The French word (from the Latin, burras, red) originally designated as a red cloth covering for writing desks. Later the desk itself. In America the name designates the commonly known "dresser."

BURJAR: A large upholstered arm chair made by Thomas Chippendale.

BURL: A tree knot or protruding growth which shows beautifully patterned grainings when sliced. Used for inlay or veneer.

BUTTERFLY TABLE: Small folding table with splayed legs, generally turned. The top has wing brackets underneath to support drop-leaf wings on either side.

BYZANTINE CHAIR: A three cornered chair originated in the Orient and later used in Italy.

C

CABINET: Originally a glass fronted cabinet intended for the display of objets d'art.

CABLE: A molding design resembling intertwined rope.

CABOCHON: A gem-shaped ornament of convex, hemispherical form.

CABRIOLE: A type of leg which swells outward at the knee and inward at the ankle.

CAMELBACK: A sofa back of irregular, curved shape characterized by a large central hump.

This design was often used by Chippendale and Hepplewhite.

CANAPE: A sofa or divan, usually associated with the Louis XV design period.

CANDLESTAND: A small (usually pedestal) and lightweight table with a round top built to chair height. Once used as a portable surface for candles.

CANE CHAIR: First produced in England. It was very popular because it was cheap, light and durable. It was first used in America in about 1690. (See Section II.)

CANOPY: A covering, attached to tops of bed posts, consisting of a wood frame covered with fabric.

CANTED: Sloping at an angle.

CANTERBURY: A portable magazine rack named after the Bishop of England.

CANTONNIERE: A bed hanging used in France from the middle of the 16th century. It hung outside the bed curtains to prevent drafts.

CAPITAL: The top part of a column.

CAPPING: A turned ornament used to make furniture more decorative.

CARLTON TABLE: An 18th century writing table with an adjustable top.

CARTONNIER: A piece of furniture which took various forms. It usually stood at one end of a writing table to hold papers.

CARTOUCHE: An elliptical tablet or scroll containing the name of a king, queen, or deity. Also a sculpture or back ornament in the form of an unrolled scroll.

CARVER CHAIR: Modern term for a 17th century "Dutch" type arm chair made of turned post and spindles.

CARYATID: The top member of a pedestal or leg, used as a support, in the form of the human figure conventionalized.

CASEGOODS: Pieces made largely, but not necessarily wholly, of wood and having certain storage facilities.

CASSAPANCA: A wooden bench with a built-in chest under the seat.

CAST IRON FURNITURE: Very popular throughout the 19th century in varying forms from garden furniture and plant stands, to umbrella racks and doorstops. The cast iron bed was manufactured into the 20th century and remains popular today. (See Section II.)

CAUSEUSE: A small settee popular in early French furniture.

CEDAR CHEST: A rectangular storage chest with hinged lid and made of solid cedar or cedar veneer surfaces to prevent moths invasion of woolens. Also, a bride's hope chest in 20th century. Still very popular.

CELLARET: A case on legs or a stand for wine bottles.

CERTOSINA: Ivory inlay, of Italian origin, no longer in wide usage.

CHAISE LOUNGE: A French "long chair." A double chair. Also referred to as a "fainting couch," it is often used in bedrooms.

CHAMFER: A beveled, angled cutting away of the top portion of any edge.

CHANNELING: A grooved or furrowed effect in wood.

CHASED: A metal surface ornamented by embossing, engraving, or carving.

CHESTERFIELD: Applied to furniture, it denoted a type of sofa. This is a common term in England and Canada.

CHEST-ON-CHEST: A highboy made by placing a small chest of drawers on a large one.

CHEVAL GLASS/MIRROR: A full-length mirror mounted on swivels in a frame capable of being locked in various positions. Traditionally cheval mirrors had candle holders mounted on each side and were used in dressing rooms.

CHEVRON: A V-shaped ornament borrowed from military lexicon.

CHIFFONIER: A French word denoting a lady's work table, derived from chiffons, meaning rags. It is also used to designate a highboy.

CHINA CABINET: Seldom found in America before 1790. A "bookcase" used for displaying china. In early examples, the lower portion is often a shallow cupboard on legs or a buffet. Today, china cabinets usually have glass fronts.

CHINOISERIE: Painted or lacquered Chinese designs in furniture.

CINQUEFOIL: Five petaled design.

CLAW AND BALL: Foot of carved animal or bird claw clutching a ball, generally terminating a cabriole leg.

COAT OF ARMS: Heraldic insignia, as on a family escutcheon.

COFFEE TABLE: Long, low table used in front of a sofa.

COFFER: A chest or box covered in leather or some other material and banded with metalwork.

COLONNADE: A range of columns connected by a horizontal entablature, or cornice, at top.

COMMODE: A chest with doors.

CONNECTICUT CHEST: Low chest, on legs, usually containing a double set of drawers.

CONSOLE: A table, usually small, having curved or otherwise ornamented supports.

CORBEL: A piece of stone, wood, etc. projecting from a wall, to support a cornice, arch, etc.

CORNICE: The top or finishing molding of a column or piece of furniture. (Also see Window Treatment - Section V.)

CORNER CUPBOARD: Triangular cupboard made to fit into a corner. It is usually a dining room china cabinet but may also be a curio cabinet for any room.

CORNUCOPIA: The horn of plenty, symbolizing peace and plenty, used as design motif.

COTTAGE FURNITURE: A term used in the Victorian period for mass produced simplified forms, frequently painted with decorative designs; often ornamented with spool turnings.

COUCH: A 17th and 18th century term for daybed. Not used as a term for sofa or settee until recent times.

COURT CUPBOARD: A small cupboard used for storing silver, china, or other precious goods.

COVER: The external fabric of an upholstered piece.

CREDENCE: An early Italian cabinet used for carving meats or displaying plates. It was the forerunner of the sideboard.

CREDENZA: A sideboard or buffet with drawers or doors.

CRESTING: Shaped and sometimes perforated ornament on the top of a structure, as in the cresting of a chair.

CROFT: A small filing cabinet of the late 18th century, it had many small drawers and a writing surface.

CROSS STRETCHER: X-shaped stretcher in straight or curved lines. Found on tables, a few chairs and in America on highboys and lowboys.

CUPID'S BOW: A term used to describe the typical top rail of a Chippendale chair back which curves up at the ends and dips slightly in the center.

CURULE LEGS: X-shaped legs used on a folding chair with no back.

CYMA CURVE: A curved molding with a reversed curve as its profile.

D

DAVENPORT: An upholsterer in Boston, named Davenport, made such handsome and luxurious overstuffed couches that people began to speak of these couches as "Davenports." This word has been replaced by the word sofa.

DAVENTRY: A small chest of drawers with a sloping top for writing.

DENTILS: A classic, decorated design consisting of rectangular blocks with spaces between.

DIAPER-WORK: Surface decoration consisting of a system of reticulations each of which contains an ornamental unit, as a flower or leaf.

DISC FOOT: A flat, disc-shaped foot used on tables or chairs.

DOLPHIN: One of the heraldic fishes represented as either embowed, counter embowed or extended. Symbolic of love and diligence.

DOVER CHEST: Early American hope chest, usually made of maple, oak.

DOWEL: Headless pin, usually made of wood, used in the construction of furniture. (See Sec. II.)

DOWRY CHEST: Made to store the trousseau of a prospective bride. American examples include the Hadley chest, the Connecticut chest, the painted Pennsylvania-German chest, the Lane Company cedar chest.

DRAUGHT CHAIR: Early English equivalent of a wing chair.

DRESSER: A species of a sideboard. Also for the service of food or the storage of dishes. The term used today indicates a chest for the storage of cosmetics or clothing.

DROP FRONT: Hinged front of desk which lowers to form a level writing surface.

DROP LEAF: Table built with hinged extension leaves which lower when not in use.

DROP SEAT: A concave seat the middle and front of which are lower than the side.

DRUM TABLE: Circular top table on a tripod base with a deep skirt that may contain drawers.

DUMB WAITER: A dining room stand with normally three circular trays increasing in size toward the bottom. Also, a pulley type elevator that brought food up from the basement kitchen to the first floor dining room.

DUSTBOARD: Horizontal board placed between drawers of a commode or similar piece to exclude dust.

DUTCH DRESSER: A cabinet with open shelves on upper portion, drawers or cupboard below.

DUCK FOOT: Webbed foot attached to a table leg which curves outward.

DUTCH FOOT: A simple pad used as the foot on cabriole legs. Sometimes confused with a duck foot.

E

EBENISTE: An ordinary French term for a cabinet maker.

EBONIZE: To stain wood to look like ebony.

ECLECTIC: Word coined last half of the 20th century; infers artful mixture of decorating styles.

EGG AND DART: A classic design, consisting of alternating eggs and darts, used mostly in cornices.

ENCARPA: A festoon of fruit and flowers commonly used to decorate friezes, other flat spaces.

ENDIVE: A carved leaf design following the lines of the endive plant.

ESCRITOIRE: A writing desk containing, with other drawer compartments and pigeon holes, one or more secret ones. The English word "secretary" was derived from this.

ESCUTCHEON: Name applied to a shield upon which a coat of arms or other devices are emblazoned.

ETAGERE: Originally a small work table consisting of shelves or tray sets one above the other. More recently, an open shelf for what-nots. May be of varying heights.

EVOLUTE: Recurrent wave motif for a band, frieze or cornice.

F

FAN PATTERN: Description of the back of a chair when fitted with ribs somewhat resembling the stalks of a half-open fan.

FARTHINGALE CHAIR: An armless upholstered chair for ladies wearing enormous skirts of early Stuart era.

FAUTEUIL: A French arm chair which, unlike the Bergere, has open spaces between the arms and seat.

FESTOON: A garland or length of foliage, flowers or branches entwined or bound together, usually hanging in a curve between two points.

FIDDLE-BACK: A chair splat shaped in manner of the violin's contour.

FILIGREE: Interlaced wirework decoration of scrolls and arabesques.

FINIAL: A decorative finishing device, usually foliated, for the terminals of projecting uprights.

FIRE SCREEN: First made to give protection from the intense heat of large open fires. Two kinds were made. The Pole screen with the screen on a tripod base and the Horse or Cheval screen which consisted of two uprights, each on two legs, enclosing a panel.

FLAMBEAU: A carved decoration in the shape of a flaming torch.

FLEMISH SCROLL: A baroque form with the curve broken by an angle.

FLEUR-DE-LIS: A French emblem in the form of a conventionalized floral design.

FLUTING: A grooving on any horizontal or perpendicular surface.

FLYING DISK: A flat disk with two outspread wings. A prominent Egyptian motif.

FLY RAIL: A folding bracket supporting a drop leaf in a table.

FOIL: A Gothic term denoting the intersection point of the junction of circular areas, as in trefoil.

FOLIATED: Decorated with leaf designs of an intricate pattern.

FRET: A kind of Greek ornament formed of bands or fillets variously combined. A piece of perforated ornamental work.

FRIEZE: In architecture, the entablature between the architrave and cornice. The term is applied to the broad border which sometimes runs around the top of a room between wallpaper and cornice.

FOUR POSTER: A colonial bed with posts extended upward, may or may not hold a canopy.

FRENCH BED: A bed in which the ends roll outward. It has no posts.

FUNCTIONALISM: Furniture design based on use rather than on ornamentation alone.

G

GADROON: A carved molding of olive or ruffle form used in the edges of table tops and chairs.

GARGOYLE: A grotesque carved figure, or head, which originally carried rainwater from the gutters.

GARLAND: An architectural ornament representing foliage, flowers or fruits plaited and tied together with ribbons.

GATELEG TABLE: A table where the folding leaf is upheld by a leg swinging out like a gate. A development of the Jacobean period, it was popular in Colonial America.

GEOMETRIC PANELS: Forming or consisting of regular lines, curves and angles.

GESSO: A bas-relief decoration, made out of plaster, which, after hardening is painted or gilded.

GIRONDOLE: A round, convex mirror used as a wall ornament.

GLASTONBURY CHAIR: An X-framed, ecclesiastical Gothic seat with sloping paneled back. Arms had a drooping curve in which a priest's vestments rested.

GLYPH: A short, vertical groove or channel. It was common in Doric architecture.

GOBELIN: Name of a French tapestry and the Parisian factory which produced it.

GRIFFIN: A chimerical beast employed in decoration in early Georgian.

GRILLE: Metal lattice work used in a great many 18th century bookcases.

GUERIDON: A small table, or tabouret, with round top for holding candles or small articles.

GUILLOCHE: An ornament formed by two or more intertwining bands or interlacing figure "8's" frequently enclosing rosettes or other details.

H

HADLEY CHEST: A colonial chest with a drawer. Sometimes used as a hope or dowry chest.

HANDKERCHIEF TABLE: A single leaf table with leaf and top triangular in shape. Closed, the table fits in a corner, opened, it is a small square.

HASSOCK: Large upholstered cushion used as ottoman. Circular or square.

HIGHBOY: A high chest of drawers, deriving its name from haut bois, which in French means "high wood."

HIGH RELIEF: This term refers to deep carving of any plane surface of any material.

HITCHCOCK CHAIR: American chair, 1820-1850, made with oval top rail and cane seat. Named for designer, Lambert Hitchcock.

HOOD: A shaped top on cabinet work. It usually overhangs the vertical lines.

HOPE CHEST: Colloquial American term widely used for dowry chest.

HUSKS: Ornamentation of flowers or foliage usually used in pendant manner.

HUTCH: Enclosed structure, often raised on uprights, or an enclosed structure of more than one tier.

I

IMBRICATIONS: Ornaments which take the form of fishes' scales or the segmented edge of tiles that overlap.

INLAY: A design of contrasting woods, ivory, or other materials, set into a surface. (See Sec. II.)

INTAGLIO: A design or illustration made by cutting into the surface of the material.

INTARSIA: An Italian type of decoration, similar to marquetry where a design is sunk into an entire surface. (See Section II.)

IONIC: Designating or of a Greek style of architecture characterized by ornamental scrolls on the capitals.

J

JAPANNING: European and American version of Oriental lacquering often substituting paint for the layers of varnish.

JEWELLING: Ornamental carving in the shape of jewels. It was common during the Renaissance.

K

KAS: An early American cabinet, of Dutch origin, made with painted or paneled wood.

KIDNEY DESK: A desk or a table with curved front and a top shaped like a kidney bean.

KLISMOS: A Greek chair design featuring a concave back and legs.

KNOB TURNING: A turning resembling a series of knobs or bosses.

KD (KNOCKED DOWN): Applied to pieces shipped unassembled or only partially assembled.

L

LACCHE: The word lacche is used in Italian to cover all painted decoration applied to furniture whether or not it has the hard glass of Oriental lacquer.

LADDER-BACK: A chair-back in which horizontal cross-rails, used instead of a splat, give a ladder effect.

LAMBREQUIN: A short piece of hanging drapery, often imitated in metal or wood for decorative purposes.

LATTICE: An openwork wood decoration in a crisscross diagonal or square pattern.

LAURELLING: A decorative feature using the laurel leaf motif as its basis.

LAZY SUSAN: A revolving tray or stand of wood or metal.

LINENFOLD PANEL: A design for a panel consisting of a combination of straight moldings in the shape of folds of linen.

LINTERS: Short cotton fibers clinging to cotton seed after it has been ginned. Used for early mattress filling.

LOTUS: The conventionalized Egyptian water lily as found in classic ornamentation.

LOVE SEAT: A small sofa or sleeper sofa designed to accommodate two persons.

LOWBOY: A table with drawers and in most cases, relatively short legs.

LOW RELIEF: This term refers to shallow carving of any plane surface of any material.

LOZENGE: A diamond-shaped decorative panel. It was the Middle English word for stone.

LUNETTE: An ornament or mural decoration shaped like a half moon.

LYRE: A stringed instrument of the harp class. Its form was used as a decorative motif by Duncan Phyfe and others.

M

MARLBOROUGH LEGS: A heavy, straight leg used by Thomas Chippendale and others.

MARQUETRY: Inlay work. Decorations formed by patterns of woods, metals, ivory or tortoise shell sunk into the surfaces of furniture. (See Section II.)

MEDALLION: A decorative plaque made of wood or metal.

MELON-BULB: Jargon and comparatively modern term for the swollen member on legs or posts of furniture.

MENUISIER: The term corresponds roughly to the English carpenter or joiner.

MIRROR STAND: An adjustable mirror mounted on a shaft and tripod base, resembling a pole-screen; popular at the end of the 18th century.

MODILLION: An enriched block, or horizontal bracket, used in series under a Corinthian or composite cornice and sometimes, with less ornament, under an Ionic order.

MOLDING: Ornamented or shaped strips, either sunk into or projecting from a surface. Used mostly for decoration.

MORRIS CHAIR: A large, easy chair with arms usually extending beyond the back and adjustable beyond the back and adjustable to various angles. It was named for its inventor, William Morris.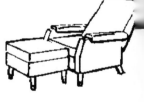

MOTHER-OF-PEARL: Inlay of nacreous shell slices, often used on early 19th century American fancy chairs, tables, mirrors, etc.

MOTIF: A dominant feature or theme in artistry or craftsmanship.

N

NESTED TABLES: Three or four identical lightweight tables sized from small to largest, each one nesting under the next.

NIELLO: The art of decorating metal plates by incising designs on them and filling incised lines with alloy.

NULLING: A projecting detail of a carved ornament, similar to gadrooning.

O

OBJET D'ART: A small object of artistic value.

OCCASIONAL TABLE: A term applied loosely to any small table.

OGEE: A compound curve, the directions of which are opposite to those of the Cyma curve.

ONLAY: Ornament applied to the surfaces of woods or other kinds of material.

OPEN STOCK: Individual pieces which can be sold separately or grouped (correlated) to form sets to the buyer's taste.

ORMOLU: A metal resembling gold. Used as mounts and decorative effects on furniture.

OTTOMAN: Low upholstered seat, without arms or back, used as a footstool.

OVOLO: A continuous ornament in the form of an egg which generally decorates the molding called "quarter-round." Eggs are often separated from one another by pointed darts.

OXBOW, OXBOW FRONT: The reverse serpentine curve, somewhat resembling the curve of an oxbow. Often used in the finest 18th century New England case furniture such as chests of drawers, secretaries, etc.

P

PALMETTE: A carved or painted ornament resembling a palm leaf; an anthemion.

PAPIER MÂCHÉ: Molded paper pulp used for many small articles and particularly suitable for japanning and polishing.

PARQUETRY: Furniture inlaid with a geometrical cube design in the manner of a parquet floor.

PATERA: A dish like ornament often worked in bas-relief on a frieze.

PATINA: A surface texture produced by age, wear or rubbing.

PEDESTAL TABLE: A table on a round center support.

PEDIMENT: The space or structure above a cornice. The classic pediment, seen in the conventional Greek temple, was triangular in shape. It is found on the tops of secretaries and grandfather's clocks, usually as a "broken pediment."

PEMBROKE TABLE: A long square-sided table with oval or square ends, the leaves at the side of which drop almost to the floor. Named for Lady Pembroke.

PENDANT: A hanging ornament, usually in a matched or parallel series.

PENNSYLVANIA DUTCH: The name applies to German settlers in Pennsylvania. Their furniture is distinctive since their cabinet makers worked in soft woods, which they painted and often decorated with floral patterns and other motifs from the vocabulary of peasant design.

PIE CRUST TABLE: A table so named because the edge is finished off in a series of serpentines or curves, as cooks crimp the edges of a pie.

PIER GLASS: Large, window-height mirror suspended above a table between two windows.

PILASTER: Flat column superimposed on any plain surface to serve as a support for a cornice or a pediment.

PINEAPPLE: Carved pineapple-shaped ornament found frequently in early 19th century American bed posts.

PINNACLE: A carved ornament at the top or crest of a piece of furniture.

PLAQUE: A flat, thin ornament, usually made of metal or porcelain and inserted into wood.

PLINTH: Square or octagonal base of a chest or other column, solid to the floor. Primarily, a stand for a plant, sculpture, or other 3-dimensional item.

POPPY-HEAD: Decorative finial of a bench or desk end as in ecclesiastical woodwork.

PORTIÈRE: A curtain hung in a doorway.

POUDRESSE: Small table with mirrored lid covering space for cosmetics.

PRESS: Broadly, a tall, enclosed, and doored structure comparable to a wardrobe.

PRIE-DIEU CHAIR: A high-backed chair of Italian origin with a narrow shelf, rail or pad upon which the user may rest his arms while kneeling in the seat.

PULL-UP CHAIR: A term for a small light arm chair. Sometimes called an "occasional chair."

Q

QUATREFOIL: An ornamental figure, foliation, perforation or panel divided by cusps, or featherings, into four foils, leaves or lobes.

QUIRK: A narrow groove channel molding sometimes called a sunken fillet.

R

RAIL: The horizontal piece in framing or paneling. In a chair back the top member supported on the stiles.

RAKE: The angle or slant of a chair back or of a non-vertical table leg.

RECLINING CHAIR: An upholstered chair or rocker that reclines.

REEDING: The reverse of fluting. A decoration consisting of parallel lines formed by beaded mountings projecting from the surface. Sheraton, Adam and Phyfe used it.

REFECTORY TABLE: A long, narrow table originally used in dining rooms of religious orders. It was later shortened in length and provided with underleaves.

RELIEF: Any ornamentation raised above the surface or background.

RESTORATION: A proper renewal of a piece by a candid replacement of hopelessly damaged or missing parts.

RIBBAND-BACK: A chair with an entwined ribbon motif ornament.

RINCEAU: A classic ornamental device composed of intertwining stalks of acanthus or other foliage.

RISING SUN: When a fan-shaped ornament is carved half-circle and the resulting spray of stalks suggest sun rays.

ROCOCO: A style of decoration distinguished by a profusion of meaningless, but often delicately executed, ornaments in imitation of rock work, shells, foliage and massed scrolls.

ROLL-TOP DESK: Similar to a cylinder-top desk but the writing table and fittings are enclosed by a curved slatted panel.

ROMANESQUE: Decorative scroll work or other intricate ornamentation derived from triangles, circles and other geometric figures. It sprang from the round arch and general massiveness of Romance architecture and reached its highest form in the 12th century.

ROMAYNE: Renaissance ornamentation featured by human heads on medallions.

ROSETTE: An ornament resembling the rose. A painted or sculptured architectural ornament with parts circularly arranged like rows of leaves in a circle around a bud.

ROUNDABOUT CHAIR: Corner chair with triangle front and usually a circular back.

ROUNDEL: Circular ornament enclosing sundry formal devices on medieval and later woodwork.

RUNNER: The curved rocker of a rocking chair, once made solely of wood but now largely of metal.

RUSH SEAT: A seat woven of rushes. Used in America from the earliest times, generally with simple furniture. (See "Wicker. Cane. Willow." - Section II.)

S

SABRE LEG: A term used to describe a sharply curving leg in the classical style which has also been called scroll shaped. It is generally reeded.

SADDLE SEAT: A chair seat hollowed out to resemble a saddle.

SALTIRE: A straight, X-shaped stretcher used on chairs or tables.

SAWBUCK TABLE: A table with an X-shaped frame either plain or scrolled.

SCALLOP: A carved ornament in the shape of a shell used widely on rococo pieces.

SCONCE: A general name for a wall-light consisting of a backplate and either a tray or branched candle-holders. Usually metal.

SCOOP SEAT: A chair with a seat which has been hollowed or formed to fit the body.

SCROLL: A spiral or convoluted line used for ornamentation.

SCROLL FOOT: A foot in the form of a spiral line; not fully articulated with part above it.

SECRETARY: A drop front desk, often with book shelves above and drawers below.

SEGMENTAL: A less than semicircular, unbroken pediment with an abruptly ending curve.

SEIGNORIAL CHAIR: An imposing highback seat for the master of a house.

SERPENTINE FRONT: Front of a commode, desk or bureau shaped in a waving curve.

SERRATED: A saw tooth or zigzag ornament that is one form of a notched dentil.

SERVING TABLE: A long, narrow table with drawers for silver, napery and crystal.

SETTEE: A long ornately carved 17th century seat or bench with a high back and often with arms. Today, usually length of a love seat.

SETTLE: Colonial all wood bench or settee with solid arms. The pilgrims brought it from England.

SHAKER FURNITURE: This furniture, while provincial, is of such sheer simplicity, so pure in line, so lean and functional in form, so well proportioned and soundly constructed, that it is much prized today. Made by the early 19th century Shakers, it is usually in pine, maple, walnut or fruitwoods.

SHIELD BACK: A chair back shaped like a shield.

SIDEBOARD: A dining room piece, with a long flat top and a superstructure, equipped with drawers.

SKIRT: A wood or fabric flounce at bottom of a furniture piece.

SLANT-FRONT DESK: A frame or chest of drawers with a top section as an enclosed desk for writing, the hinged lid sloping at a 45-degree angle when closed.

SLAT BACK: Type of back, used in early American chairs and settees, composed of horizontal slats attached to back parts.

SLEEPY HOLLOW CHAIR: Large upholstered chair with hollowed seat, high back and solid low arms.

SLIP-SEAT: A removable upholstered seat for a chair, used especially in dining and light pull-up chairs.

SOFA: The sofa was first introduced into Italy in the late 17th century. In fact, many Italian and early French sofas resembled a row of chairs joined together. Long sofas with carved wooded backs, and usually rush seats, were popular in the 18th century.

SOFA TABLE: A small, narrow, rectangular table with two front drawers in the apron and hinged leaves at each end. First made in America about 1800. More recently, a narrow table to be placed alongside the back of sofa.

SPADE FOOT: A rectangularly shaped tapered foot resembling a spade.

SPANDREL: An arch form bounded by a horizontal and vertical frame such as was used by Sheraton in some chair backs.

SPINDLE: A slender turned baluster, often tapered or molded.

SPINET DESK: A writing desk designed after a small musical instrument of the colonial period. When the instrument wore out, the keyboard was removed and the cabinet used as a writing desk, for which the recessed space, formerly housing the keys, was happily adapted.

SPIRAL LEG: A leg carved in the shape of a rope twist or a spiral.

SPIRAL TURNING: A column twisted like strands or filaments of rope.

SPIRAL WAVE: A series of turning, wavelike scrolls used as decoration.

SPLAT: The central member of a chair back, also called a "splad." (See chair parts - Sec. II.)

SPLAYED: A pitched spread or slant; a surface canted outward, beveled or angled.

SPLINT SEAT: A seat made of oak or hickory strips interlaced. Used in country furniture through the 18th century.

SPOOL BEAD: A continuous turning having the form of a series of connected beads.

SPOON BACK: A chair back which is spooned or shaped to fit contours of human body.

STAMPS: Various names and letters are often found stamped on French furniture made in the 18th century or later. These stamps are a most important means of identifying the makers of individual pieces of furniture.

STEP TABLE: A table resembling a one-step stair commonly used at the end of a sofa. The top shelf being shorter and higher.

STRAPWORK: A narrow band folded, crossed, and sometimes interlaced. Also an ornament consisting of a narrow band in convolutions similar to those of a leather strap thrown at hazard.

STRAW-WORK: A method of decorating furniture with tiny strips of bleached and colored straws to form landscapes, geometrical patterns, etc. in the 17th century.

STRETCHER: The underbracing of chairs and tables taking and "H" or "X" form.

STRIPPING: Removing the old surface or finish from a piece of furniture.

SUITE: A complete set of matched furniture.

SWAG: A festoon of flowers, fruit or draperies resembling a garland.

SWING LEG: A hinged or folding leg used to support the drop leaf of a table.

SWIVEL CHAIR: A chair which revolves on a stationary platform or on legs.

T

T-CUSHION: A "T" shaped back or seat cushion made to fit around arms of a chair, love seat, or sofa.

TABOURETTE: A stool or small seat, usually without arms or back, used as a stand.

TAMBOUR: A desk with a secretary (shelved) top and sliding panels replacing the grille.

TAPER LEG: A leg which diminishes in thickness as it approaches the foot.

TAVERN TABLE: Sturdy, rectangular table on four legs, usually braced with stretchers. Much used in 18th century taverns.

TESTER: Top framework of a high-post canopy or draped bed, of wood or fabric.

THERM LEG: A square or four cornered tapered leg used on chairs or tables.

TIER TABLE: An occasional (usually pedestal based) table with 2 or 3 tiered round tops of graduated size.

TILT-TOP: A small table, with the top hinged to a pedestal base permitting it to hang vertically when not in use.

TORCHERE: A floor lamp designed to throw light upward. In early times, it was any stand that held a light.

TRAIL: Undulating bands of formalized leaf, berry or floral pattern.

TREE-OF-LIFE: Carved tree or vine design with fruit and often birds or animals in foliage.

TREFOIL: A three-leaved or three-cusped ornament usually contained within a circle.

TRESPOLO: Elegant three-legged tables usually designed to stand against a wall.

TRESTLE: A braced frame, forming the whole support for a table top.

TRIPOD: A three legged stand for a pedestal table. Adam and Chippendale favored it.

TRIPTYCH: A three part, hinged mirror or small screen inspired by alter pieces.

TRIVET: A three legged stand or small table normally flanking a fireplace. It now often refers to a wall decoration or a heat-resistant stand for hot objects.

TROMPE: d'oeíl. A French phrase meaning "fool the eye". Usually a realistically painted surface which gives a three-dimensional effect.

TRUMPET LEG: A leg shaped like a trumpet and having its characteristic flared profile.

TRUNDLE BED: A low bed of colonial days which, during the daytime, was rolled under a larger bed. Just as popular in 21st century.

TUCKAWAY TABLE: A hinged leaf gate-leg table with cross legs which fold into each other as compactly as if tucked away.

TUDOR ROSE: A decorative motif compounded of the White Rose and the Red Rose.

TULIP: A design in the shape of a tulip, carved or painted on American furniture, especially Shaker.

TURNING: The shaping of legs or trim obtained by using a lathe. It is one of the most venerable wood working processes.

U

URN: A vase-shaped receptacle also used for ornament, especially on sideboards, or as finial of a broken pediment.

UPRIGHTS: The outer vertical posts of a chair.

UPHOLSTER: To fit, as furniture, with coverings, padding, springs, etc.

V

VALANCE: A horizontal cross section of draperies.

VANITY: A low, drop-center ladies' dressing table with an attached mirror and drawers and matching pull-up bench.

VARGUENO: A fall or drop front desk of Spanish origin popular in the 16th and 17th centuries.

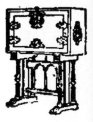

VENEER: Thin sheets of wood applied to the surface for decorative effect or to improve the appearance of furniture. (See Section II.)

VIS-À-VIS: A tête-à-tête chair in which two sitters face oppositely.

VITRINE: A glass-front china cabinet used mostly to display fine pieces.

VOLUTE: A spiral, scroll-like ornament on Ionic and Corinthian capitals.

W

WAINSCOT CHAIR: An Elizabethan oak chair, the back of which is paneled like the wainscoting of a wall. These chairs are massive, ornately carved with strap work.

WASH STANDS: Specially adapted for bedroom use after 1750. A cupboard or chest of drawers on four legs with a basin sunk in the top.

WELSH CUPBOARD: A cabinet with large enclosed storage base and upper part of open shelves.

WHAT-NOT: A portable stand with four uprights enclosing shelves, in use after about 1800 for books, ornaments, etc.

WHEAT: Carved ornamentations representing three ears of wheat. It was extensively used by Hepplewhite.

WINDSOR CHAIR: A chair with a wooden or rush seat, pegged legs, and back of turned spindles. Backs may be fan, hoop or comb type.

WING CHAIR: An upholstered chair with a high back, stuffed arms, and wing shaped protectors at head level protruding from the back over the arms. Introduced in America before 1725.

X

X-STRETCHER: A crossed stretcher at the bottom of a chair or table.

X-CHAIR: An ancient folding-type chair dating back to Egypt, Rome and the Middle Ages.

Y

YORKSHIRE CHAIR: 17th century carved side chair native to Yorkshire, England. Of oak, with turned front legs and stretchers, it derived from the "wainscot chair."

YORKSHIRE DRESSER: Dresser or cupboard, of oak or teal, with a low back.

Z

ZENANA: Furniture reserved for the part of the house in which women and girls were secluded in ancient Persia.

ZIG-ZAG: A molding with a series of frequent sharp turns from side to side.

IDENTIFICATION OF CHAIR SHAPES

Upholstered chairs are produced in many shapes and kinds. There are certain types, however, which have proved popular through the years and are found in the lines of most manufacturers. These styles have been given identifying names and although details, such as legs, trim and cushion treatment vary widely, the general shape of the chair remains much the same. While they do not comprise all the styles and shapes now being made, they are among the most popular and are found in the lines of the leading manufacturers of upholstered furniture.

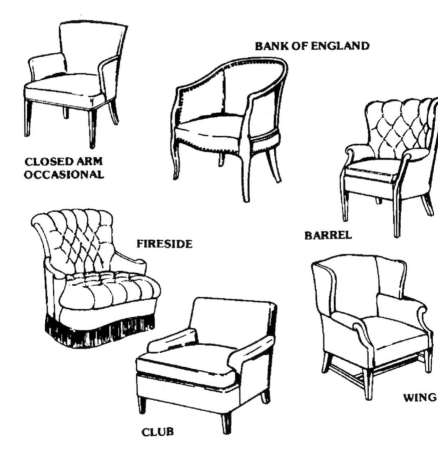

BANK OF ENGLAND

CLOSED ARM
OCCASIONAL

FIRESIDE

BARREL

CLUB

WING

COGSWELL

TUB

LAWSON

FANBACK

CHARLES OF LONDON

SHELL

COCKFIGHT

OPEN ARM PULL-UP

CORNER

WINDOW SEAT

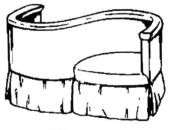

TETE-A-TETE

IDENTIFYING OCCASIONAL TABLES

There are many different kinds of occasional tables used in the living room of today and often it is difficult to remember what each type looks like. On this page, we will illustrate the most common types. Decorative details, legs, feet and minor points of construction may vary according to the period design of the piece but the general characteristics remain much the same.

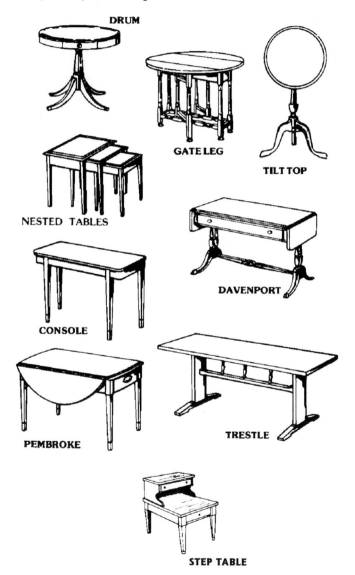

DRUM

GATE LEG

TILT TOP

NESTED TABLES

DAVENPORT

CONSOLE

PEMBROKE

TRESTLE

STEP TABLE

IDENTIFICATION OF SOFA SHAPES

Upholstered sofas and sleeper sofas are identified by their general shape, type of back, arms, legs, height from the floor and trim. The following styles are representative of sofas through the years, although most of the details, such as legs, trim and cushion treatment, vary with the individual designer. An important point to remember is that dual-purpose sleeper sofas are now widely available in the same distinctive styles as stationary sofas.

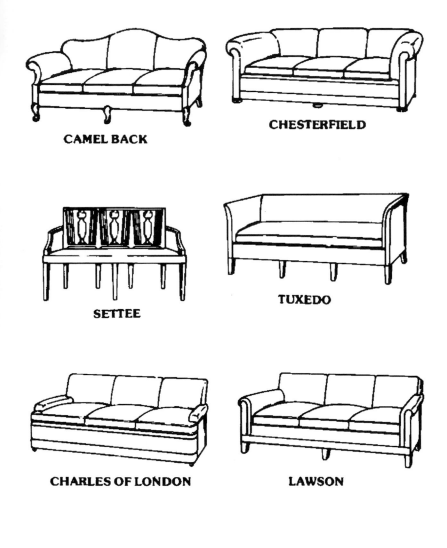

CAMEL BACK

CHESTERFIELD

SETTEE

TUXEDO

CHARLES OF LONDON

LAWSON

DICTIONARY OF FURNITURE WOODS

This list, alphabetically arranged for convenient reference, names and describes furniture woods in use. For your guidance, "grain" denotes arrangement and direction of the wood elements, "texture" refers to their relative coarseness, and "figure" describes the grain pattern.

A

ABOUDIKROU: (Africa). A wood resembling mahogany and somewhat related to sapele.

ACACIA: Has narrow sapwood and vari-colored heartwood ranging from yellowish brown to shades of red and green.

AFARA: This is the English name for korina, one of the more exotic woods.

AFRICAN PADAUK: (Central Africa). Fancy wood marked with ripples on deep golden red, bright plum red, or deep violet.

ALDER, RED: (U.S.). Hard, strong wood which seasons easily, works well, is easily stained to imitate walnut and mahogany. It has maple-like figure. Used for plywood cores, occasionally for exposed surfaces.

ALLECEDA: (Philippines). Coined name for wood of the bean family. Light brown to brown.

ALMON: (Philippines). Pale reddish to tan wood used for veneer. Usually has a broken stripe figure.

AMARANTH: (Central & South America). A strong, tough and extremely hard wood it is capable of high finish and polish. Owes its ornamental value to unique purple, sometimes blood red, heartwood. Used mostly for inlays, panels, and small carved pieces.

AMBOYNA: (New Guinea, East Indies). Durable wood with frequent burls, beautifully mottled patterns. It takes a high polish. Color varies from light red-brown to orange.

APPLEWOOD: (America). A fine fruitwood used in colonial times for furniture and inlays.

ASH: Several native varieties are used in furniture. White ash is a ring-porous, hardwood of great strength. Extensively used for furniture frames and hidden parts. It bends well and stays in place after manufacture. Brown ash has strong grain character and is used for veneers. Black ash is similar to white but lighter in weight and softer. Ash burls have closely twisted, interlaced figure.

ASPEN: The European white poplar once cultivated in the eastern U.S. and now plentiful in the west. Once highly prized for bedroom pieces. White-yellow, with simple straight figure, to light brown at crotch. Lustrous satiny surface.

AVOIDURE: (West Africa). It has a milky white to slight yellowish shade, with satiny lustre. Typical figure is a ropy mottle.

AYOUS: (West Africa). White to creamy yellow, sometimes tinted with brown. Stripes in veneer are regular, like mahogany.

B

BASSWOOD: A creamy white wood of soft, fibrous structure with poor finishing quality and no figure. Used principally for cores and cross banding.

BEECH: (Europe and America). A tough wood with very small pores, rarely figured. Its color is light reddish brown of various shades. Extensively used for frames, bent chair backs, rocker runners, drawer slides.

BIRCH: One of the strongest American cabinet woods which is widely used by the furniture industry. Similar to maple, it is heavy, of average stiffness and hardness for hardwood, and is above average in toughness. The texture is even, the grain fine and close. It is easy to work and is adaptable to fine finishes. Yellow birch, which has creamy white sapwood and yellowish brown heartwood, is used in furniture. Sweet birch is also used. When rotary cut, the outer part of the log yields white wood and the inner part yields "red birch" which can be kept separate. "Unselected" birch is the run of the log, some white, some red, some mixed. It is widely used for frames, drawers, partitions and slides in natural state. It can be stained and finished to resemble many expensive and imported cabinet woods.

BLACK BEAN: (Australia). A hard wood showing, in veneer, a handsome sheen. Varies from pale straw yellow to mellow chocolate or blackish color, with narrow broken lines of lighter color.

BLACK GUM: This is a synonym for tupelo which is described further on in this section.

BLACKWOOD: (Tasmania and Australia). Similar to acacia and has similar properties.

BOSSE: (Africa). Well-figured wood used for veneers. Varies from pink to light reddish brown.

BOX ELDER: (U.S.). Soft, light wood, a species of maple. Used for cheap furniture only.

BOXWOOD: (Florida). Tough hard textured wood. Because of its peculiar yellow color, it is often used for inlays.

BRAZILIAN ROSEWOOD: (Brazil). Reddish brown wood streaked with darker purplish lines to darker brown shades, varying from deep purplish to black.

BUBINGA: (West Africa). Predominating shades from pale to deep flesh red or purple which is sometimes broken by light colored narrow strips.

BULLET WOOD: (Brazil, Guiana and Venezuela). Reddish brown, sometimes purplish cast. Strong and durable but its chief decorative value is in color rather than in figure.

BURMA PADAUK: (Burma). A harder wood of finer texture than African padauk. Color ranges from yellowish or golden red to dark red streaked with brown.

BUTTERNUT: It is also called white walnut. A soft wood, yellow-gray in color. Used only for decoration, where strength is not a factor.

C

CAPOMO: (Central America). Pale cream wood with a stripe figure. See satine rubanne.

CARAPATHIAN ELM BURL: (Europe). Light reddish brown wood with dark brown buds and deep veinings. Used in table tops, drawers, chair backs.

CATIVO: (Central and South America). Firm, straight grained wood which takes a smooth finish. Heartwood is medium to light brown, often streaked.

CEDAR, RED: A durable wood noted for its fragrance and used principally for lining cedar chests, closets and drawers.

CHERRY: Warm, reddish brown color, resembling maple in character. Now popularly known as fruitwood, it is strong and durable, does not warp. Widely used for French Provincial stylings and in lesser degree for Colonial style furniture.

CHESTNUT: Native wood, rather light in weight, with coarse open grain and prominent figure on flat cut surface. Grayish brown to near white in color. Used for fumed-finish furniture, occasional pieces and as core for veneers, practically free from warping. Not in common use as most commercial stands have been wiped out by blight.

CIRCASSIAN WALNUT: (Europe). Comes from the arid Black Sea region where, in their struggle for life under unfavorable conditions, the trees twisted and gnarled becoming highly figured.

CLARO WALNUT: Also called California walnut. Moderate to heavy black stripe of irregular pattern on background of gray, tan or dark brown. Bold figure due to variations in grain and pigment.

COCOHOLO: (Central America and Mexico). Has fine uniform grain. Ranges from shades of red, rose, orange or purple. Veneer sometimes shows a rich, mottled effect.

CORE: The tough central section of wood to which veneers are laminated.

COTTONWOOD: Native wood of medium strength. Has no figure. Rotary cuts used for veneer cores, kitchen furniture.

CYPRESS: Native wood of U.S. southern states. Usually durable but has no figure or pattern.

D

DAO: See paldao reference further on in this section.

DOUGLAS FIR: Light, strong, native wood especially suited for paneling because of its freedom from warping and shrinking. Has attractive, variable grain. Used for linings, backings, drawer bottoms.

E

EAST INDIAN ROSEWOOD: (Asia). Long used in China for carving. Color varies from light red-violet to deep purple, sometimes tending toward black, often cut by streaks of light nut brown or deep brown. Red-violet or deep purple tints predominate.

EAST INDIAN SATINWOOD: (Southern India and Ceylon). A very hard wood used widely in native furniture. Golden yellow to light brown, with soft stripes and rich mottles.

EBONY: (Ceylon, India and Africa). Has gray sapwood, deep black heartwood. Hard and fine grained, takes a high polish. Used for veneers and inlays, musical instruments.

ELM: Tough native wood principally used for frames of upholstered furniture and also for kitchen furniture. Gray elm used as veneer for interior trim of homes. Grain is similar to ash.

ENGLISH HAREWOOD: (British Isles). Actually "harewood" comes from a maple tree which has a leaf like a sycamore. It is called sycamore in England. Color ranges from gray white to reddish white, but is often dyed in different colors.

EUCALYPTUS: (Australia). Member of the myrtle family. Wood often shows an interesting blister figure.

F

FAUX STINE (FALSE SATINWOOD): Used in veneers. Amber to golden brown. It is really a cypress crotch wood.

FIBER: A paper product used in "woven" furniture. It is formed into strands with wire core.

FRUITWOOD: Name applies to some apple, cherry, pear woods grown domestically or imported from Europe for veneers.

G

GABOON: Golden to brown with pinkish cast. Soft wood with straight figure also called okoume. Used in Europe for commercial plywood. Crotch figures cut for face veneers.

GONCALO ALVES: (Eastern Brazil). From the sumac family. Color varies with growing conditions. Usually light brown softly streaked with dark tone.

GREYWOOD: Artificially dyed English harewood. Sometimes called silver greywood because of metallic sheen. Produced in this country from maple.

GRANADILLO: West Indian ebony. Yellow to rich dark brown wood, marked with dark stripes and grain figures.

GUMWOOD: See red gum described at length further on.

H

HACKBERRY: Native American wood, now quite widely used in the south, resembling elm. It has a natural blonde color.

HICKORY: Native wood of the walnut family. Hard, tough and heavy. Used for rustic furniture.

HEMLOCK: (U.S.). Pale buff wood with reddish tinge. A moderately strong, light wood.

HOLLY: Hard, white wood with no figure, used with figured woods for contrast.

I

IIMBUYA: Also called Brazilian walnut. Olive to chocolate brown color. Used in veneers.

INDIAN LAUREL: (India and Burma). Naturally dark brown wood that bleaches to light brown, sometimes with grayish cast, with slightly darker wavy streaks. Veneer is richly figured.

IROKO: Also called kambala, sometimes erroneously called African oak or African teak. A heavy hard wood, its color varies from light golden brown to rich warm brown, but bleaches on exposure. Occasionally used for veneers.

ITALIAN WALNUT: Harder than other European walnut woods, has dark rich color and uniform figure. Used during and since Italian renaissance.

K

KAMBALA: (West Africa). Commonly called iroko but not in wide general usage.

KELOBRA: (Mexico and Central America). Walnut brown with various shadings. Used as veneer only. Also called guanacastle and genisero.

KINGWOOD: (Brazil). A straight grain hard wood. Rich violet to almost black, often broken by streaks of golden to dark brown. The colors become richer with age.

KOA: (Hawaii). From trees of acacia family. Formerly and erroneously known as Hawaiian mahogany. Durable and resistant to dents. Generally used in musical instruments and cabinet veneers. Color varies from golden brown to dark brown or red. Butt wood is beautifully figured.

KOKO: A chocolate brown wood similar to dark walnut. Has wavy figure of straight and curving lines with dark and light shading tones.

KORINA: (Africa). A recently developed trade name for an African wood which is an acceptable substitute for prima vera. There are two types. Only the creamy white is imported as korina.

L

LABURNUM: (Southern Europe). Also called Corsican ebony. Once used as veneer. Sapwood yellowish, heartwood brown with greenish tinge. Not strong or durable. Has distinct rings and rays, takes a high polish.

LACEWOOD: (Australia). A durable wood, medium soft but does not easily dent. Color varies from flesh pink to light leather brown broken with silvery flecks, further enriched by high lustre.

LARCH: Native soft wood with striped figure. Finishes smoothly and takes high polish. Resists decay well.

LAUAN: (Philippines). Reddish brown hard wood somewhat similar in character to mahogany. When quarter sawed, has beautiful ribbon figure. Once marketed as "Philippine mahogany."

LAUREL: (Burma and India). See Indian laurel.

LETTERWOOD: (Guiana). Also known as snakewood. Reddish brown in color with irregular darker patches. Used for inlays and small cabinetwork.

LIMBA: French name for korina. In England it is called afara.

LINDEN: Occasional designation for basswood native to the U.S.

LOCUST: (U.S.). Also called honey locust. Heartwood is reddish or bright brown with thin layer of pale yellow sapwood.

LOVOA: (Tropical Africa). Belongs to mahogany family but resembles French and Circassian walnut. Formerly called African walnut. Also known as tiger wood. Ordinarily yellow brown to dark nut brown, veneer showing golden lustre. Veneers are quartered, bringing out a straight stripe with strong contrasts.

M

MACASSAR EBONY: (Celebes and Borneo). Black or streaked. A hard and durable wood, used as long ago as the 17th century B.C., historians say.

MADAGASCAR ROSEWOOD: (Madagascar). Has a close straight grain and ranges generally from bright rose, with a tinge of maroon, to deep violet. Finished surface has a high lustre.

MADRONE: (California, Mexico). Fine burl figures with overall red-brown appearance.

MAGNOLIA: Similar to yellow poplar but harder and heavier; straight grained, uniform texture.

MAHOGANY: The popularity of mahogany, often called the aristocrat of cabinet woods, dates back to the Chippendale era of the 18th century. There are three general types of mahogany. West Indian mahogany is the hardest and strongest but it is scarce. Tropical American grows from southern Mexico to Columbia and Venezuela, Brazil and eastern Peru. It is somewhat milder textured than the West Indian. A third type comes from the west coast of Africa. It is not quite so firmly textured as American mahogany but is highly figured. It supplies most of the mahogany veneers used in this country. Mahogany is strong and tough, uniform in structure and close, moderately open grained, depending upon the locality where it is grown. It holds its shape to an exceptional degree and possesses excellent physical and woodworking qualities. It is receptive to the finest of finishes. Freshly cut, mahogany ranges from a light pink to yellow, but on exposure to light and air, quickly turns to a reddish brown or sherry color. It has an interlocking grain which on the quarter usually reveals a straight stripe or ribbon figure. Some trees show broken stripe, rope, ripple, mottle, fiddleback and blister figures, and various combinations of these. The outstanding figure in mahogany is the crotch and swirl obtained from sections of the trunk immediately beneath a fork or crotch. Mahogany does not produce clearly defined annual growth rings. Consequently the shell or leaf pattern in flat cut mahogany is due to the interlocking grain.

MAKORE: (Africa). Also called African cherry. Resembles cherry as known in U.S.

MANSONIA: (Africa). Resembles walnut closely. Extensively used in England as substitute for walnut.

MAPLE: Hard, or "sugar," maple is one of the most popular of today's furniture woods. It is strong and elastic. It wears well and has good shock resisting qualities. It is one of the hardest of the common woods. The grain is usually straight, although occasionally there are wavy, curly and bird's eye patterns which are much prized for veneers. The natural color of maple ranges from white to amber, but some logs have a reddish cast. In most instances, the characteristic "maple shade" used in today's furniture is the result of staining. On a cross section piece, the pores are tiny holes evenly distributed over the surface. Less desirable qualities are that it warps easily unless properly seasoned, and occasionally splits. Maple is sometimes finished to simulate cherry wood, which has a similar grain and figure. It can also be bleached white. Today, maple is used for much of the better, inexpensive furniture in both Modern and Colonial reproductions because the wood is so hard and dense it does not readily absorb impurities. It has been used for making frames for reed furniture, rockers, dowels, and stretchers. It was used as an inlay for mahogany during the 18th century. Bird's eye maple is a highly priced stock which is quite rare and is generally reduced to veneers. Its characteristic "bird's eye" figure is due to buds which could not force their way through the bark. When such a tree is converted into lumber, the saw cuts through these abnormal growths exposing crumpled edges of tilted annual rings formed around the buds.

MOVINGUI: (West Africa). Light yellow wood with open grain and prominent pores. Veneers show figure formed of lighter and darker rings.

MYRTLE BURL: (California and Oregon). Light cream to rich brown with curly grained effect, intricately woven. Often used for panels.

N

NARRA: Rare Philippine wood resembles satinwood in quartered stripe figure. It is a species of padouk and comes in red and yellow. Used only for decorative veneers.

NEW GUINEA WOOD: (Papua, Oceania, East Indies). A species of dao or paldao. A plain striped and highly figured wood. Color varies from brown to light gray with black lines.

O

OAK: Oak comprises a large proportion of all wood used in furniture making. Moderately heavy, hard, strong and tough, it scores high in wearing qualities. Oak is a ring-porous wood with well-developed yearly rings and is rich in "pith" or "medullary" rays. It therefore has a pronounced grain that is emphasized when quarter sawed, when the surface flakes are enlarged. Oak, however, is difficult to work and for that reason is utilized for the simpler furniture styles, notably William and Mary and Colonial where carving and shaped members are not characteristic details. Two varieties of oak are mainly used, red and white. Both are of about the same quality and appearance.

OJOCHE: See capomo previously described in this section.

OLIVE: (Mediterranean countries). Close, fine grained wood light yellowish brown in color with irregular wavy dark lines and mottles. Takes fine polish. Used in inlays and marquetry.

ORIENTAL WOOD: (Australia). A member of the laurel family. Comes in many natural colors, some of them tints and shades from gray to odd colors like salmon red, walnut brown.

P

PADOUK: (Burma). A highly durable wood, ranging from pink through vermillion shades and dark cherry red to reddish brown, often with dark streaks. Often called Andaman padouk.

PALDAO: (Philippines). Also called dao. Has a great variety of grain effects, unusual figure and ranges in color from gray to reddish brown.

PARTICLE BOARD: Widely used for core stock. (See Wood By-products in Section II.)

PEARWOOD: The wood of our familiar pear trees. Wood of younger trees is whitish with tint of soft brown; in older trees, it is yellowish brown to reddish brown. Gnarled markings give veneer attractive figure, richly mottled.

PECAN: A type of hickory native to south central U.S. It has a strong grain pattern resembling walnut and is used with hackberry for solid exposed parts in combination with walnut furniture.

PEROBA: (South America). Pale rosewood with darker streaks; color fades to brown in strong light. White peroba is pale golden olive with fine grain.

PINE: Soft wood, white or pale yellow. No figure. Grain character obtained by rotary cutting. Knotty pine is used extensively for paneling and plywood, cabinets and doors. Sometimes used as solid wood. Dries easily and does not shrink or swell much with changes in humidity.

PLANE: European sycamore. Used for veneer and inlays. Grain like American sycamore.

PLYWOOD: Thin layers of wood glued together with the grains of each layer crosswise to its neighbor. Strong. Resists splitting, warping and cracking. (See Section II.)

POPLAR: See yellow poplar described further on.

PRIMA VERA: (Mexico and Nicaragua). Sometimes called white mahogany. Whitish to straw yellow, with glossy effect, lined with pale brown.

R

RATTAN: (Asia). A vine used in weaving wicker furniture. It does not take color but can be varnished or lacquered. (See "Wicker. Cane. Willow." - Section II.)

RED GUM: Has a fine-grained, smooth, close texture. It is fairly tough but has little resilience. A diffuse, porous wood, the pores of the red gum are quite uniform in size and regularly distributed. The natural color of the wood (the heartwood is a rich reddish brown) is in itself attractive but it takes stain so well it is often used to imitate mahogany and walnut. Widely used, too, for legs, posts and framework of furniture otherwise of genuine walnut. When red gum is properly finished, it is only by careful examination that the difference can be determined by inspection of the pores. In mahogany and black or Circassian walnut the pores are so large they can be distinctly seen on a smoothly cut end surface, appearing as fine groves running parallel to the grain. They are even visible through varnish as dark lines. In red gum, the pores are much smaller and can be seen only with a magnifying glass.

REDWOOD: (California). One of the most durable woods, extensively used for furniture cores because of stability, machining and gluing qualities, high strength and light weight. Reddish brown with attractive grain and texture. It has limited use as veneer on drawer fronts and cabinets. Popular in outdoor furniture because of high resistance to decay and insects, weathers well.

ROSEWOOD: (South America and India). Dark chestnut or red brown wood streaked and grained with black. Takes a fine polish. Has a milk rose aroma.

S

SABICU: (Cuba). A wood which resembles mahogany. It is pink to red in color.

SANDALWOOD: (India). Hard, yellowish brown, close-grained wood. Has characteristic fragrance which increases with age. Used principally for inlays.

SAPELE: (West Africa). A wood of the mahogany family. When quarter-cut, it shows a straight stripe from medium to narrow width. Also known as "tiama."

SATINE RUBANNE: (South America). Name means "satin ribbon." Also known as capomo. Tough, strong, elastic and durable wood with straight grain. Finished wood has attractive ribbon markings. Used for banding, inlays, overlays. Sapwood is yellowish white. Heartwood has various shades of rich red and yellow.

SATINWOOD: (India, Ceylon, Australia). Light orange wood with beautiful feathered figure. Wood is hard and close grained, has a tendency to darken with age. Takes a fine polish. Used for veneer inlays and cabinet work.

SPRUCE: Unusual combination of lightness and strength. Easy to dry and glue. Gaining in favor as core material.

SYCAMORE: Hard, cross-grained wood with a tendency to warp. Reddish brown rays. Quarter sawing produces striking flake or splash figure. Its veneer is used in plywood drawers.

T

TAMO: (Japan). Japanese ash. Varies in color from straw yellow to light brown sometimes with a suggestion of steel gray. Figures in the veneer are beautiful and varied, ranging from peanut size to dazzling fields of similar design spread irregularly, making fantastic patterns.

TANGUILE: (Philippines). Hard wood similar to lauan. Has been marketed as "Philippine mahogany." Dark red-brown.

TEAK: (Java, Burma, Thailand and India). When cut it is yellow or straw shade to dark brown. Colors enrich with age. Generally straight grain, though often richly figured. Fragrance like rosewood.

THUYA: (Algeria). A very hard wood. Color varies from light to dark brown. Generally used as burl veneer.

TIGER WOOD: See Lovoa reference which is listed above.

TULIPWOOD: (Brazil). A species of rosewood. Lustrous yellow of varied shades, streaked with deep purplish or blood-red stripes.

TUPELO: Also called black gum. A soft wood easily worked, it has involved grain with interwoven fibers. Tough and wear resisting. Used mostly for interior trim of houses, cores and cross-banding in plywood.

V

VIOLETWOOD: See amaranth which is described above.

W

WALNUT: American walnut was introduced into England by William and Mary. Some fine examples of Dutch and Flemish furniture of the period, done in walnut and well preserved, are found in Hampton Court. One of the leading qualities is its remarkable fidelity. Drawers centuries old continue to slide smoothly. Soft and pleasing of grain, walnut is admirably suited to carving. While the trunks of walnut trees are straight-grained and provide little figure, wood of decided grain is obtained from stumps, most every one of which shows a wavy grain where roots spread out from the tree. Good stumps, about one in a hundred, are carefully dug, sent to the mills and quartered. These quarters are made into veneer in such a manner that full advantage is taken of the grain. Figured walnut is also obtained from the "burl," a huge growth like a mole found generally at the roots but often on the trunk. Burls weigh as much as a ton and are prepared like stumps. The pleasing rotary figure in veneer is obtained by cutting a walnut or other log around as you would unroll a spool of ribbon. Crossing of the annual growth rings at wide intervals produces the characteristic wavy pattern. The heartwood of American walnut is light brown to chocolate brown.

WICKER: In todays vernacular we refer to wicker not as a material but as a construction technique. (See "Wicker. Cane. Willow." - Section II.)

WHITEWOOD: A synonym for yellow poplar described below.

WILLOW: (Mississippi Valley). A rather soft wood which takes walnut and mahogany stain well. Used as solid wood only. Willow withes are used in weaving wicker furniture.

Y

YELLOW POPLAR: (U.S.). Even textured, straight-grained with a pale, yellow heart wood of greenish cast. It is widely used for cores and to a lesser extent for crossbandings and face veneers.

YEW: (Europe). Hard, durable, elastic, close-grained wood, resembling mahogany. Reddish brown color. Used for veneer and cabinetwork.

YUBA: This is a species of oak prevalent in Tasmania.

Z

ZEBRAWOOD: (West Africa, Cameroon). So called because, when quartered, it shows brown and black stripes on its light yellowish to brown ground, resembling the zebra. Also called zebrano.

DICTIONARY OF FABRICS

Many fabrics carry trademarks which must not be confused with the name denoting the general character of the fabric. As far as possible only the general terms, and not the trademark names, are given here. Because many fabrics are used for both upholstering and draperies, this listing includes definitions and terms from both of these categories. Upholstery and drapery materials can be divided into four major types according to content. These comprise: Animal Origin (Wool, silk, mohair, felt, leather), Vegetable Origin (Cotton, linen, jute), Chemical Origin (Rayon, plastics, glass, nylon, polyester, polypropylene), Metallic Origin (Fabrics made of aluminum, silver or gold threads usually in combination with one of the above materials), and Mixed Origin (Combinations of the above types such as silk and wool, cotton and polyester, rayon and nylon, etc.) (See Sec. II.)

A

ACETATE: A synthetic fiber. Fabrics made from this fiber often have a luxurious feel and luster.

ACRYLIC: A manmade fiber. The properties of this fabric make it adaptable to many uses.

ANGORA: Yarn from fleece of the Angora goat. It is woven into mohair.

ANILINE: Term applied to dyes derived from coal tar. Used in coloring fabrics.

ANTIMACASSAR: Small pieces of lace or needlework used in Victorian period to protect upholstering on backs and arms of chairs or sofas.

APPLIQUE: Design made by sewing one material on another.

ARMURE: Drapery fabric with designs woven on a rep foundation, or a figure weave. Plain or mixed colors usually of cotton. Armure Silk is an application of armure weave using silk warp and cotton weft.

ARRAS: Wall tapestry or hanging of the type originally made in Arras, France. Shakespeare often used the word to denote a partition.

ARTIFICIAL LEATHER: A substitute for leather made by coating a cotton fabric with a nitro-cellulose preparation and embossing the surface to imitate leather.

AUBUSSON: Fine handwoven flat tapestry from the French district of the same name.

B

BAGHERRA: A knitted or woven velvet with an uncut pile.

BAIZE: A coarsely woven, reversible fabric with a felt-like surface.

BARKCLOTH: A woven fabric with a rough texture primarily used for draperies.

BASKETWEAVE: Plain under-and-over weave used in the weaving of baskets. Used occasionally for colonial fabrics.

BATIK: Hand printed material, colored by dipping into dyes of various hues. The parts which are not to be colored in each particular shade are made resistant by wax.

BATISTE: A soft, sheer fabric usually in white. It can be woven of cotton, silk, linen, wool or synthetic fabrics.

BEAUVAIS: Tapestry used on walls and as furniture upholstering; made originally at Beauvais.

BEDFORD CORD: Lengthwise corded material of cotton, worsted or silk first made in this country in New Bedford, Mass.

BENGALINE: A finely woven fabric with a raised horizontal rib.

BLOCK PRINT: Design printed by blocks of wood or metal instead of rollers.

BOBBINET: Curtain material made with round hole mesh. Closeness of mesh and fineness of thread determine the quality. Used for sheer curtains.

BOUCLE: French word for curled. Indicates a curled nap, with loops, for a rough appearance.

BROADCLOTH: A textured cloth with a plain or twill weave and a lustrous finish.

BROCADE: Originally heavy silk with elaborate pattern in silver or gold threads. Brocade has an embossed appearance. BROCHE: A French term meaning brocade which is described above.

BROCATEL: A variation of brocade with a higher relief or repousse effect with warp and filling yarns unequally twisted and an extra set of yarns for backing. Jacquard pattern stands out in raised or blistered effect.

BUCKRAM: Once a rich, heavy woven cloth but now a stiffened material, usually cotton sized with glue, which is used to reinforce draperies and valances.

BURLAP: Coarse cloth woven from jute. Used to cover furniture springs.

BUTCHER'S LINEN: A coarse, homespun linen weave cloth originally used for French butcher's smocks.

C

CALICO: A plain weave, lightweight fabric that is printed with small figured patterns.

CAMBRIC: A fine closely woven white or solid color cotton fabric with glazed appearance on the right side. Primarily used for curtains.

CANDLEWICK: Material used for bed spreads which has design of clipped fuzzy yarn tufts.

CANVAS: A closely woven cloth usually of linen, hemp or cotton.

CASEMENT CLOTH: Broad term which covers many drapery fabrics usually light, plain, neutral color. Weaves are plain twill, satin striped.

CASHMERE: The soft, glossy hair of the Kashmir goat which is spun and then knitted or woven into soft fabrics. Can be combined with other natural fibers to produce luxurious fabrics.

CHALLIS: Soft fabric of silk, worsted or rayon. Plain colors or printed with small figures.

CHAMBRAY: A fine quality plain weave fabric with a linen like finish that is woven in solids, checks and stripes.

CHENILLE: Fabric made by weaving a thick, soft weft and a small hard warp which binds weft threads tightly together. Split into strips, this forms the chenille yarn used for weaving. The cut edges of yarn form a plush-like surface.

CHIFFON: A thin gauze fabric of plain weave made of silk. Used mainly for curtains.

CHINO: A coarse cotton fabric woven of combed yarns in a twill weave.

CHINOISERIE: A French term denoting fabrics with oriental or Chinese design influence.

CHINTZ: Originally any printed cotton fabric, the same as calico. Now a drapery or clothing fabric which usually has a glazed surface.

CIRE: A shiny patent leather effect produced on fabric by the application of wax, heat and pressure.

COPTIC CLOTH: Heavy cotton upholstery fabric with a tiny pattern. Plain rustic weave.

CORDUROY: From French "Corde du Rois" (a king's cord). A kind of cotton or rayon velvet with ridges or cords in the pile. Made with an extra weft of mercerized yarns which float on the surface at intervals. Floats are cut, making tufts stand up in a corded effect. Surface brushed and singed.

COTTON: A natural fiber from the seed case of a cotton plant. Cotton is a versatile fabric and produces a wide range of weight, texture and pattern. Durable, pliable and dyable.

CRASH: Term applied to several fabrics having coarse, lumpy, uneven yarns of rough texture. Drapery fabric. Natural or colors. Made of lute, rayon, linen or cotton or a combination of them.

CREPE: General term covering many kinds of crinkled or uneven surfaced materials. Wool crepe or crepon.

CRETONNE: Printed drapery fabric of cotton or linen in all variety of weaves and finishes.

CREWEL EMBROIDERY: Embroidery worked in colored worsted yarns with long loose stitch on cotton, linen or wool fabrics.

D

DAMASK: Named for the ancient city of Damascus where elaborate floral designs were woven in silk. Damask is flatter than brocade and is reversible. Pattern changes color on the wrong side.

DENIM: From the French town of Nimes, "serges de Nimes." Heavy cotton twill made of coarse yarns. Denim is sold by weight. Drapery denim is finer and has a softer finish than Jean denim; usually yarn-dyed and woven in small geometric figures. Weave: twill or figure.

DENIER: Weight of a fiber thread. It is expressed in grams per foot.

DIMITY: Crisp light weight cotton fabric usually woven with a stripe or check pattern.

DOBBY WEAVE: Cloth with small geometric pattern woven on loom with special attachment.

DOTTED SWISS: Sheer, plain weave cotton fabric embroidered or woven with dots at intervals. Used for clothing and curtains.

DOUPPIONI: A slubbed yarn made from silk.

DRILL: A heavy twill cloth with denim characteristics. Often used as a foundation for leather-like coated fabrics.

DUCHESS: Curtain material with an applique design.

E

EMBOSSING: Fabric pressed between engraved rollers with heat to give a raised effect, similar to embossed stationery. Washing or steaming removes the design. Embossed velvet, or plush, is a fabric made by weaving the pile high then shearing it to different levels.

EMBROIDERY: A decoration in needlework executed by hand on fabric already woven.

F

FAILLE: Ribbed fabric of silk, rayon or cotton, with stripes, produced by alternating fine and heavy warps.

FELT: Wool, mohair or mixed fibers, pressed into a compact sheet without weaving.

FILET: Square meshed net or lace. Once handmade it is now mostly machined.

FILLING: Same as weft or woof. Yarn for the shuttle. Each crosswise yarn is called a "pick."

FLANNEL: A soft fabric of plain or twill weave with a napped surface on one or both sides.

FLOCK: Short, clipped fibers glued to wood, paper or fabric to provide a suede-like surface.

FRISÉ: Pile fabric of uncut loops. Designs may be produced by contrast of cut and uncut loops, by different colored yarns or by printing the surface.

FUSTAIN: A stout, twilled cotton fabric with velvet-like pile.

G

GABARDINE: A firm, tightly woven fabric with a close diagonal twill weave surface and flat back.

GALLOON: Narrow binding of cotton, wool or silk, usually showing fancy weaves.

GAUZE: A sheer, thin open weave fabric that is sometimes finished with a stiff sizing.

GENOA VELVET: A figured velvet with a satin ground, multicolored pile.

GIMP: Ornamental braid, used to cover upholstery tacks. It is sometimes stiffened with wire.

GINGHAM: Made of cotton yarns dyed before weaving. Originally a clothing fabric, it is used now for draperies and slip covers.

GLAZED CHINTZ: Both chintz and plain color fabrics are treated with paraffin and calendered. Used for curtains, lampshades, slip covers and upholstery.

GOBELINS: Royal (handmade) tapestry works in Paris. Machine woven tapestry is incorrectly called Gobelin.

GRASS CLOTH: Coarsely woven fabric of vegetable fibers used as wall coverings and draperies.

GRENADINE: Curtain fabric, of leno weave, plain or with woven dots, in silk, rayon or wool.

GRENFELL CLOTH: Closely woven cloth for draperies and upholstery it is water repellent.

GROS POINT: Needlepoint embroidery similar to but larger than petit point.

H

HAIR CLOTH: A fabric composed of cotton warps and filling threads of horsehair.

HAND-WOVEN: A term which indicates some part of weaving done by hand.

HERRINGBONE: A pattern made up of rows of parallel lines which in any two adjacent rows slope in opposite directions.

HOMESPUN: Loosely woven fabric made to resemble hand woven colonial material. Also called "peasant weave."

HOPSACKING: A rough-surfaced cotton, linen or rayon fabric with a plain basket weave pattern.

HUCK: A heavy linen or cotton fabric with a honeycomb effect that is used for toweling or for embroidery.

I

INDIA PRINT: Cotton fabric with hand-blocked (or simulated) designs in bright colors.

INGRAIN: Flat weave cloth woven of multicolors and threads dyed before weaving.

IRISH POINT: Net curtain material with applique design like duchess.

J

JACQUARD WEAVE: A general classification. Formal, highly decorative, includes damasks, tapestries, brocades and all cloths with elaborate figures woven on a Jacquard loom. Used extensively in upholstered furniture, both traditional and comtemporary.

JASPE: French term for streaked or striped.

JUTE: Silver grey or yellowish brown fiber.

K

KAPOK: Soft, light fibers from seed pod of a tree in East and West Indies. Called "silk floss." Uses: mattresses, pillows, and life preservers.

KNITS: The interlocking of a series of loops made from a single yarn to form an elastic fabric.

L

LACE: A fine, openwork fabric with patterns of knotted, twisted, or looped threads on a ground of net or mesh. Largely confined to draperies and curtains.

LAMBELLE: A lightweight damask texture having fine mercerized warp threads and slightly coarser weft threads of contrasting color.

LAMPAS: Originally an East Indian printed silk. Now applied to decorative fabric having rep ground with satin-like figures formed of warp threads and contrasting weft figures.

LAWN: Light, thin curtain fabric of highly polished cotton yarn. Originally of linen. Sometimes used for baby clothes.

LEATHER: See Section II, "Leather."

LINEN: A fabric made from the bark of a flax plant. Woven into cloth it is noted for its smoothness, strength, coolness and luster. Also durable, pliable and dyable.

LINSEY-WOOLSEY: A coarse fabric made of wool combined with cotton or flax.

LISERE: French silk cord fabric, made with weft of brocaded flowers, warp of Jacquard figures.

LUSTER: Gloss finish applied to fabric by heat and pressure.

LYCRA: A tradename which has become synonymous with a man-made fabric with inherent and great properties of elasticity.

M

MADRAS: A marquisette type fabric with an overall design in print or color. Colors often bleed.

MARQUISETTE: A type of open weave rather than a distinct fabric. It is used for draperies and curtains. Marquisette fabrics are made of rayon, nylon, silk or cotton.

MATELASSE: French, meaning to cushion or pad. Hence a quilted surface produced on the loom. A figured or brocaded cloth with a raised pattern.

METAL CLOTH: Any fabric of any material with decorative interwoven metallic threads.

MOHAIR: Made from the hair of the Angora goat, long and silky. Also called Alpaca, it is a pile fabric with a back of cotton or wool and pile of mohair. Cut and uncut loops.

MOIRE: A fabric, especially silk, having a watered or wavy pattern.

MOLESKIN: Heavy cotton, napped fabric used for foundation for some artificial leather and lined materials.

MONK'S CLOTH: Rough, canvas-like drapery material, made of heavy cotton yarns often containing some flax, jute or hemp. Also called friar's cloth; it wears unusually well and is used for hangings, soft covers, and upholstering.

MOUSSELINE: A lightweight muslin-like cotton with a crisp finish that is closely woven of highly twisted yarns.

MUMMY CLOTH: Light textured cotton or silk fabric with an irregular warp figure.

MUSLIN: A plain weave cotton fabric; sometimes printed; varying in crude to fine texture.

N

NAP: Not to be confused with pile. The downy or fuzzy appearance of cloth produced by raising the fibers to the surface as in flannel.

NATURAL FIBERS: Fibers produced from natural sources (silk, wool and cotton) as opposed to synthetic fibers (rayon, nylon and others).

NEEDLEPOINT: Patterns known as "needlepoint" are hand worked with a needle using wool, cotton or silk.

NETS: Fabrics of loose, open construction with threads that are tied where they cross. Largely confined to draperies and curtains.

NINON: A type of light, transparent celanese (plain weave) used for sheer curtains.

NOIL: Short fibers removed during the combing of a textile fiber and spun into yarn.

NOTTINGHAM: Flat lace used for curtains and table cloths. Originally handmade now machine made.

NYLON: A synthetic material adapted for fashioning into filaments of extreme toughness, strength and elasticity, then knitted into fabrics.

O

OILED SILK: A thin waterproof silk fabric which has been soaked in oil and dried.

OLEFIN: A trade name, this fiber is a product of the petroleum industry. It is a lightweight highly durable fiber.

ORGANDY: A fine lawn cloth, chemically treated to produce crispness and stiffness, it is used for clothing and curtains.

ORGANZINE: A thrown silk of continuous fiber made from the unbroken cocoon.

P

PAISLEY: A multicolored design, woven or printed, usually on natural fabrics.

PANNE: A term applied to plush, velvet, mohair or silk which has been flattened by steaming and pressure so that pile lies close to back, giving a shiny appearance.

PEAU de SOIE: A soft, closely woven satin with a mellow luster usually made of silk.

PERCALE: A finely woven cotton cloth used for sheets. It is also printed and glazed like chintz.

PETIT-POINT: Needlework usually on cotton, silk or linen, using a very fine stitch.

PICK: The weft. Comes from one passage of loom's shuttle.

PILE: A general classification. Fabric having a surface made of upright ends, as in fur. Pile may be made of extra woof yarns as in velvets and plushes, or of extra warp yarns as in velveteens and corduroys. Piles may be uncut as in Brussels carpet. Warp pile can have loops on both sides as in terry cloth or Turkish toweling. Used in both traditional and modern pieces.

PILING: Narrow decorative fold of fabric on the edges of draperies and upholstery.

PLAIN WEAVES: A general classification of fabric. The coarser kinds of plain weaves are widely used in modern and colonial furniture. The finer weaves are used as traditional draperies.

PLASTIC: A manmade material of chemical origin, produced in different types such as vinyl, saran, nylon and others.

PLISSE: Cotton fabric, chemically treated to give a crinkled surface.

PLUSH: Cut or uncut pile fabric having a pile of greater depth than velvet.

POINT d'ESPRIT: A bobbinet with a small dot or woolen figure similar to dotted Swiss.

POLYESTER: This is a synthetic polymer. The fiber is strong and durable but pills and soils easily. It blends easily with natural fibers such as cotton for strength and versatility.

POLYURETHANE: See Section II, "Furniture Fabrics."

PONGEE: A plain weave drapery fabric, of silk or cotton.

POPLIN: Fine, cotton ribbed fabric, usually mercerized. Launders and wears well unless the weave is loose.

PRINTED FABRICS: General classification. These include both glazed and unglazed materials. They are used extensively for draperies, boudoir furniture, slip covers and modern pieces. Examples: chintz, cretonne, percale. Printed linen was originally block-printed by hand.

Q

QUILT WEAVE: A weave that simulates quilting and its padded effect.

R

RADNOR: Upholstery fabric with small surface design on close-weave background.

RAMIE: A fiber, similar to flax, obtained from the stalk of a plant native to China.

RATINE: Tapestry woven fabric with nubby or bumpy surface.

RAW SILK: Silk fibers as they are taken from the cocoon before the natural gum has been removed.

RAYON: A lustrous textile fiber made by converting cellulose (wood pulp or cotton linters) into a filament by means of a chemical and mechanical process. More lustrous and stiffer than silk, not so strong but less expensive.

REP: Closely resembles poplin. Rep has a heavier cord (filling yarn) and is a wider fabric used for hangings and upholstering. A Jacquard figure introduced on a rep background is called armure.

REPEAT: One complete repetition of a pattern. A process used in rugs, wallpaper and fabrics.

ROLLERPRINT: Fabric of natural or synthetic fiber, with a design printed on it by rollers.

S

SAIL CLOTH: Light cotton canvas or other material of close weave.

SANFORIZING: A patented pre-shrinking process.

SARAN: A type of plastic extruded as yarn and then woven into fabric. Widely used for webbing in outdoor furniture, and auto seat covers, it is also known as velon.

SATEEN: Mercerized cotton fabric of satin weave. Better grades resemble satin made of silk.

SATIN: A lustrous surface fabric with broken twill weave. Usually woven of silk threads but may be made of rayon.

SCHIFFLI: A type of shuttle embroidery done on a sheer fabric by a machine. This machine can be hand-guided to create patterns of great complexity.

SCREEN PRINT: Design printed by screen process. Designs are hand applied.

SELVAGE: Tightly woven edge that prevents fabric from raveling.

SCRIM: A coarse type of voile used principally for sheer curtains.

SHADE CLOTH: Opaque stiffened cloth used for window shades because of light deflection capacity.

SHANTUNG: Nubby fabric, originally woven from Chinese silk, now made also from rayon or cotton.

SHEETING: Plain cotton muslin, percale or linen supplied in wide widths, long lengths.

SICILIAN SILK: A damask fabric with a silk warp and cotton or linen weft, forming a plain ground with a satin figure.

SILK: Soft, natural thread obtained by unraveling the cocoons of Japanese silk worm. Also applied to fabrics woven of silk thread.

SISAL: A tough tropical fiber, woven in porch rugs and, during the 20th century, into mats to cover furniture springs before upholstering.

SIZING: Any chemical substance applied to a fabric to provide greater stiffness, smoother surface, increased strength. Can be permanent (glue, clay) or temporary (starch).

SLEY: A general term used to designate the number of warp ends per inch of fabric.

STAPLE: Average length and fineness of a fiber such as cotton, wool, flax, synthetics.

SUEDE CLOTH: Cloth with a napped surface made to resemble suede.

SWISS: Finely woven, sheer cotton fabrics for sheer curtains or clothing.

SYNTHETIC FIBERS: Fibers made through chemical and machine processes; also called manmade fibers.

T

TAFFETA: A name applied to several types of canvas-like fabrics. May be made of silk, cotton, linen, rayon in mixed fibers.

TAMBOUR EMBROIDERY: Machine embroidery in chain-stitch to resemble hand work done on tambour frames.

TAPA: Native fiber cloth made from mulberry bark by South Sea island natives and printed by block designs in vegetable dyes and fantastic patterns.

TAPESTRY: Originally a handwoven fabric made with a bobbin worked from the wrong side on a warp stretched vertically or horizontally. A machine reproduction of tapestry is a yarn dyed figured fabric composed of two sets of warp and filling yarns woven on a Jacquard loom.

TARLATAN: Thin gauzy fabric of cotton, glazed to supply stiffness. Used mostly for curtains.

TERRY CLOTH: An absorbent toweling fabric, woven or knitted with a loop pile.

TEXTURE: Characteristic structure and feel of fabric (soft, smooth, rough, for example).

TICKING: A heavy, strong cotton fabric used to cover mattresses. There are many grades.

TIEBACKS: Loops of fabric, plastic, metal or wood to hold curtains in position.

TOILE: A finely woven cotton or linen with transparent qualities.

TOILE de JOUY: Eighteenth century French fabric printed in a classical design pattern.

TRAPUNTO: Quilting which raises a design on the surface, giving a padded effect.

TRICOT: A low-priced cotton or rayon tapestry with right and wrong sides different.

TWEED: Upholstering fabric similar to clothing tweed but heavier in texture and weight.

TWILL: A heavy cotton fabric used for embroidery bases. Parallel diagonal-lines effect.

U

ULTRASUEDE™: A manmade luxurious fabric with no bias. Beautiful colors, fairly thick, supple and sturdy. Has a fine suede-like appearance.

UTRECHT VELVET: A furniture plush of velvet or mohair, the pile of which is flattened into a pattern by pressure, the upstanding pile forming a soft velvet surface.

V

VAT DYE: A process of dying any material to obtain permanent color.

VELCRO: A trade name for a 2-sided reusable fastening device widely used in upholstering of cushions.

VELOUS OR VELOURS: General term for pile fabrics made with a short pile.

VELVET: Broad and inclusive term covering all warp pile fabrics except plush and terry.

VELVETEEN: A fabric with short cotton pile made in approximate imitation of silk velvet.

VINYL: A non-woven plastic capable of being embossed or printed to produce any desired finish such as leather grain, wood, floral or textured designs. There are three types of vinyl fabric: (1) Quilted, consisting of a vinyl face sheet, a layer of cushioning and a fabric backing, electronically welded together to form a quilt, trapunto or embroidery designs; (2) Supported, tough vinyl plastic face sheet laminated to a fabric backing. "Elastic" types have a stretchy backing easy to tailor. They come in various weights and patterns; (3) Unsupported, all-plastic materials with no fabric backing. Easy to cut and tailor, readily adaptable to furniture.

VOILE: An organdy-like fabric made of yarns which have more than the normal amount of twist.

W

WAFFLE: Cotton cloth with raised waffle-like pattern, padded effect.

WALL CLOTH: Coated fabrics used on walls. Pattern is printed or embossed. Durable and washable.

WARP: Set of yarns which run lengthwise of cloth. They run across the weft or woof.

WEAVE: An ancient art where cloth is formed by interlocking strands of yarn. Weaves can be classified in three general types: plain (plain and basket weaves); floating weaves (textiles and satin); and pile weaves (cut and uncut weaves). The pattern is created by the weave of the fiber.

WEBBING: Tight fabric, usually woven of jute but may also be of linen or synthetic yarns. Widely used during the first 75 years of the 20th century for furniture bases and spring supports.

WEFT: One of sets of yarns running crosswise and interlaced with the warp to produce a fabric. Also called woof, filling, pick, or shoot.

WHIPCORD: A ribbed material formed by floating the warp threads over several large filling.

WOOL: Each breed of sheep produces its own unique type and grade of wool but all wool shares the quality of warmth and elasticity that makes it adaptable to blending with other fibers. It can be combined with natural or manmade fibers for strength, beauty and smoothness.

WORSTED: Smooth tightly woven woolen fabric made from exceptionally long fibers. Gabardine and serge are examples.

Y

YARN DYED: Fabrics woven of yarn dyed before it is put on the looms.

Z

ZIBELINE: A thick woolen cloth with a flattened, hairy nap. The cloth resembles sable fur.

ZIPPER: A slide-fastening device, originally used exclusively for clothing, but now used widely in upholstering of cushions.

GLOSSARY OF FLOOR COVERINGS

This glossary is divided into two alphabetically arranged sections, soft flooring and resilient/hard flooring, with each word conveniently reference according to category. Some terms, though no longer current, have been retained as these items have had a significant part in the history of flooring.

SOFT FLOORING

A

ACRYLIC: (surface carpet fiber). Soft appearance, good resilience, colorfast, crush-resistant. Resists mildew and sun. Not fire resistant. Generates static electricity. May "pill" with hard wear.

AUBUSSON RUGS: (carpet term). These tapestry-like rugs, which date from the 16th century, are named for the town where they have been made since the time of the Moors. Their characteristic colors are pale, almost faded. These rugs had heavy linen warps until about the 19th century when cotton was substituted for linen. These rugs are still being produced today in traditional or modern designs.

AXMINSTER CARPETS: (carpet term). Its origins date to the second half of the 18th century when seamless, handknotted carpets were first made in Axminster and elsewhere in England. Similar handknotted carpets were manufactured in America by the 1790's. Machine woven Axminster carpets were developed in the 19th century. The patterns of these carpets often imitated Oriental rugs. Machine or spool looms are still producing these carpets.

B

BERBER CARPET: (carpet term). Named for the resemblance to the off-white, heather look cloaks used by the Berber tribes of North Africa. Loop sizes vary from small to large nubby looks. Patterned styles available in multi-level loop or cut loop. Flecked yarns used; available in pastels and dark tones as well as natural.

BINDING: (carpet term). Strip sewn around carpet edge to prevent unraveling. Carpet finished with binding is referred to as a rug.

BRAIDED RUGS: (carpet term). A rug made from strips of new or used cloth, usually cotton or wool, that are folded in at the edges and then braided. The braided strips are usually sewn together with carpet thread.

BROADLOOM: (carpet term). Term originally used to indicate carpet produced in widths wider than six feet. Standard widths today are six, twelve and fifteen feet.

BROCADE: (carpet term). Denotes a carpet having a raised pattern formed by heavily twisted yarn tufts on a ground of straight fibers.

BRUSSELS AND WILTON CARPETS: (carpet terms). English weavers used handlooms to produce Brussels (looped-pile) and Wilton (cut-pile) carpeting beginning in the mid-18th century. Erastus Bigelow invented the first power loom for weaving these two types of carpet in 1846.

BURNS: (carpet care). Should be taken care of immediately. First clip off the damaged fibers. Then sponge with a soapless cleaner and blot dry. Extensive damage can be repaired with patching or retufting by a professional.

C

CARPET BACKING: (carpet term). Fabrics or yarns forming the back of the carpet that hold surface yarns together. Tufted carpets have two backings: a primary backing to which the pile yarns are inserted, and a secondary backing of fabric laminated to the carpet back for strength and stability.

CARPET CARE: (carpet care). Keep all information relating to your carpet in a file for handy reference. This includes: your original sales receipt; warranty; pamphlets on care and cleaning, padding and installation information; along with a swatch of your carpet and padding.

CARPET ODOR: (carpet care). New carpets and padding can have a detectable odor. These usually disappear within a few days with ventilating and vacuuming.

CARPET PADDING: (carpet term). Also referred to as lining, cushioning or underlay. Placed under carpet to extend carpet life by helping to absorb crushing forces on the pile. It also adds underfoot comfort and further insulation against noise, heat and cold. Some carpets are made with sponge or latex foam rubber padding permanently attached. Several types of separate padding available with varying densities, thicknesses and weights. Seek professional advice to choose the appropriate combination for each application as determined by traffic patterns and warranty requirements.

CUT-LOOP, SCULPTURED OR CARVED: (carpet texture). Multi-level with sheared taller loops and uncut shorter loops forming a sculptured pattern. Sometimes referred to as random shear. Hides footprints, dust and dirt well. Wears well on stairs.

CUT PILE, PLUSH, VELVET OR SAXONY: (carpet texture). The richest looking of the textures. All yarn loops are cut so that yarns stand upright and form an even surface. It is easier to clean than uneven textures, but tends to show dirt and lint readily. Saxony generally has a shorter pile than plush and hides footprints better, while plush is softer with a nicer sheen. It is also subject to shading when yarns are bent, making them reflect light in different directions. It can be reduced by vacuum cleaning the yarns in the same direction. Generally Saxony for formal settings, plush for informal.

D

DENSITY: (carpet texture). Generally, the greater the density, the better the quality and the longer the carpet will wear. A brush of the hand over the surface of the pile will indicate if it is thick, tight and springy. Folding a corner of the carpet will reveal how much backing shows through the pile-less visible backing means greater density. A short or medium-height dense pile will wear best in traffic areas.

DHURRIE CARPETS: (carpet term). Made of cotton or silk, these flat woven carpets are traditional to India. Colors are soft and patterns varied.

DRYCLEANING: (carpet care). Home kits now available for spot cleaning.

F

FELTED: (separate carpet padding). Padding made of animal hair, jute fibers or any combination thereof. Some are coated with rubber. It is sturdy, with a firm walk or feel. Felted pads tend to mat and can mildew if exposed to continued wetness and are not generally used today.

FIBER BLEND: (surface carpet fiber). Two or more fibers blended in carpet surface yarns take advantage of the outstanding characteristics of each. For example, a blend of 70 percent wool and 30 percent nylon, looks and feels like wool, but has some of the toughness of nylon. A carpet label must show the percentage by weight of each fiber. Less than 20 percent of any fiber would not be enough to affect carpet quality, and would have been added merely as a selling point.

FLOCKED: (carpet construction). In the flocking process, closely packed short lengths of fiber, usually nylon, are embedded upright in adhesive on a backing. The resulting dense mass of upright fibers forms a carpet with good resilience and compression resistance. Flocked carpet often is used in commercial areas.

FLOORCLOTHS: (carpet term). Floorcloths were in use as early as 1750. They were a step forward from the painted wooden floor, less expensive than carpets yet gave the illusion of a carpet. Good quality floor cloths were made from four to six coats of oil-based paint applied to both sides of a canvas and followed by a decorative pattern either by stencil or original art. Some floorcloths were block printed in factories during the 19th century. Currently, artist painted floorcloths are quite popular. They are finished with varnish on both sides and impervious to surface wear and spills. Non-skid floor pads are required. Available from 2' x 3' to room size.

FRIEZE, TWIST OR TEXTURED: (carpet texture). Yarns are tightly twisted and sometimes heat set to increase resilience and durability and to give a nubby appearance. The texture is known as frieze(pronoounced "free-say"). It wears well and hides footprints, dirt and dust. If it has a level surface, it is not difficult to clean. Well suited for high-traffic and informal areas.

FUZZING: (carpet care). Hairy effect on carpet surface caused by wild fibers, slack yarn twists, or by fibers slipping out of yarn either during carpet use or wet cleaning. Shearing by the manufacturer or a professional cleaner will correct the problem. Continuous filament yarn carpets become fuzzed when filaments snag or break.

H

HOOKED RUGS: (carpet term). Hooked rugs were once a New England specialty. They are as American as apple pie. They reached their peak popularity during the 19th century and their designs were of rural scenes, animals, flowers, birds and people. Yarn or rags are pulled through a coarse canvas backing to create pile and pattern. Hooked rugs go well with a country theme.

I

INDENTATIONS OR CRUSHING: (carpet care). Furniture and traffic can crush a carpet's pile. Frequent vacuuming in high traffic areas and rustproof glides under heavy furniture can help the problem, as well as rearranging the furniture to change traffic patterns. Furniture indentations can often be remedied by gently rubbing with the edge of a ruler. If still matted, hold a steam iron an inch above it, just long enough for the fibers to absorb the steam. Be <u>extremely</u> <u>careful</u> not to melt synthetic fibers! Then fluff the pile with your hand.

J

JUTE: (carpet backing). A plant fiber previously used in backings for woven and tufted carpets. Strong, durable and resilient, it absorbed and retained adhesives well to help bonding between layers of backing in tufted carpets. It was subject to mildew in excessively damp locations.

K

KILIM: (carpet term). A flat, woven, usually reversible carpet. Also kelim.

KNITTED: (carpet construction). Similar to woven in that pile and backing yarns are interlocked in one operation. May be produced in any width (while other methods make carpet in standard widths only). Less than one percent of carpet production in the U.S. is knitted.

L

LEVEL LOOP PILE: (carpet texture). Uncut loops of yarn of uniform height form the carpet surface. This texture wears well and tends to hide footprints, but it shows dust and lint readily. Recommended for high-traffic areas and informal settings. Easy to vacuum.

LEVEL TIP SHEAR: (carpet texture). The surface is level with some loops cut and some uncut. Tends to show dirt and lint readily, hides footprints better than plush, but not as well as level loop pile. Easy to vacuum.

M

MODACRYLIC: (surface carpet fiber). Sometimes used alone in scatter rugs. In larger carpets it is blended with acrylic because its self-extinguishing properties increase flame resistance. Alone, lacks good resilience. Elura and Dynes are trade names.

MULTI-LEVEL LOOP PILE: (carpet texture). All yarns are uncut loops, and the loops are of several different levels. This texture hides footprints, dust and dirt better than level loop carpets. Broad range of applications.

N

NAVAJO INDIAN RUGS: (carpet term). These tightly woven rugs are made by the tribes of American Indians who live in the Southwestern part of the United States. The Navajos learned carpet weaving from the early Spanish settlers. Their rugs are woven in natural colored wools, often from their own sheep. The symbolic patterns are striking and the rugs are vivid with black, reds, blues and yellows usually on a grey or beige background.

NEEDLEPOINT RUGS: (carpet term). Needlepoint rugs date back to the 15th century and are the most elegant of floor coverings. The stitching is made with wool yarn on a linen canvas backing. The rugs were usually made of squares which were then sewn together. Now it is possible to buy a canvas in large sizes to make these lovely rugs.

NEEDLE-PUNCHED: (carpet construction). A core of fiber sheet and layers of loose fibers on each side are interlocked by a machine punching thousands of needles through them. A dense, felt-like carpet results. Usually a thin layer of latex is added as backing. Needlepunch carpet is durable and moderately priced. Used in indoor-outdoor or kitchen carpet, and sometimes in styles suitable for bedrooms or living rooms. About six percent of production in U.S. is needle-punched.

NYLON: (surface carpet fiber). Soil-resistance is poor to excellent, depending upon particular nylon fiber and how it's used. Has good resilience, excellent wear-resistance and good color-fastness. Nylon carpet made from short fibers, instead of continuous filaments, may fuzz or "pill" under hard wear. Abrasion-resistant and has low moisture-absorbency. Naturally resists moths and beetles, but will melt in extreme heat. Trade names: Anso, Antron, Cadon, Caprolan, Enkaloff, etc.

O

ORIENTAL RUGS: (carpet term). Woven by hand in the Near or Far East. The colors and design of these rugs denote the region in which the carpet was made. These carpets are knotted and have a short pile. Flat woven carpets, usually called kilims are also made. The glowing colors and the durability of these rugs make them a timeless investment. Many machine made rugs, made using Oriental rug designs, are also referred to as Oriental rugs.

P

PILE: (carpet term). Raised surface of yarn loops, may be cut or uncut.

PILLING: (carpet care). Small balls of fiber can appear depending on the type of carpet fiber and traffic. Clip with scissors. Never pull.

POLYESTER: (surface carpet fiber). Has a soft, luxurious appearance, good wear resistance and color-fastness. Resilience is somewhat less than nylon, so denser pile construction is needed for the same performance. Abrasion-resistant, some static tendencies and high ease-of-care properties. Trade names: Avlin, Dacron, Fortrel, Encron, Kodel, Trevira.

POLYESTER PNEUMACEL: (surface carpet fiber). Firm and resilient. Non-flamable. Mold and mildew resistant.

POLYPROPYLENE OR OLEFIN: (carpet backing). Used as backing in tufted carpets. Strong and durable and resists mildew. Also a (surface carpet fiber). Used for indoor-outdoor and commercial use because it is not damaged by moisture. Good wear and abrasion-resistance, excellent resistance to water-based stains, excellent color-fastness. Relatively low resilience.

R

RAG RUG: (carpet term). A carpet woven using strips of cloth or the selvages of fabric. The strips are cut on the bias and twisted together to make a ribbon which is then woven on a cotton or linen warp. Popular in early American homes.

RAYON: (carpet surface fiber). Used in some carpets. Poor durability.

REMNANT: (carpet term). Piece of carpet at the end of a carpet roll, usually measuring less than nine feet long.

RIPPLING: (carpet care). High heat and humidity can cause temporary rippling in wall-to-wall carpeting. If the ripples do not disappear when normal humidity returns, have a professional restretch the carpet with a power stretcher, not with a knee-kicker.

RUBBER AND VINYL: (carpet backing). Sometimes substituted for the usual secondary backing of tufted carpet. Provides additional resilience and helps prevent carpet from stretching or wrinkling.

RUBBER OR URETHANE: (separate carpet padding). Latex foam, sponge rubber, bonded urethane or prime urethane (which is the strongest on the market and non-allergenic) has a fiber facing on one side to keep it from stretching. Unaffected by humidity and does not attract vermin.

RUG: (carpet term). Smaller than room size, finished edge carpet laid loose on the floor.

S

SHAG: (carpet texture). Carpet having looped or cut pile yarns one and one half inches and longer with a random, tumbled appearance. Popular in the 70's. Hides footprints, dust and dirt. A new contemporary look shag with exciting new textures and up-to-date colors is gaining in popularity.

SHEDDING OR FLUFFING: (carpet care). Some new carpets will shed bits of fiber for a period of time. These will be gradually removed through vacuuming and are not an indication of poor carpet quality. Shedding is more common with wool than with synthetics.

SISAL FLOORING: (carpet term). Rugs and mats woven from sisal, a strong fiber from the leaves of an agave plant. Available dyed and hand-painted.

SNAGS: (carpet care). Occur when sharp-edged objects grab carpet fibers. Fixed by clipping.

SOILING: (carpet care). A build up of soil particles in the carpet fibers. Remedied by thorough, frequent vacuuming with professional cleaning recommended every eighteen months.

SOIL RETARDANT: (carpet term). Having a chemical finish either applied to or inherit in the carpet fibers that inhibits soil from adhering to those fibers.

SPILLS OR STAINS: (carpet care). Spills and stains need immediate attention. Their severity is affected by type of carpet fiber, color of carpet, age of stain and cause of stain. See carpet warranty for recommended cleaning steps.

SPROUTING: (carpet care). Occasionally a tuft will rise or sprout above the carpet surface. Never try to pull it out. Clip with scissors.

STAIN RESISTANT: (carpet term). Having a chemical finish either applied to or inherit in the carpet fibers that inhibits specific stains from penetrating those fibers.

STATIC ELECTRICITY: (carpet care). Cooler outside temperatures combined with low humidity can create static electricity. A humidifier or anti-static spray will help control static buildup. Some carpets have built-in anti-static protection.

STRETCH: (carpet term). The give in carpet when it is pulled over the pad onto tackless strips.

T

TACKLESS INSTALLATION: (carpet term). Another name for wall-to-wall installation. Carpet is laid over the pad and stretched over strips of wood with implanted tacks that hold the carpet to the wall.

TAPESTRY CARPETS: (carpet term). In 1832, Richard Whytock, Scotland, invented a weaving process using preprinted woolen warp threads wound on large drums that formed the face of looped or cut-pile carpets. His invention permitted a limitless number of colors and reduced the amount of expensive wool needed to weave a pile carpet.

TEXTURE RETENTION: (carpet care). The ability of carpet tufts to keep their visible shape under foot traffic. Following appropriate guidelines for carpet care will minimize texture loss.

TUFTED: (carpet construction). Process in which a high-speed machine with hundreds of needles inserts pile yarns through the primary backing fabric forming loops, or tufts. An adhesive coating is applied to anchor the tufts permanently. Then a secondary backing is bonded to the first for reinforcement and dimensional stability. Over 90% of the North American made broadloom carpet is tufted. Quality is indicate by the number of tufts per square inch. If two carpets have the same size yarn, the one with more tufts per inch has the higher qualify.

W

WALL-TO-WALL CARPET: (carpet term). Carpeting can either be made from natural (animal or vegetable) fibers or man-made fibers. How well a carpet wears depends on the type of fiber used, the density and height of the pile and whether it has been well laid on a level surface either with a good underlay or a foam backing.

WOOL: (surface carpet fiber). The traditional leader in higher-price, luxury lines. It resists soil, is easy to clean, and is warm, soft and comfortable. It has resistance to wear, excellent resilience, and good ability to take dyes. Look for "Moth Proof" on wool carpet labels.

WOVEN: (carpet construction). Similar to woven fabrics, the surface and backing yarns are interlaced to produce a sturdy textile for the floor. About 3 percent of carpet made in the U.S. is woven. The principle types are velvet, Wilton and Axminster, each named after the type of automated loom on which it is manufactured. Another type sold in the U.S. is the Oriental, and is always imported, and made on a hand loom.

RESILIENT / HARD FLOORING

A

ASPHALT TILE: (resilient flooring). Low cost, permanent resilient flooring available in a wide variety of colors. Resists alkalis well so may be installed on, above or below grade. Non-grease resistant and thus not recommended for kitchens.

B

BACKING: (resilient flooring). Material to which plastic sheet flooring and linoleum is bonded during manufacture. Usually made of specially treated felt.

C

CERAMIC GRANULE: (resilient flooring). Developed primarily for industrial and commercial uses, it consists of ceramic coated quartz granules embedded in a clear plastic resin. Especially long wearing, it resists heel marks, grease and other stains. This type of flooring is seamless, reducing collected dirt.

CERAMIC SURFACE: (resilient flooring). Term describing vinyls and woods treated with a ceramic type finish that looks, feels and wears like ceramic.

CERAMIC TILE: (hard flooring). Tile made from clay or other organic materials; finished by kiln firing. May be glazed or unglazed. Suitable for residential, commercial or exterior use. Available in a wide variety of styles from smooth finishes to stone looks. Easy to maintain; most are non-skid.

CORK: (resilient flooring). A forerunner in resilient flooring and formerly one of the most resilient of all smooth-surface floors. Many colors including several natural shades. Available unfinished, waxed, resin-reinforced waxed and vinyl impregnated as either tiles or sheets. Does not wear well in heavy traffic areas. Preferred use is as a wall covering.

COVE BASE: (resilient flooring). Concave "link" between floor and wall when resilient flooring is installed. Provides sanitary baseboard treatment, eliminates dust catching cracks and corners.

CUSHIONED SHEET: (resilient flooring). Formerly a term used for vinyl sheet with a foam underlay. Known for its warmth, sound absorption, and addition to resiliency.

E

EMBOSSING: (resilient flooring). Treatment of flooring designs to enhance pattern effect, heighten resemblance between flooring and material it simulates. Embossed inlaid flooring has part of surface indented for a three-dimensional effect.

G

GAUGE: (resilient flooring). The thickness of overall material in resilient flooring - common service, standard and heavy. All types or patterns not made in each gauge.

GRADE-LEVEL: (resilient flooring). Location corresponding to ground-level. Some types of resilient flooring are not suitable to high moisture and alkalinity conditions, so grade-level is an important consideration.

H

HARD FLOORS: (flooring term). Hard surfaced, durable flooring. Brick, terrazzo, marble, stone and slate are some examples.

I

INDEXED DESIGN: (flooring term). Specially designed tile patterns which nearly eliminate seam visibility.

INLAID COLOR FLOOR: (flooring term). Millions of color granules are applied layer upon layer through hand-cut stencils. These tiny granules create the pattern from the backing right through to the wear layer. A handcrafted look of extraordinary depth and richness.

L

LAMINATED FLOORING: (flooring term). Layered flooring (surface, core and balancing) produced by pressing together several materials at high temperatures with high pressure and sealed with a plastic-like substance. Available as panels, planks or tiles in wood, marble, tile and other looks. Easy care, fade resistant and durable (some water resistant). Quality varies with manufacturer; check individual warranties for specifics.

LINOLEUM: (resilient flooring). One of the first resilient floor coverings; introduced in the 1800's. No longer manufactured in the U.S., it was available in sheet or tile form and in numerous design effects. Popular in kitchens because it resisted grease, but not used in cellars because of low resistance to alkalinity and moisture in below grade concrete sub-floors. Sometimes incorrectly used to describe vinyl resilient flooring.

M

MARBLE: (hard flooring). A hard limestone flooring which takes a high polish. Marble look also available in tiles.

MOSAIC TILE: (hard flooring). Small, patterned ceramic tiles mounted on a backing material for ease of installation.

P

PARQUET FLOOR: (wood flooring). Inlaid wood floor of geometric design.

PATTERN REPEAT: (flooring term). The distance from a point in a pattern to the point where it occurs again, measuring lengthwise.

PICKLED FLOOR: (wood flooring). A "whitened" wood floor with a more casual look.

PLANK FLOORING: (wood flooring). Made of long boards wider than three inches.

R

RESILIENCE: (resilient flooring). Ability of a flooring material to spring back to original shape or thickness after being crushed or walked upon.

RESILIENT FLOORING: (flooring term). Available in so many types, styles, kinds and colors, it almost defies description. The terms "smooth-surface floor coverings" or "resilient flooring" are often used to classify permanent types of flooring (tiles, strips or sheet goods) usually cemented to the sub-floor. Resilient flooring should not be confused with felt-base rugs and floor coverings, which are laid loose on the floor. Included in the resilient category are plastic and vinyl sheet flooring, asphalt, rubber, solid vinyl, linoleum, cork, vinyl-corks and similar products.

ROTOGRAVURE VINYL FLOORING: (resilient flooring). Decorative floor covering with a pattern printed by rotogravure and protected with a clear vinyl plastic. Unlike true resilient flooring, it is not permanently cemented.

RUBBER FLOORING: (resilient flooring). A synthetic rubber tile or sheet mechanically reinforced for durability with a smooth, platelike surface. When installed with special adhesives, it may be laid on, above or below grade-level. Available in ribbed, coin or other raised pattern.

S

SELF-ADHERING: (resilient flooring). Vinyl tile with a self-stick backing. It is similar to sheet in maintenance and is usually no-wax. Self installment is possible, bringing with it considerable savings. Today's peel & sticks are much better in quality than past products.

SLATE: (hard flooring). A hard rock, the thin smooth layers of which are embedded in cement or mortar to produce a patterned floor.

STRIP FLOORING: (wood flooring). Wood flooring made of long, three inch wide tongue-and-groove boards that are end matched.

SUPERIMPOSED PATTERN: (resilient flooring). Sheet vinyl with a printed pattern superimposed under clear sheet.

T

TERRAZZO: (hard flooring). A highly polished, smooth, multicolored floor made by embedding chips of marble or stone in a cement binder. Generally poured and set on site, but also available as tiles.

U

UNDERLAY: (resilient flooring). Flexible lining material used under resilient flooring during installation. It absorbs normal movement of wood subfloors, prevents splitting of resilient flooring. Two types are made: an asphalt treated felt (lining felt) and air-filled foam-cushion (used under laminates).

V

VINYL ASBESTOS TILE: (resilient flooring). This was a fire-retardant floor tile in clear, brilliant colors. Installation ranged from basement to attic; some were available with adhesive backing. Asbestos is now considered a hazard to health.

VINYL SHEET: (resilient flooring). The successor to linoleum, usually available in 12 x 16 foot rolls. It has few seams, making it ideal for kitchens and baths. Requires no waxing and resists marks. Can be found in a variety of colors and patterns.

VINYL TILE: (resilient flooring). A durable, colorful material, also known as "solid vinyl" or "homogeneous" tile, with the same high resistance to staining, wear and common chemicals featured in vinyl sheet. It has clean colors, can be found in intricate patterns, and its density inhibits wear.

W

WOOD FLOORING: (flooring term). Most wood flooring is made from the hard, compact wood or timber of various hardwood trees such as maple, cherry, oak, mahogany, pecan, beech, etc. Available as either solid wood flooring or laminated flooring, most is prefinished at the factory providing a uniform finish and making installation easier. Some available with no-wax, ceramic surface finish that provides greater wear and stain resistance.

GLOSSARY OF WINDOW TREATMENTS

B

BALLOON SHADES: The Balloon shade is constructed on the same principle as the Roman shade. Balloon shades, however, require more fabric so that when it is in the raised position the shade billows into soft poufs of fabric along the bottom edge. Headings determine the look of this shade. With a gathered heading, the shade has a puffed look in the lowered position. The pleated heading falls into inverted box pleats and is flat in appearance in the lowered position. Shorter versions of both pleated and gathered headings may be used effectively as valances over roller shades, curtains or shutters.

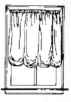

BLINDS: Mini-blinds, vertical blinds, and Venetian blinds now come in many colors and fabrics. They look well on windows and fit in with decorative looks in all areas. They allow greater light entry, without screening or filtering it by adjusting the amount of light penetration. Blinds can give the illusion of height and width to different shaped windows. With slats of steel, wood, plastic or fabric, blinds can become almost as much a part of the architecture as the windows themselves.

C

CAFE: These curtains cover half the window's height and are usually simple, hemmed curtains of patterned material. Most installations use two sets per window, mounting one set above the other as illustrated. Adding a valance also helps.

CASEMENT WINDOWS: Often require special curtain treatment. Those that swing inward are generally fitted with shirred sheer curtains fastened to the top and bottom of the windows. Those that swing out are usually fitted with straight hanging curtains or draperies. To present a uniform appearance from the street, all windows on the same floor should have the same kind of curtains or lined draperies.

CORNICES: Cornices are boxlike shapes sometimes used instead of valances. They are generally from four to seven inches deep and made of wood or metal. Some are painted to match the woodwork or the draperies. Others are covered with drapery material, mirrors, carved or molding designs, or with applied plaster decoration. They add to the apparent height of short windows.

COTTAGE SET: Cottage curtains combine straight curtains of cafe type with tie-backs. Tie-backs, which experienced a greater popularity before the increase in use of traverse rods, do not usually overlap.

D

DRAPERIES: May also be referred to as "over-curtains," "over-draperies" and "drapes." Draperies are generally of heavier material, lined and weighted at the bottom, and tailored to fit the particular window.

Draperies are used in three principal lengths: (1) In informal rooms such as dens, sunrooms and breakfast rooms, draperies can hang to the lower edge of the window apron and/or sill; (2) In formal rooms, they may be long enough to permit spreading the ends on the floor or "puddling"; (3) In the vast majority of cases, the draperies should hang to the floor. All lengths can be used with or without valances. Standard lengths are 36 inches, 45 inches, 54 inches, 63 inches, 72 inches, 84 inches, 90 inches and 95 inches.

Draperies can be made of almost any material, ranging from such informal materials as cotton, linen, monk's cloth and chintz to the more formal brocades, velvets and damasks. The edges may be finished with ruffles, bandings, braids or edgings according to the type of fabric.

F

FABRIC SELECTION: The kind of fabric and the pattern can greatly affect the design and success of your window treatment. The following points should be considered in making any selection of fabrics:

Vertical patterns or stripes make a window appear taller and narrower.

Horizontal patterns or stripes make a window seem shorter and wider.

Small floral or geometric designs tend to increase the apparent size of the windows.

Large floral or geometric designs make a window seem smaller.

Generally large patterns are best for large rooms and small ones for smaller areas.

The length should determine the scale of the pattern.

The carpet should harmonize with the drapery fabric and texture.

The texture, design and the care factor should all be taken into consideration. Kitchen curtains should be washable and of a durable fabric. Cotton is an excellent fabric for the kitchen. Formal room draperies can be made of a more expensive fabric such as silk, brocade and satin since they do not receive hard usage and are usually constructed to last for several years. However, buy the best quality of fabric you can afford for any area of your home and select a color and design that you love - you'll never tire of your selection if you follow these two simple rules.

H

HEADINGS: The heading is the top of the drapery, especially that part which extends above the traverse rod. When hung with hooks, the heading should be long enough to cover the rod. Shirred curtains or draperies should extend one to two inches above the rod.

L

LACE: Lace curtains came into prominence with the popularity of French and American country furniture. They can be used on windows, as a valance, on glass doors and cabinet doors, and as an outside shower curtain to give a soft, yet light and airy look. There are many distinctive designs in the lace fabrics. Copies of old lace curtains are now available with designs of animals, flowers, trees and hearts.

LAMBREQUIN: A lambrequin can be described as a cornice that not only goes across the top of the window but extends down each side to the bottom of the apron or to the floor. Draperies or curtains are hung inside the three-sided box like structure. The lambrequin can be painted or covered with the fabric of the draperies or a contrasting fabric.

P

PANEL: Panel curtains are straight, draped curtains of floor or sill length. Each panel should run the full width of the window. Two pairs, or two panels, are illustrated. Using several curtains of this style improves effect of fullness.

PASSE MENTERIE: Decorative trimming, tassels, rosettes, gimps, and fringes of all sorts.

PRISCILLA: These curtains are fluffy, ruffled and feminine and can be either floor length or sill length, as shown. Overlap can be partial, as shown, or complete. Tie-backs are of same ruffled material as curtains.

PUDDLING: When draperies fall past the floor in a puddle shape. A plush, luxurious look for formal rooms.

R

ROMAN SHADES: Roman shades are similar to a fabric roller shade in that they have a tailored look but they have a more elegant appearance. The Roman shade hangs smoothly when down but in a raised position the fabric falls in graceful folds. This accordion effect is created by rings and cords attached on the back of the shade. This is an economical window treatment since it only requires enough fabric to fill up the window.

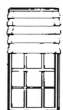

S

SCREENS: These are effective window treatments to hide an unattractive view. They can be hardboard panels with a cutout or lattice design to filter light. Panels that fit inside the window can be painted with an outdoor scene and hinged for opening. Large expanses of picture windows can be broken up with wall-to-wall louvered panels. Mirror glass fitted into the lower part of a window lets in light at the top but also makes the room seem larger. Plants can also be effective screens that let in light but are still attractive and conceal the view.

SHADES: Roller shades consist of muslin, coated plastic, jute, matchsticks, bamboo and linen. Laminated shades consist of cotton, rayon or linen fabrics bonded to shade cloth. Shades can be either translucent or transparent, for light control, or opaque for darkening effects. Shades add to the architectural grace of a house. Special types are available for almost every kind of window. They help reduce heat loss and screen out noise. Solid color shades are predominately pastel tan, green, white and off-white. Pale shades diffuse light while darker ones reduce or even eliminate it. Shades in stripes and floral patterns enhance decorative effect. Vertical stripes make windows seem taller; horizontal ones create the illusion of wider windows. Shades were traditionally pulled down from the top of the window but "bottom-up" ones permit unusual window treatments. Consider trims, painting, applique and stenciling for dressing up window shades.

SHEERS: These are curtains of thin material which cover the window. They assure privacy but are still thin enough to admit light and air. They may be used alone or in combination with draperies of heavier, opaque material. They may hang straight or be tied back (if used without draperies); they may be severely plain or have ruffled edges. If hung inside the window casing, they should reach to the window sill. If hung on the outside casing, with or without over draperies, they should still hang to the bottom of the apron or even to the floor in very formal rooms. They are made of such materials as marquisettes, nets, organdy, silk or synthetic gauze.

SHUTTERS: Shutters look secure and attractive both from the outside and the inside of a window. They can be finished natural, painted, stained or have a fabric center. Shutters can cover an entire window or only the bottom section. If only half the window is shuttered, the top valance can be made of wood or fabric.

T

TASSELS: Tassels are small works of art. They add a touch of beauty and elegance wherever they are used -- as tie-backs for draperies, on the end of cornices, on pillows, to hang on an armoire door handle or on a fringed round hassock. They are made of velvet, silk, cotton and synthetic fabrics. Look for old European ones in antique shops and flea markets. See Passe menterie.

TIE-BACK: Loops of fabric, plastic, metal or wood to hold curtains in position. Place either above or below the center of the window to avoid the appearance of cutting the window space in half. Usually, the higher the tie-back, the taller the window appears.

TIER: Tier curtains are composed of two or more sets of overlapping short curtains. Each tier usually once ended in a ruffled flounce, but tailored tiers are now more popular than the ruffled.

TRAVERSE DRAPERIES: These are hung on a traverse rod so that they may be drawn together at night. They should be made with a fullness ratio of two to one or more, depending upon the fabric, and can be used with underneath sheer curtains. Special hardware is required.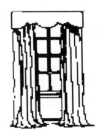

V

VALANCES: Valances are the top or horizontal portion of the drapery treatment. They were originally used to hide the drapery poles and fixtures, but have survived for decorative reasons. Valances of light material can be shirred or ruffled and are most frequently used in bedrooms. They are customarily four to six inches in depth for ordinary size windows. With heavier materials, tailored or draped valances of varying shapes and styles are commonly used. The illustrations that follow show the most popular styles. Simpler types of valances are most effective although period rooms may require special treatment. Flat, shaped valances are usually lined with heavy material for stiffness. These should be from eight to twelve inches in depth and should never exceed one sixth of the total window depth. Shade color valances, installed on curtain rods, now offer pleasing mix-match combinations.

MEASURING WINDOW TREATMENTS

The first step in making curtains and draperies is measuring the window. This will be the basis for the design and to determine the necessary yardage.

If you are going to have your curtains or draperies custom-made, have a professional come and measure. If you are making the window covering, buy the correct rod and install it before you measure. For accuracy, use a wooden or steel rule.

Select your fabric. Check to see if both the lining and the fabric are preshrunk. If it is a patterned fabric the repeat is important in determining the yardage.

To determine the width of the draperies, measure the length of the rod including the returns, (the distance from the corner of the rod to the bracket on the wall), and the overlap (the distance at the center of a two panel treatment where one panel overlaps the other, usually about three inches per panel). For pleated headings, you will need 2¼ times the rod length plus 2" per side for the side hems. For shirred curtains, allow two times the rod length for heavy fabrics and three times for light fabrics.

To determine the finished length of each panel, measure from the bottom of the rod for a shirred curtain, or from ½" above the traverse rod for pinch pleats to the desired length. Allow 10" for floor length panels and 6" for the window sill or apron length. To these measurements you must also add for the heading. For standard rods, allow 1½" for the casing. For larger rods, measure the circumference of the rod, add 1" and divide this number in half. For pleated headings, add ⅝".

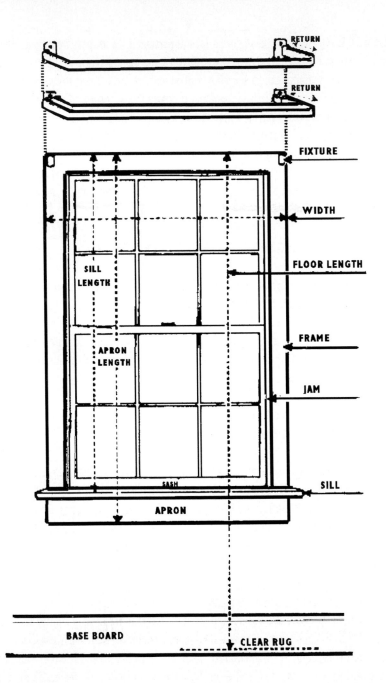

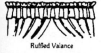

Ruffled Valance

Pleated Valance

Shaped Valance

Scalloped Valance

Cascaded Valance

Festooned Valance

Swag Valance

Square Cut Valance

A Salute to the Furniture Industry and its Constituents...

The people of the world have always placed beautiful, fine furniture among their most treasured possessions. The individuality and patina of the wood grain makes each piece unique; the lustrous fabrics bring each piece to life; while modern manufacturing techniques make furniture accessible to all. This updated 21st Century edition of Furniture Facts© is dedicated to the people of the Furniture Industry who share the belief that the harmonious home is the basis of our culture and must be nourished to perpetuate...and in that spirit offer value to benefit that end.

Thank you... **Dr. Richard R. Bennington, Professor of Business, High Point University, High Point, North Carolina**

Dr. Bennington's interest and attention to details and voracious quest for knowledge in his field of expertise--all phases of the industry--makes him truly one of the furniture industry's best allies. He has developed a unique field of study for High Point University and with his dedication and smiling countenance, is a boon to the industry. Certainly, his numerous suggestions and contributions to updating Furniture Facts© for the 21st Century edition were appreciated beyond measure.

Thank you to the furniture manufacturers and their staffs who responded promptly and enthusiastically with beautiful illustrations for the 28th Edition:

Ashley Furniture, Incorporated
Ashley, Wisconsin

Drexel Heritage Furnishings Incorporated
Drexel, North Carolina

Ethan Allen Incorporated
Danbury, Connecticut

Lane® Home Furnishings Collections
Altavista, Virginia

La-Z-Boy® Incorporated
Monroe, Michigan
as well as La-Z-Boy Business Furniture Division
      La-Z-Boy Healthcare Division

Ligne Roset
New York, New York

Henredon Furniture Industries, Incorporated
Morganton, North Carolina

Hickory White
Hickory, North Carolina

Thayer Coggin/TCI Incorporated
High Point, North Carolina

As we enter the year 2000, there are over ten thousand furniture manufacturing and related industry companies in the Western Hemisphere. Regretfully, only a small representation was possible within these covers.

*Thank you...*In addition to credits given throughout <u>Furniture Facts©</u>, the following people and companies were generous with their time and expertise: John F. Lawhon, Selling Retail International™ Inc., Tulsa, Oklahoma; Philip Meyer, ABC Carpets, Pleasant Hills, California; Jan Muschler, Director of Operations, Ligne Roset, St. Louis, Missouri; Lana Rusch, SRI™ and Karen Litchfield, Metcalf Designs, Tulsa, Oklahoma. Many other furniture, carpet and floor covering retailers, manufacturers, designers and industry associations throughout the United States, Canada and Great Britain have made important contributions. And, our sincere appreciation extends to those who have contributed technical data, photography, articles, and reference material from the past editions of <u>Furniture Facts©</u>, especially Annette Wagoner, Editor and Lori Altman, illustrations, 27th Edition.

Catherine D. Lawhon
EDITOR

In March 1912, Edward Hudson Lane, with his father, founded The Standard Red Cedar Chest Company and sawmill at Altavista, Virginia which later became the Lane Company. By 1922, the thriving company boldly launched a national ad campaign (see early advertisement, right) and the name Lane became synonymous with "hope chests." Historically, the "hope chest" or dower chest contained the heirloom handmade linens and quilts for the bride's new home.

The distinctive chest shown, below right, is from Lane's Williamsburg Collection.

Today, Lane Home Furnishings Collections include occasional tables, casegoods, upholstery and accent pieces.

Editor's note: Historical information, like the Lane story, can add value to what is sold, without raising the cost. At the same time, interesting facts and background information about the products sold can make selling more fun, exciting and rewarding for retail salespeople and Interior Designers -- and their customers.

A random sampling from the La-Z-Boy Inc. dual-purpose chair collection making the case in point that function can be delivered in style. "Oasis℗" (above left) is aptly named, featuring a ten-motor massage and heat system, corded telephone, and a thermoelectric beverage cooler. The cooler, located in the arm, stores six cans. The other arm conceals the phone and massage/heat control wand. "Carlyle" (above right): Reminiscent of art deco era; light enough to be a pull-up chair, but actually is a recliner. "Kramer" and "Riley" (below) demonstrate variations of contemporary casual style.

Hickory White of Hickory, North Carolina, is one of America' oldest and most respected makers of fine furniture. Shown above and on the next page, are a range of Hickory White's versatile designs for bedroom, living room and dining room which illustrate old world quality and craftsmanship; good examples of all that was good historically in fine furniture with all the benefits of improvements made possible by modern technology.

Upscale executive office furniture by La-Z-Boy Business Furniture Gallery. Their RJPlusII System, above, offers many design mix and match component options: cherry, veneers, and matching carefree laminates. Next page above, the La-Z-Boy Dakota Series features 27 configuration elements with which to efficiently customize and maximize the business environment. Below right, La-Z-Boy Pacific Collection. The La-Z-Boy desk chair shown is designed for health and comfort in the workplace with adjustable arms, height and width; contoured foam seat and back; casters for mobility.

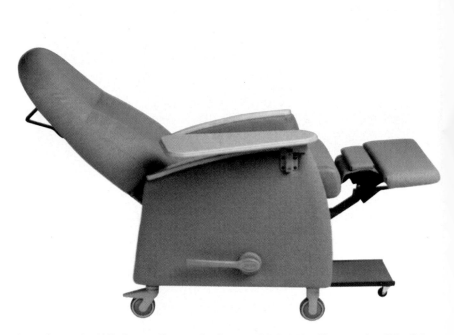

According to the U.S. Census Bureau, by the year 2050, 394 million people will be living in the United States and nearly 79 million of them will be over age 65; 18 million will be over 85. Furniture manufacturers have already begun to design products which make life easier for caregivers and the elderly. The HealthCare Division of La-Z-Boy, Inc. calls the example above their "workhorse" because it has the most function and mobility features. It is designed to maximize a caregiver's time and efforts, and still exceed the comfort expectations of patients. Interior designers now consider retro-fitting homes to accommodate frail limbs, failing eyesight, and difficult joints; and people are urged to include these built-in amenities (such as grab bars in shower and bathrooms) in their retirement self-care budgets.

The **Ligne Roset** bed, above, framed in natural beech, with movable back cushions, pivotal table/tv table and slightly recessed mattress, is an island of comfort in the European manner designed by Peter Maly.

ABOUT THE COVER AND SECTION ART...

Selected from Parisian archives, this original black and white

"plate 79" was the depiction used to present a furniture

collection in the early 1800s and reads:

Muebles et Objects de goût.

Restauration (1814-1818).

Drexel Heritage Furnishings, Inc. of Drexel, North Carolina combines drama and luxurious comfort in the traditional setting above. The muted color scheme is an enticing background for the striking upholstered furniture.

Below, Drexel Heritage Furnishings, Inc. merges many textural elements in The Corbel Collection unique designs.

Ashley Furniture, Inc, "Capri" sectional in top-grain leather from the Millennium™ collection. Ashley is a good example of companies who bring quality leather furniture to mid-price range budgets without forfeiting good design or amenities heretofore available only in high-end furniture.

Furniture Facts: Modern technology and the expanded resources of the development of a global economy has had a dramatic effect at the medium-price levels of furniture manufacture. It has resulted in better designs and better quality. Since this improvement will continue, keeping up-to-date with those companies in the forefront of this development is essential for the retail furniture salesperson and Interior Designer. The room groupings above from Bassett® Furniture Industries, Inc. are handsome examples of these developments.

Above, Ethan Allen Inc.'s "Country Colors Collection" with its nature inspired hues, reflects the clean lines of Shaker furniture with contemporary amenities.

Below, British Classics Collection by Ethan Allen for the home workplace. The rich timeworn patina of the maple furniture adds warmth to designs that recall snug Victorian reading rooms and jurist offices with touches of spirited Caribbean.

Inspired by Art Deco and Moderne design, Ethan Allen's Avenue Collection blends geometric appeal with custom details. The Bogart chair shown in the living room setting above is pure "retro." The Ethan Allen dining room group with its uniquely designed roundback chairs artfully melds past and present.

For near half-century, the Thayer Coggin firm has produced cutting-edge, avante-garde furniture. The Milo Baughman design (below) the "Limited Edition" day chaise, is one of 500 pieces in the company's commemorative collection. Each piece is signed and numbered and offered with a letter of authenticity signed by the legendary designer Baughman, who has designed exclusively for Thayer Coggin since its inception.

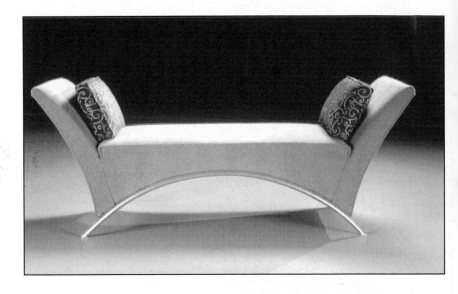

Right, the "harrison" club chair designed by Ransom Culler for Thayer Coggin, Inc. brings into play the art deco look of the 1920's while incorporating the comfort possible today.